STUDY GUIDE TO ACCOMPANY

CALIFORNIA CIVIL LITIGATION

FIFTH EDITION

SUSAN BURNETT LUTEN

Australia • Canada • Mexico • Singapore • Spain • United Kingdom • United States

Study Guide to Accompany California Civil Litigation, Fifth Edition
Susan Burnett Luten

Vice President, Career and Professional Editorial: Dave Garza

Director of Learning Solutions: Sandy Clark

Acquisitions Editor: Shelley Esposito

Managing Editor: Larry Main

Senior Product Manager: Melissa Riveglia

Editorial Assistant: Lyss Zaza

Vice President, Career and Professional Marketing: Jennifer McAvey

Marketing Director: Debbie Yarnell

Marketing Manager: Erin Brennan

Marketing Coordinator: Jonathan Sheehan

Production Director: Wendy Troeger

Production Manager: Mark Bernard

Senior Content Project Manager: Glenn Castle

Art Director: Joy Kocsis

Technology Project Manager: Tom Smith

Production Technology Analyst: Thomas Stover

For product information and technology assistance, contact us at
Professional & Career Group Customer Support, 1-800-648-7450

For permission to use material from this text or product, submit all requests online at **cengage.com/permissions.**
Further permissions questions can be e-mailed to
permissionrequest@cengage.com.

Library of Congress Control Number: 2008927612

ISBN-13: 978-1-4283-1848-9

ISBN-10: 1-4283-1848-8

Delmar
5 Maxwell Drive
Clifton Park, NY 12065-2919
USA

Cengage Learning products are represented in Canada by Nelson Education, Ltd.

For your lifelong learning solutions, visit **delmar.cengage.com**

Visit our corporate website at **cengage.com**

Printed in Canada
1 2 3 4 5 6 7 12 11 10 09 08

NOTICE TO THE READER

Publisher does not warrant or guarantee any of the products described herein or perform any independent analysis in connection with any of the product information contained herein. Publisher does not assume, and expressly disclaims, any obligation to obtain and include information other than that provided to it by the manufacturer.

The reader is notified that this text is an educational tool, not a practice book. Since the law is in constant change, no rule or statement of law in this book should be relied upon for any service to any client. The reader should always refer to standard legal sources for the current rule or law. If legal advice or other expert assistance is required, the services of the appropriate professional should be sought.

The publisher makes no representation or warranties of any kind, including but not limited to the warranties of fitness for particular purpose or merchantability, nor are any such representations implied with respect to the material set forth herein, and the publisher takes no responsibility with respect to such material. The publisher shall not be liable for any special, consequential, or exemplary damages resulting, in whole or part, from the readers' use of, or reliance upon, this material.

CONTENTS

INTRODUCTION

This *Study Guide* is intended to supplement and enhance the learning experience provided by the accompanying text, *California Civil Litigation,* Fifth Edition. *California Civil Litigation* is intended to provide the paralegal with a comprehensible and comprehensive explanation of relevant legal principles and their practical applications.

Many students suffer from a lack of confidence in their abilities simply because they have not had an adequate opportunity to work through the material in the text. This *Study Guide* is intended to develop student confidence by providing that opportunity. The *Study Guide* presents the material in a format that is different than but complementary to that of *California Civil Litigation*, to reinforce and provide additional learning experiences for the student. The *Study Guide* also provides opportunities for review and self-testing of the concepts presented in the text, as well as for on-line examination of codes and analysis of cases relevant to the chapter topics.

This *Study Guide* follows the same chronological approach as the text—beginning with fundamental principles, followed by the inception of a lawsuit, and progressing through discovery, trial preparation, trial, and appeal. It emphasizes civil litigation in California state and federal courts. Local rules are discussed only in general and by way of example: the paralegal is cautioned to check local rules with the court clerk of the relevant jurisdiction before undertaking any work on behalf of a client.

Like the text, this *Study Guide* does not include family law or probate, and only mentions administrative law. It does not include eminent domain or unlawful detainer, which have their own complex statutory schemes. It does include elements of the law school classes of civil procedure and evidence, which represent a year and a semester, respectively, of law school. These pages are not a substitute for these classes or for the accompanying text.

Text and *Study Guide* Objectives

A paralegal has to know about litigation because the paralegal practices litigation. The text and this *Study Guide* explain, and demonstrate, the chronology of a case, explain, and show, the issues presented, and provide opportunities for self-testing, research, and to produce the relevant workproduct. If the student can do all of this, then he is ready to work in the profession. The objective of the text and this *Study Guide* is to provide the student with realistic paralegal experiences.

This course—the text, this *Study Guide*, and the *Online Companion*—are the tools to learn the trade, to learn how to do the things paralegals do every day, and using the resources they have available to them.

The Fifth Edition

The fifth edition of the text has been completely updated and revised to encompass changes in the law and procedure since the last edition publication. These revisions reflect the reorganization of relevant codes and rules. They also include updated research projects, including citation of recent cases.

Study Guide Chapter Format

The *Study Guide* is intended to add depth to the student's learning experience. Each chapter in this *Study Guide* includes the following features:

1. **Chapter Outline.** An outline following the organization of the text presents the text material in a concise format.

2. **Chapter Objectives.** Following the Chapter Outline, each chapter contains a review of the Chapter Objectives set forth at the beginning of each chapter in the text.

3. **Review Exercises.** Each chapter includes a series of fill-in-the-blanks Review Exercises covering the chapter objectives and the major topics covered in the text and the *Study Guide* outline.

4. **Key Words and Phrases.** Each chapter contains a list of key words and phrases from the chapter, with blanks for the student to provide definitions learned from the text.

5. **Online Projects.** Each *Study Guide* chapter includes Online Projects. These require the student to locate statutes, rules, court opinions, and official forms on-line, and apply them.

6. **Additional Research.** Each *Study Guide* chapter contains a number of additional citations to California court opinions on topics related to those in the chapter, for additional reading, assignment, or discussion.

7. **Quiz.** The student can test his understanding of the material covered in the chapter in an objective question format before moving on to the next chapter.

8. **Alternate Assignments.** Two cases continuing throughout the *Study Guide* chapters present assignment alternatives to *Murphy v. Johnson* in the text. These alternate assignments involve more complex fact patterns for state and federal courts as well as personal injury and other tort causes of action, so that the student can be exposed to a complete spectrum of practice.

The Study Guide also includes two appendices: a deposition transcript from one of the Alternate Assignment cases, and a description of office procedures and file organization for law offices.

Online Companion

In addition to the learning opportunities in the text and *Study Guide*, the course includes an Online Companion, located at http://www.westlegalstudies.com. The Online Companion contains additional examples of pleadings, discovery, motions and briefs, another deposition transcript, and examples of correspondence with clients, courts, and opposing counsel. The on-line exhibits augment those found in the text and illustrate practical approaches to everyday problems.

The Online Companion is organized into a series of sections, based on a variety of fact patterns and substantive areas that illustrate the type of workproduct produced every day by paralegals. Each section poses questions about the workproduct that focus attention on the myriad issues addressed daily in the legal environment. For example, one section focuses on correspondence with clients, counsel, and the courts, illustrating a variety of common communications, from termination of representation to letters to court clerks and opposing counsel. Another section presents a motion for protective order, illustrating not only the format and procedural points made in the text but also the correspondence leading up to the motion and how it is used to support the motion, and law and motion calendaring problems. A motion made in an administrative law case presents ethical problems as well as demonstrating how litigation is conducted in an agency setting.

Even if the Online Companion is not used as part of the student's course, it is an important resource and may help to clarify points made in the class presentations and the text.

For the student, the Online Companion is like having a set of client files sitting in an in-box waiting for review for various work assignments. Just as a working paralegal might be asked to review the pleadings in a new case, a motion to compel in a case with which he has had no experience, or to check the caption style of an appellate brief against the California Rules of Court, the Online Companion presents a diversity of workproduct and fact patterns.

The student using the Online Companion on his own might complete a few chapters of the text and Study Guide, then browse through the Companion to see what aspects of it apply to the course material. The student can focus his attention on some of the issues presented by reading and then working through the questions posed in the Companion sections; then he can return to the Companion from time to time as more chapters are read and digested.

The Online Companion also links to a variety of Web sites useful for research, information, and support services. An instructor might ask a student to explore a Web site provided in the Online Companion as a starting point, or to perform a particular task based on a particular site. A student working on his own will be able to explore some of the most reliable and useful sites to get an idea of the breadth and depth of information available.

How to Use the *Study Guide*

Litigation is a difficult course for novice paralegals because it requires mastery of several disciplines. In addition, by the time the student has completed the course, employers will expect that the student not only knows the underlying theories but is able to produce usable workproduct for clients.

Obviously, this is a daunting prospect. The text contains the theory, and exhibits illustrating the types of workproduct needed at various points in the case. It also contains a case to work on.

A student approaching the material should first read the chapter in the text and work through the discussion questions at the end of the chapter. Then, he should review the Chapter Outline in this *Study Guide* to make sure that he understands the material from the text. Then, he should complete the *Study Guide* key words and review exercises. The Chapter Outline can also be used as an outline for the classroom work, if the instructor follows the chapter format for lecture and discussion.

The Online Projects and Additional Research provide the student with another type of learning experience. The amount of time available for the litigation course rarely permits research on the topics presented. The Online Projects provide an opportunity to research an issue on-line to see how to approach the issue in practice. They also remind the student to check on-line resources to see whether forms in the text are current, and to look for additional forms related to the chapter topics. This section of each *Study Guide* chapter provides a view of the law beyond the theory and concepts in the text, and brings it into perspective.

Each chapter of the *Study Guide* includes a Quiz. The Quiz should be taken after the student completes all of the reading and assignments. The results of the Quiz will reveal any areas which have not been mastered and require further reading.

Finally, each chapter concludes with Alternate Assignments, which provide workproduct experience relevant to the subject matter of the chapter. They follow two cases: one emphasizes federal practice, while the other includes tort causes of action.

The same caveats to the use of the text are appropriate here. This is not a practice book; it is not a research or form book. It is meant only as a learning tool. Since the law is in constant change, no rule in this book should be relied upon for any service provided to any client. The student should refer to standard legal research sources for the answers to specific questions.

Learning to think like an attorney means discipline, no compromises, and no easy answers. This *Study Guide* is intended to build the student's confidence in his abilities in an ever-changing and demanding profession.

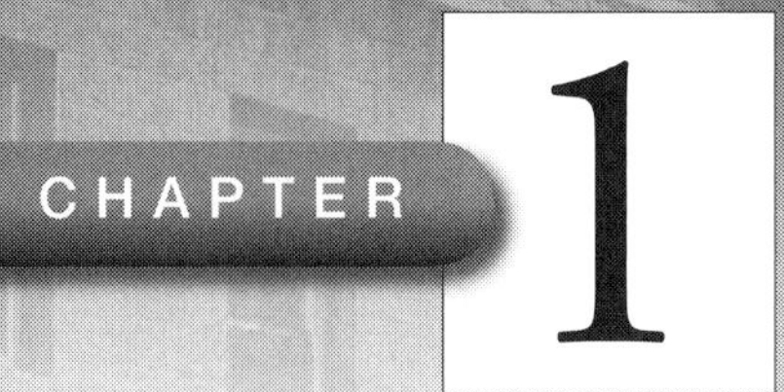

LITIGATION OVERVIEW

After completing the chapter reading, Discussion Questions, and Online Projects, review the material in the following Chapter Outline, then complete the Chapter Objectives, Review Exercises, and Key Words and Phrases. When these are mastered, complete the Online Projects, Additional Research, Quiz, and the Alternate Assignments.

CHAPTER OUTLINE

I. Litigation Is a Process Defined by Statutes and Rules.

A. The four most important sources of litigation statutes and rules for California State Courts

1. California Code of Civil Procedure (CCP)
2. Evidence Code (EC)
3. California Rules of Court (CRC)
4. local rules adopted by each jurisdiction

B. The four most important sources in federal litigation practice

1. Federal Rules of Civil Procedure (FRCP)
2. Federal Rules of Appellate Practice (FRAP)
3. United States Code (USC)
4. local rules adopted by each jurisdiction

II. The Litigation Process

A. The prelitigation phase extends from the first contact with the prospective client through factual and legal research to evaluate the merits of the case.

B. Pleadings filed with the court set forth the facts of the case, the remedies sought, and the defenses asserted.

C. The pleadings may be attacked for technical legal reasons.

D. Virtually all cases involve discovery to develop the facts and evidence required for trial.

E. Procedural and substantive disputes during the litigation may be resolved in "law and motion."

F. The case management judge (state court) or the trial judge (federal court) manages the case's progress and sets trial dates.

G. As discovery is completed and the trial date approaches, the parties focus their energy on trial preparation.

H. The evidence is presented at trial for a judgment based on a determination of the facts and law.

I. Post-trial motions may obtain compensation for attorneys' fees and costs of trial, to obtain a new trial, or to alter the judgment.

J. A losing party may appeal the trial court judgment to a court of appeal, whose decision may be appealed to the supreme court.

III. Types of Paralegal Employers Include Law Firms, Public Agencies, and Nonprofit Corporations.

A. Litigation law firms

1. These firms may be one lawyer or hundreds.
2. These firms may bill by the hour or on contingency.
3. Most law firms are either sole proprietorships, partnerships, limited liability partnerships, or corporations.
   a. Paralegals cannot participate in the ownership of law firms.
4. Most litigation law firms have specialized practices.
   a. Common areas of specialty are personal injury and commercial or business litigation.
   b. Firms may also represent plaintiffs or defendants exclusively.

B. Public (government) agencies may employ paralegals to

1. draft and apply laws and regulations.
2. assist in litigation.

C. Nonprofit corporations employ paralegals to assist in litigation.

IV. Paralegals Can Contribute at All Stages of Litigation.

A. A lawyer may increase profitability by delegating billable tasks to paralegals capable of professional-quality work but not paid as much as lawyers.

B. A lawyer may increase the quality of the work performed for the client and reduce the client's cost by delegating tasks to paralegals who have specialized training or experience.

C. Key aspects of the paralegal's role

1. The more efficient the paralegal, the more profitable the firm.
2. The more functions the paralegal can perform for the lawyer, the more valuable the paralegal becomes to the lawyer and the firm.

3. For the paralegal to be both profitable and valuable, his work must be of excellent quality—*equal to that of the lawyer*. For the work assigned to the paralegal, the paralegal must do attorney-quality work.

CHAPTER OBJECTIVES

1. List in order the seven general phases of civil litigation.

   a. ______________________________

   b. ______________________________

   c. ______________________________

   d. ______________________________

   e. ______________________________

   f. ______________________________

   g. ______________________________

2. List three types of employers of litigation paralegals.

   a. ______________________________

   b. ______________________________

   c. ______________________________

3. What is the role of the litigation paralegal?

   ____

   ____

   ____

REVIEW EXERCISES

Fill in the Blanks:

1. Define litigation. ______________________________

____

____

2. Substantive law is ______________________________, while procedural law is ______________________________. ______________________________ is an example of substantive law; ______________________________ is an example of procedural law.

3. Sources of California procedural law for state courts are found in the ______________________________ and ______________________________. The most important source of federal procedural law is the ______________________________.

4. The prelitigation phase extends from ______________________________ to ______________________________. Factual and legal research is necessary to ______________________________.

5. Pleadings are filed with the court and set forth what three things?

a. ______________________________

b. ______________________________

c. ______________________________

6. Why might pleadings be attacked?

____

____

____

7. Discovery is intended to ______________________________.

8. Discovery disputes that cannot be resolved by the attorneys are usually resolved in a legal process called ______________________________.

______________________________ is presented at trial; the

________________ is the outcome of the trial, which is based on the application of the ________________ to the ________________.

9. Typical post-trial motions address the following three issues:

a. ________________

b. ________________

c. ________________

10. A losing party may ________________ a judgment.

11. Paralegal employers may be law firms or ________________ in the public sector, or ________________ representing special interests.

12. Litigation firms may bill in one of three general ways:

a. ________________

b. ________________

c. ________________

13. Litigation law firms may be sole proprietors, or one of three types of entities:

a. ________________

b. ________________

c. ________________

14. Common areas of specialization in law are ________________ and ________________.

15. The business consideration for law firms employing paralegals is whether the paralegal's work is ________________. That factor can

be enhanced by delegating tasks from ____________________ to

____________________.

16. What are the three essential events in litigation?

a. ____________________

b. ____________________

c. ____________________

KEY WORDS AND PHRASES

Provide a Definition for Each of the Following:

Substantive laws: ____________________

____

Civil procedure: ____________________

____

Local rules: ____________________

____

Local local rules: ____________________

____

Party: ____________________

____

Plaintiff: ____________________

____

Judgment: ____________________

____

Defendant: ____________________

____

Pleadings: ______________________________

____

At issue: ______________________________

____

Discovery: ______________________________

____

Law and motion: ______________________________

____

Contingency fee: ______________________________

____

Limited liability partnership: ______________________________

____

Corporation: ______________________________

____

Sole proprietorship: ______________________________

____

Partnership: ______________________________

____

Law clerks: ______________________________

____

Legal assistant: ______________________________

____

Paralegal coordinator: ______________________________

____

Paralegal manager: ______________________________

____

Alternative dispute resolution (ADR): ______________________

____

Mediation: ______________________

____

Partner: ______________________

____

Associates: ______________________

____

Administrative law: ______________________

____

ONLINE PROJECTS

1. Access the Professional Rules of Conduct at the official State Bar of California Web site **(http://www.calbar.ca.gov/)**. Look over Rule 1–320. What does this rule communicate about how law firms are set up and how their personnel are compensated?

2. Access the official State Bar of California Web site **(http://www.calbar.ca.gov/)**. Locate the article referenced for learning about the legal system, entitled "A Guide to Legal Literacy." Focus on the stages of a civil case before trial and during trial, and the role of an attorney. What does this article communicate to the public about the role of the lawyer in a legal dispute?

3. Access the Web site located at **http://www.weblocator.com/**, and locate the *California Law Guide* and the essays on the California court system and the process of a lawsuit. Using the essay, draft a time line of civil litigation, highlighting important terms.

4. Access the Web site for the Superior Court of California County of Santa Clara **(http://www.scselfservice.org/)**. Locate the Self-Service Center discussion about civil litigation. Prepare an outline based on the discussion, annotating it with the various resources referenced.

5. Review the introductory pages to the judicial council forms at **http://www.courtinfo.ca.gov/**. These forms will be referenced and used throughout this course. How are forms accessed? How are they completed on-line? Is there an efficient way to locate recently changed forms?

ADDITIONAL RESEARCH

The following are cases accessible on the official California courts Web site **(http://www.courtinfo.ca.gov/)** on various topics of interest relating to this chapter.

Perkins v. Superior Court (1981) 117 CA3d 1 (pleading)

Guardian North Bay Inc. v. Superior Court (2001) 94 CA4th 963 (demurrer)

Barrenda L. v. Superior Court (1998) 65 CA4th 794 (discovery)

Medix Ambulance Service Inc. v. Superior Court (2002) 97 CA4th 109 (law and motion)

People v. Roberts (1997) 55 CA4th 1073 (trial)

QUIZ

1. The process of civil litigation is
   a. a discipline.
   b. a remedy.
   c. civil procedure.
   d. torts.

2. The sources that govern the litigation process are
   a. statutes, codes, and rules.
   b. rules and codes.
   c. the state and federal constitutions.
   d. civil procedure.

3. Local rules apply to
   a. all of the courts in that jurisdiction.
   b. only the courts of that state.
   c. only the courts of that region.
   d. codes, statutes, and rules of the state.

4. Local rules may govern
   a. where cases are filed.
   b. when papers are filed.
   c. methods for rendering decisions.
   d. a, b, and c.

5. Every case must have
   a. pleadings, discovery, and trial.
   b. pleadings, discovery, and appeal.
   c. pleadings and discovery.
   d. pleadings.

6. Discovery involves
   a. fact gathering from parties.
   b. fact gathering from nonparties.
   c. a and b.
   d. neither a nor b.

7. The litigation is controlled by the
   a. pleadings, trial, and appeal.
   b. pleadings, trial, and post-trial motions.
   c. pleadings and discovery.
   d. pleadings.

8. Law firms can be
   a. only partnerships consisting of lawyers.
   b. corporations consisting of lawyers and nonlawyers.
   c. partnerships or corporations consisting of lawyers and nonlawyers.
   d. partnerships or corporations consisting of lawyers.

9. Legal assistants
   a. are paralegals.
   b. are lawyers awaiting bar results.
   c. are associates.
   d. cannot manage law firm personnel.

10. Paralegals
   a. cannot improve the quality of attorney workproduct because they are not lawyers.
   b. cannot improve firm profitability because they are not lawyers.
   c. can do their work as well as the same work done by attorneys.
   d. can do all of the same work as attorneys.

ALTERNATE ASSIGNMENTS

1. Your supervising attorney has informed you that the president and major stockholder of a prospective corporate client has called inquiring about the firm's ability to undertake the immediate representation of the client in litigation to enforce a contract.

Review the job description in Exhibit 1–1 in the text, and indicate which skills will be of immediate importance as the prospective client is interviewed. Are there any skills not mentioned in the job description that may be important before or during the interview?

2. Your supervising attorney has informed you that a local business woman has called inquiring about the firm's ability to defend her in an action brought by her former attorney for unpaid fees, and to prosecute an action against the attorney for malpractice and personal injuries.

Review the job description in Exhibit 1–1 in the text, and indicate which skills will be of immediate importance as the prospective client is interviewed. Are there any skills not mentioned in the job description that may be important before or during the interview?

CHAPTER 2

ETHICS IN LITIGATION

After completing the chapter reading, Discussion Questions, Online Projects, and Assignments, review the material in the following Chapter Outline, then complete the Chapter Objectives, Review Exercises, and Key Words and Phrases. When these are mastered, complete the Online Projects, Additional Research, Quiz, and the Alternate Assignments.

CHAPTER OUTLINE

I. California Attorneys Are Subject to Ethical Rules.

A. The California Rules of Professional Conduct

1. are adopted by the board of governors of the State Bar of California and approved by the California Supreme Court.
2. are mandatory.
3. subject an attorney who willfully breaches the California Rules of Professional Conduct to disciplinary action, including disbarment.

B. Attorneys are also bound by sections of the Business and Professions Code applicable to lawyers.

C. California courts have also developed standards for professional conduct in case law.

D. There are additional guidelines promulgated by voluntary organizations.

E. Attorneys must pass a professional responsibility examination as part of the bar exam.

F. Paralegals must indirectly follow the Rules of Professional Conduct.

G. Paralegals are governed directly and indirectly by Business and Professions Code sections 6450–6.

II. Attorney Rules of Professional Conduct

A. Unauthorized practice

1. An attorney may not aid anyone in the unauthorized practice of law.
    a. If a paralegal intended to offer legal services to the public, any attorney who aids or assists the paralegal would be subject to discipline.
2. Attorneys cannot form a law partnership with nonlawyers.
3. Attorneys may not share legal fees directly or indirectly with nonlawyers.
    a. This rule does not prohibit gifts to the referral source, but the gift must not be compensation, and must not be given for the purpose of encouraging future referrals.

B. Advertising and solicitation

1. Attorneys may advertise, but only if the advertisements are true, not misleading, and are clearly advertisements.
2. No solicitation may be made directly to a prospective client who does not have a history with the firm.
    a. If an attorney must advise a past client of a change in the law, or an aspect of his matter which should be evaluated, solicitation is permitted.

C. Relationships between attorneys

1. Once a party is represented by counsel, no attorney may communicate directly with the party without the consent of counsel.
    a. If the party is a corporation, an attorney may not communicate with the corporation, or any officer, director, or employee of the corporation.
    b. This rule is not intended to limit communications between the parties, which are encouraged, since they may lead to settlements of disputes.
2. While lawyers may not share fees with nonlawyers, they may share fees with other attorneys.
    a. An attorney who intends to share a fee with another lawyer
        (i) must disclose the fee split to the client and obtain written consent.
        (ii) must assure the client that the fee will not be increased as a result of the split.
3. Attorneys may not compensate other lawyers for referring cases, but they may give gifts to referring counsel, provided the purpose of the gift is not to promise additional rewards for future referrals.

D. Relationships with clients

1. An attorney may not take a case that he is not competent to handle.
2. An attorney may not take a case that is not meritorious.
    a. An attorney is prohibited from advising a client to violate the law.
3. An attorney may not represent a party when the attorney has a relationship with the opposing counsel.

4. An attorney may not contract with the client to limit the attorney's liability for malpractice.
   a. If malpractice claims are made, the attorney may not settle the claim with the client without advising the client that the client may seek advice from an independent counsel.
5. Attorneys must keep clients reasonably informed about developments relating to the attorney's employment, and comply with reasonable requests for information.
6. An attorney representing an organization.
   a. must advise the client when a conflict has developed between the client and the client's spokesperson.
   b. may advise the client if the attorney believes that the client's spokesperson's decision-making is not responsible, but if the problem is not resolved, he must withdraw.
7. Attorneys must communicate written settlement offers to their clients.
8. Attorneys owe a duty of confidentiality to clients.

E. Terminating the client relationship

1. An attorney must return all documents and files immediately, and must cooperate in a transition with new counsel.
2. An attorney must withdraw if he has reason to believe
   a. that the client will file an unmeritorious claim.
   b. that continued representation will cause the attorney to violate the rules of conduct.
3. An attorney may withdraw
   a. if he has a dispute with the client over fees.
   b. if he has a dispute with cocounsel.
4. If an attorney represents a client in a tribunal that requires permission to withdraw, the attorney must obtain that permission.
5. An attorney must also take reasonable precautions before withdrawing, including:
   a. notice to the client
   b. allowing time for the client to obtain new counsel
   c. returning all fees which have not been earned

F. Financial relationships with clients

1. Commingling attorney funds with client funds is prohibited, very dangerous, and can have serious consequences.
2. An attorney may not keep any of his own funds in the client's trust account, except an amount adequate to pay bank charges against the account.
   a. The attorney is required to keep all unearned funds in the trust account.

G. Advocacy and representation

1. An attorney may not threaten criminal, administrative, or disciplinary charges to obtain an advantage in a civil matter.

2. An attorney may not mislead a court by making a false or misleading statement.
   a. He may not knowingly misquote the law, or cite a case that is no longer valid.
3. An attorney must not assist a witness in hiding to make himself unavailable as a witness, and must not pay a witness for testimony.
4. An attorney may not directly or indirectly attempt to influence a juror outside of the courtroom.

III. Attorney Voluntary Professional Guidelines Have Common Themes for Paralegals.

A. A paralegal must
1. maintain high professional standards.
2. always represent himself to be a paralegal and not an attorney.
3. protect the client's interests ahead of his own.

IV. Statutes Governing Paralegals (B&Pc Sections 6450–6)

A. "Paralegal" means a person who holds himself out to be a paralegal and
1. is qualified by education, training, or work experience.
2. either contracts with or is employed by an attorney.
3. performs substantial legal work under the direction and supervision of an attorney.

B. Paralegal tasks include
1. case planning, development, and management.
2. legal research.
3. interviewing clients.
4. fact gathering and retrieving information.
5. drafting and analyzing legal documents.
6. collecting, compiling, and utilizing technical information to make an independent decision and recommendation to the supervising attorney.
7. representing clients before a state or federal administrative agency if that representation is permitted by statute or rule.

C. A paralegal shall not
1. provide legal advice.
2. represent a client in court.
3. select, explain, draft, or recommend the use of any legal document to or for any person other than the attorney who directs and supervises the paralegal.
4. act as a runner or capper.

5. engage in the unlawful practice of law.
6. work for a natural person other than an attorney to perform paralegal services.
7. induce a person to engage in a business venture.
8. negotiate fees with the attorney's client.

D. Paralegal qualifications include

1. a certificate of completion of a paralegal program approved by the American Bar Association, or
2. a certificate of completion of a paralegal program at, or a degree from, a postsecondary institution that requires the successful completion of a minimum of 24 semester, or equivalent, units in law-related courses and that has been accredited by a national or regional accrediting organization or approved by the Bureau for Private Postsecondary and Vocational Education, or
3. a baccalaureate or advanced degree in any subject, a minimum of one year of law-related experience under the supervision of an attorney with three years' experience, and a written attorney declaration that the person is qualified to perform paralegal tasks, or
4. a high school diploma or general equivalency diploma, a minimum of three years of law-related experience under the supervision of an attorney who has been an active member of the State Bar of California for at least the preceding three years or who has practiced in the federal courts of this state for at least the preceding three years, and a written declaration from this attorney stating that the person is qualified to perform paralegal tasks.

E. Continuing paralegal education

1. Paralegals shall certify completion every three years of four hours of mandatory continuing legal education in legal ethics.
2. Every two years, all paralegals shall certify completion of four hours of mandatory continuing education in law.
3. Certification shall be made with the paralegal's supervising attorney. The paralegal shall be responsible for keeping a record of the paralegal's certifications.

F. Statutes also prohibit the paralegal from dealing directly with clients, require ethical duties consistent with those of attorneys, and provide for recovery of damages against violators who harm consumers.

CHAPTER OBJECTIVES

1. What rules govern lawyers' professional conduct?

____

____

What are the potential consequences for lawyers who violate them?

____

____

2. What rules govern paralegals' professional conduct?

____

____

What are the potential consequences for paralegals who violate them?

____

____

3. What are the requirements for someone to represent himself or herself as a paralegal in California?

____

____

REVIEW EXERCISES

Fill in the Blanks:

1. What is the unauthorized practice of law? ______________________

2. What types of advertising and solicitation are permitted by the Rules of Professional Conduct?

____

____

____

3. How do the Rules of Professional Conduct limit relationships between attorneys?

4. How do the Rules of Professional Conduct encourage attorneys to take only those cases that they have experience in handling?

5. What communications with clients do the Rules of Professional Conduct encourage?

6. When is withdrawal mandatory?

7. When is withdrawal permissible?

8. What is commingling of trust account funds, and why is it prohibited?

9. How are paralegals defined by the Business and Professions Code?

10. What are the continuing education requirements to remain a paralegal under California law?

KEY WORDS AND PHRASES

Provide a Definition for Each of the Following:

Unauthorized practice of law:

Attorney discipline:

Fee splitting:

Commingling:

ONLINE PROJECTS

1. One of the most important court opinions relating to paralegals is *In Re Complex Asbestos Litigation* (1991) 232 CA3d 572. It is the foundation upon which many of the principles relating to attorneys and paralegals are based. Access this case through the official California courts Web site **(http://www.courtinfo.ca.gov/)** and read it carefully. It is a long opinion, and you may find it helpful to outline it as you read it.
   a. As you read the opinion for the first time, make a list of the things that paralegal Vogel did that you think are consistent with the Rules of Professional Conduct, and a list of his actions that you believe are inconsistent with the Rules of Professional Conduct.
   b. What does the court hold is/are the ethical obligation(s) of paralegals?
   c. What could the law firms have done to avoid this situation? What sections of the Professional Rules of Conduct, located at the official State Bar of California Web site **(http://www.calbar.ca.gov/)**, have been violated?
   d. Business and Professions Code sections 6450–6 **(http://www.leginfo.ca.gov/)** were not adopted until years after *In Re Complex Asbestos Litigation.* If they had been in effect at the time, and had the persons involved in the case followed them scrupulously, would the situation have been avoided? What does that analysis tell you about attorney and paralegal ethics?

2. Business and Professions Code sections 6450 through 6456 **(http://www.leginfo.ca.gov/)** are currently the most important statutes pertaining specifically to paralegals. Review them carefully. What damages may be recovered by persons harmed by paralegals? Why are these persons referred to in the code as "consumers" and not "clients"?

3. Locate California Rules of Professional Conduct rule 3–310 at the State Bar of California Web site **(http://www.calbar.ca.gov/)**. How might a paralegal's duties be affected by this rule?

4. Locate the Statement of Professionalism and Civility at the Web site for the Alameda County Bar Association **(http://www.acbanet.org/)**. Does this document set forth mandatory rules? How is it enforced? Why do you think it was adopted? How is it different from the Rules of Professional Conduct?

5. Review the judicial council forms at **http://www.courtinfo.ca.gov/**. Which ones relate to initiating or terminating representation? Are the forms in the text current?

ADDITIONAL RESEARCH

The following are cases accessible on the official California courts Web site **(http://www.courtinfo.ca.gov/)** on various topics of interest relating to this chapter.

Gilbert v. National Corporation for Housing Partnerships (1999) 71 CA4th 1240 (nature of conflict of interest)

Henrikson v. Great American Savings & Loan (1992) 11 CA4th 109 (ethical walls)

Abeles v. State Bar (1973) 3 C3d 603 (prohibited communications to represented party)

QUIZ

1. California attorneys are subject to
   a. mandatory ethical rules.
   b. the California Rules of Professional Conduct.
   c. rules adopted by the board of governors of the State Bar of California, and approved by the California Supreme Court.
   d. a, b, and c.

2. An attorney who willfully breaches the Rules of Professional Conduct may
   a. be disbarred by the superior court.
   b. be subject to additional standards set by the Business and Professions Code.
   c. suffer disciplinary action, including disbarment.
   d. b and c.

3. Paralegals
   a. indirectly follow the Rules of Professional Conduct, since they must be supervised by an attorney.
   b. may practice law under the supervision of an attorney.
   c. may give legal advice under the supervision of an attorney.
   d. may make "appearances" by signing documents, but not by arguing motions in court.

4. Once a party is represented by counsel,
   a. no attorney may communicate directly with the party without the consent of counsel, unless the party is a corporation.
   b. no attorney may communicate directly with the party unless to communicate a settlement offer in writing.
   c. any party may talk to the party directly.
   d. no party may communicate with the party except through counsel.

5. A paralegal can be anyone
   a. employed by an attorney who performs paralegal tasks.
   b. employed by an attorney who performs paralegal tasks for a governmental agency or a corporation.
   c. whose time is billed by an attorney for paralegal tasks.
   d. supervised by an attorney who meets the qualifications of the Business and Professions Code.

6. An attorney must withdraw if the client
   a. asks about an unmeritorious claim.
   b. asks him to violate professional rules.
   c. insists that the attorney violate professional rules.
   d. has a dispute with counsel over fees.

7. An attorney may withdraw if the client
   a. demands that the attorney pursue an unmeritorious claim.
   b. demands that he violate professional rules.
   c. communicates with another party.
   d. has a dispute with counsel over fees.

8. An attorney may not keep any of his own funds in the trust account,
   a. because all of the funds belong to clients.
   b. because the client must be billed before the funds can be withdrawn.

c. except an amount adequate to pay bank charges against the account.
d. a, b, and c.

9. A paralegal has a duty of continuing legal education
   a. only if she is employed by a government agency.
   b. if she does not have a B.A.
   c. as long as she performs paralegal tasks.
   d. as long as she performs only paralegal tasks.

10. A paralegal can contract to
   a. perform paralegal tasks directly for an attorney.
   b. perform paralegal tasks directly for a client of an attorney.
   c. perform paralegal tasks directly for a consumer of legal services.
   d. a and b but not c.

ALTERNATE ASSIGNMENTS

1. Review the *Auntie Irma's v. Rilling Enterprises* assignment at the end of Chapter 3 of the Study Guide. Assume that you, the paralegal working for the firm interviewing the prospective client, Auntie Irma's Cookie Company, have previously worked for the Rilling Enterprises in the development department.

Prepare a memorandum to your employer describing the situation, and whether you believe it presents a conflict of interest. If that is your conclusion, indicate what steps should be taken by you and/or the firm to avoid the conflict.

2. Review the *Auntie Irma's v. Rilling Enterprises* assignment at the end of Chapter 3 of the Study Guide. Assume that you are the paralegal working for the firm representing Rilling Enterprises. You previously worked for a business broker in Florida who negotiated the deal between Auntie Irma's and Enterprises.

Prepare a memorandum to your employer describing the situation, and whether you believe it presents a conflict of interest. If that is your conclusion, indicate what steps should be taken by you and/or the firm to avoid the conflict.

3. Review the *Whetstone v. Brian* assignment at the end of Chapter 3 of the Study Guide. Assume that you are the paralegal working for the firm representing Whetstone. Prior to this employment, you worked for a law firm that considered a malpractice case against Whetstone, but the client decided not to pursue it.

Prepare a memorandum to your employer describing the situation, and whether you believe it presents a conflict of interest. If that is your conclusion, indicate what steps should be taken by you and/or the firm to avoid the conflict.

CHAPTER 3

INITIATING THE CLIENT RELATIONSHIP

After completing the chapter reading, Discussion Questions, Online Projects, and Assignments, review the material in the following Chapter Outline, then complete the Chapter Objectives, Review Exercises, and Key Words and Phrases. When these are mastered, complete the Online Projects, Additional Research, Quiz, and the Alternate Assignments.

CHAPTER OUTLINE

I. Interviewing the Prospective Client

A. First contact is usually from prospective client.

1. Firm should make sure no deadlines threaten client's interests.
   a. Attorney may be liable for malpractice for failure to meet deadlines of prospective clients.
2. Calls are screened to make sure firm is interested in the case.
3. Call should reveal who referred client.
4. Call can prepare client to bring relevant documents, and firm to review relevant law.

B. The initial interview

1. The firm tries to learn as much as possible about the client and case, and build client confidence.
2. The client tries to find out if the firm will properly represent his interests.
3. Interview is protected by attorney-client privilege, even if lawyer does not take the case.

II. Evaluation of the Ethics of the Prospective Case

A. Attorneys owe a duty of confidentiality to clients.

B. Case must be meritorious.

C. Case must not present a conflict of interest.

1. Attorney could be disqualified for a conflict of interest.
2. Some conflicts can be waived after written disclosure.
3. Paralegals can create conflicts for the firm.

D. Attorney must not be a prospective witness in the case.

E. Attorney must be competent to undertake the case.

III. Business Considerations of Prospective Case

A. The case should be compatible with practice of the firm.

B. The firm should be financially prepared to undertake the case.

IV. Client's Financial Considerations

A. The prevailing party is entitled to recover a reasonable amount of costs, but usually not attorneys' fees.

1. Costs are the out-of-pocket expenses of the litigation.
2. Attorneys' fees are fees charged to compensate the firm for its time.

B. Attorneys' fees may be awarded if

1. there is a contract between the parties that so specifies.
2. such recovery is authorized by a specific statute.
3. the litigation has been undertaken for the benefit of the public.

V. Fee Agreements Must Provide for Reasonable, Not Unconscionable, Fee.

A. Four types of fee agreements

1. Hourly: the client is billed for each hour or portion of an hour worked.
2. Fixed: the client is charged a flat rate.
3. Contingent: if successful, the client is charged a percentage of the recovery, usually 30 percent to 40 percent; if not successful, no fee is charged.
4. Combination: combination of hourly, fixed, and contingency rates.

B. Medical malpractice cases are limited to percentages of recovery.

C. Written agreements required for all contingency cases and hourly cases over $1,000.

1. Contracts may require retainer, deposited in trust account.

D. Fee disputes may be resolved by arbitration.

VI. Undertaking Representation

A. Clients may change attorneys at any time, with or without cause.

B. When the client discharges the attorney, the attorney is entitled to fees for work done.

   1. The attorney may file a lien with the court to prevent distribution of a recovery without payment of his fee.

C. Attorneys also may withdraw from representation, with or without cause.

   1. Withdrawing attorney without cause has no right to his fee.

   2. Unless client agrees, attorney must obtain court's permission.

D. The change from old to new counsel is accomplished by substitution of attorneys filed with the court and served on parties.

CHAPTER OBJECTIVES

1. The initial client contact is important to the client because

____

____

____

2. Name three factors that a law firm evaluates before undertaking a prospective case.

a. ____

b. ____

c. ____

3. What are the four types of fee agreements?

a. ____

b. ____

c. ____

d. ____

4. A document called a ______________________ is used to transfer representation from one attorney to another. The old firm should immediately transfer ______________________ to the new attorney.

REVIEW EXERCISES

Fill in the Blanks:

1. What is the most immediate concern at an initial client contact?

______________________ Why? ______________________

2. During the initial client interview, the firm considers the following five factors in deciding whether or not to take the case:

a. ______________________

b. ______________________

c. ______________________

d. ______________________

e. ______________________

3. Conflicts of interest arise when ______________________.

4. Two examples of conflicts of interest are ______________________.

5. An attorney can be ______________________ if a conflict situation is not handled properly; a paralegal can also cause the firm to be ______________________ for conflict of interest.

6. An attorney must have the skill and experience required to perform the work, or have a plan to get it, or he may violate the California Rules of Professional Responsibility regarding ______________________.

7. In the initial interview, the client should understand the difference between costs and fees because ______________________________.

8. The ______________________________ is entitled to recovery of costs.

9. The law provides that attorneys' fees may be recoverable if

a. ______________________________ or

b. ______________________________ or

c. ______________________________.

10. Written hourly fee agreements are required when ______________________________; or if the lawyer will be entitled to some portion of the recovery from the case, called a ______________________________ fee.

11. When may clients change attorneys?

____

____

____

KEY WORDS AND PHRASES

Provide a Definition for Each of the Following:

Disqualification of counsel: ______________________________

____

Conflict of interest: ______________________________

____

Conflict of interest check: ______________________________

____

Costs: ______________________________

____

Attorney-client privilege: ______________________________

____

Attorneys' fees: ______________________________

____

Public interest litigation: ______________________________

____

Retainer: ______________________________

____

Trust account: ______________________________

____

Lien: ______________________________

____

ONLINE PROJECTS

1. Using the official California courts Web site **(http://www.courtinfo.ca.gov/)**, access and read carefully the court's opinion in *Wager v. Mirzayance* (1998) 67 CA4th 1187. What is an attorney's duty prior to seeking payment of fees from a client? What happens if he does not perform that duty?

2. Using the official State Bar of California Web site **(http://www.calbar.ca.gov/)**, research the form and process for fee arbitration. What is the process for seeking fee arbitration? How is a judgment entered following such arbitration?

3. Using the official California courts Web site **(http://www.courtinfo.ca.gov/)**, access and read carefully the court's opinion in *Stanley v. Richmond* (1995) 35 CA4th 1070. Is the case over? What is an attorney's fiduciary duty? What are the elements of a prima facie case for breach of fiduciary duty? What should the attorney Richmond have done differently to avoid the claim by her client? What role do the Rules of Professional Conduct play in determining the scope of an attorney's duty to his client?

4. Access the Web site at **http://www.weblocator.com/**, and locate the *California Law Guide* and the essay on hiring a California attorney. What does this article suggest about the nature of attorney-client consultations and relationships as Internet use becomes more pervasive?

5. Using the Official California Legislative Information Web site **(http://www.courtinfo.ca.gov/)**, access and read carefully the court's opinion in *Severson & Werson v. Bolinger* (1991) 235 CA3d 1569. How could the agreement between the parties have been drafted to avoid this dispute? Could bills and statements during the relationship have cured the defect in the agreement? Does a written agreement automatically avoid the problems raised in this case?

6. Using the Official California Legislative Information Web site **(http://www.leginfo.ca.gov/)**, locate Civil Code section 1717. How does this code section relate to the fee agreements with clients?

7. Using the Official California Legislative Information Web site **(http://www.leginfo.ca.gov/)**, locate Business and Professions Code section 6148. When is a written attorney-client fee agreement not required?

8. Review the judicial council forms at **http://www.courtinfo.ca.gov/**. Is the substitution of attorneys form in the text current? What is the purpose of the proof of service that is part of the official form?

ADDITIONAL RESEARCH

The following are cases accessible on the official state court Web site **(http://www.courtinfo.ca.gov/)** on various topics of interest relating to this chapter.

Carwash of America–PO LLC v. Windswept Ventures No. 1 (2002) 97 CA4th 540 (distinction between attorneys' fees and costs)

Streit v. Convington & Crowe (2000) 82 CA4th 441 (attorney competence and to whom duty is owed [contract attorney making special appearance])

Alderman v. Hamilton (1988) 295 CA3d 1033 (effect of inadequate contingency fee agreement)

Cazares v. Saenz (1989) 208 CA3d 279 (effect on fees at termination of representation)

QUIZ

1. The most basic purpose of the initial client contact is to determine
   a. whether the nature of the case is within the firm's expertise.
   b. the personality of the client.
   c. the client's ability to pay.
   d. the value of the case.

2. A purpose of the initial client conference is to
   a. get the client to sign a fee agreement.
   b. answer the client's questions, while answering the firm's questions.
   c. determine the client's ability to pay.
   d. determine the value of the case.

3. Which of the following is not an ethical consideration in undertaking a new case?
   a. The attorney may be a witness.
   b. The attorney may not be competent to handle the case.
   c. The attorney may not be financially able to take the case.
   d. The attorney may have a conflict of interest.

4. An attorney with a conflict of interest can be disqualified by
   a. his current client.
   b. his former client.
   c. both his former client and his current client.
   d. the other attorneys in the case.

5. A paralegal with a conflict of interest
   a. should not be concerned because only attorneys can be disqualified.
   b. should not be concerned because the firm is not affected by staff conflicts.
   c. should immediately be concerned because the opposing party could find out if they do a conflict of interest check.
   d. should immediately disclose the conflict to his employer.

6. Prevailing parties are awarded
   a. their costs and fees.
   b. their costs and fees, but only if they have a contract with the opposing party.
   c. their costs and perhaps their fees.
   d. their fees but not their costs.

7. Costs are
   a. the out-of-pocket expenses of the litigation.
   b. the money paid to support staff.
   c. the money paid to expert witnesses.
   d. court filing fees.

8. The following fee agreements must be in writing
   a. contingent agreements but not hourly.
   b. contingent agreements and hourly agreements over $1,000.
   c. contingent agreements over $1,000 and hourly agreements.
   d. agreements for medical malpractice cases.

9. Clients may change attorneys at any time
   a. for any reason.
   b. for good reason.
   c. for any reason if they pay the attorney's bill.
   d. for good cause if they pay the attorney's bill.

10. An attorney who withdraws from a case
    a. may do so only for cause.
    b. might not be paid unless the withdrawal is with good cause.
    c. can hold the client files until he is paid.
    d. must cooperate by filing a lien for his fee.

ALTERNATE ASSIGNMENTS

Assignments in this study guide will follow the same two cases from the prelitigation phase through trial and post-trial motions. Choose one party and prepare the assignments for that party. You may read the facts given for the other side at the end of each chapter, but it will be easier if you do not look ahead to future assignments.

1. *AUNTIE IRMA'S COOKIE COMPANY v. RILLING ENTERPRISES, INC.*

AUNTIE IRMA'S COOKIE COMPANY: Auntie Irma's Cookie Company is a corporation with its principal offices in Seaside City, California. It has several cookie shops throughout Fremont County. It has a license agreement with Rilling Enterprises, an Illinois company that permits Auntie Irma's to use the secret recipe for the Rilling Roll, a fabulously popular cookie, in Fremont County. Auntie Irma's may make and sell the Rilling Roll in Fremont County and advertise it anywhere. The license guarantees that Rilling Enterprises will not sell other licenses permitting sales within Fremont County.

The license agreement is unusual: instead of requiring a royalty of gross sales as most licensees do, it requires no royalty, only a contribution to the national advertising cooperative of 0.5 percent of gross sales, and a yearly fee of $10,000 for updated recipes and new product lines.

Auntie Irma's agreed to pay Rilling Enterprises $250,000 over five years for the license.

Lucille Fitzhugh, who owns 85 percent of Auntie Irma's stock, says that as soon as she made the last payment, Rilling Enterprises opened its own store in Fremont County and began to sell directly to the public. In addition, Fitzhugh says that Rilling breached another contract with Auntie Irma's—an exclusive license to sell the Lacy Irma, a special cookie recipe developed by Auntie Irma's. Rilling was supposed to pay a 10 percent royalty on gross sales. Although Rilling has been selling the cookie for two years, it has failed to pay the royalty or account for any sales.

Fitzhugh intends to sue Rilling Enterprises to stop it from selling the Rilling Roll directly to the public, for breach of the license agreement for the Rilling Roll, for the license agreement for the Lacy Irma, and for damages.

RILLING ENTERPRISES, INC.: Alice Rilling, the stepmother of a good client of the firm, telephoned your supervising attorney from Jacksonville, Illinois, about a licensee of Rilling Enterprises, Inc. in Fremont County, California. Rilling says that the licensee, Auntie Irma's Cookie Company, has breached its license by failing to meet minimum sales standards. Rilling says that Auntie Irma's also breached the license agreement by failing to pay the mandatory $10,000 annual fee for the past two years. Rilling says that Auntie Irma's was supposed to be trying to market and sell the Rilling Roll, but instead it was emphasizing the marketing and sales of the Lacy Irma. Rilling says Fitzhugh has threatened to sue Rilling Enterprises; Rilling says if she's sued, she wants to sue Auntie Irma's and Lucille Fitzhugh for breach of contract, for the unpaid fees, and for damages to Rilling Enterprises, Inc. and the Rilling Roll names.

Rilling will be available by telephone for an initial interview. Prepare a comprehensive list of documents for your prospective client to provide at the initial interview, as well as a checklist of specific questions to be answered during the interview. Your checklist need not exceed three pages.

2. *THOMAS WHETSTONE v. MEGAN BRIAN*

THOMAS WHETSTONE: Thomas Whetstone is a local sole practitioner attorney who usually practices business and real estate litigation. His office is located in Seaside City, California. He was licensed to practice in California 10 years ago. He has never been sued before, and no complaints have been made against him to the state bar.

Whetstone agreed to represent Megan Brian early last year in a personal injury action by Brian against another local business person, Gregory James. Brian claimed that

James had hit her and thrown her down the stairs of a building owned by James. She claimed to have suffered physical injuries, and that she was unable to work as a result of the attack.

Whetstone just recently tried the matter before a jury, but Brian lost. Brian has refused to pay him for his services, about $55,000. He wants to collect his fees.

MEGAN BRIAN: Megan Brian is a local real estate broker. She claims that while trying to show a property to a client, she was physically attacked by Gregory James, a competing broker. She claims that he attacked her on the stairs of the apartment building she was showing and threw her down the stairs, causing her physical and emotional injuries from which she has not yet recovered.

The case was recently tried to a jury by another local attorney, Thomas Whetstone. Brian lost. Now Whetstone wants his fees of more than $55,000 paid. Brian wants to avoid paying the fee and to sue Whetstone for malpractice.

Prepare a comprehensive list of documents for your prospective client to provide at the initial interview, as well as a checklist of specific questions to be answered during the interview. Your checklist need not exceed three pages.

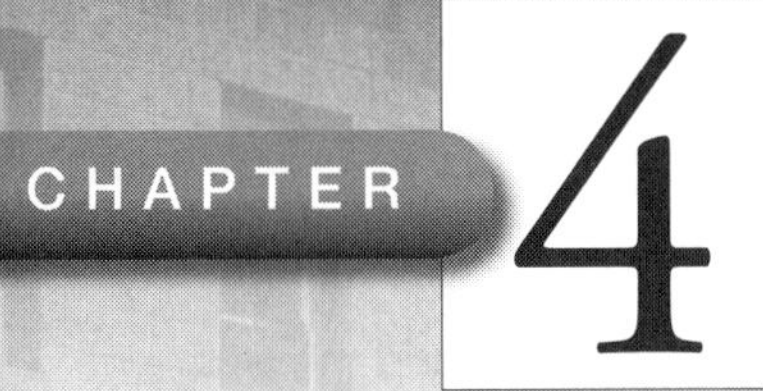

CHAPTER 4

COURTS IN CALIFORNIA

After completing the chapter reading, Discussion Questions, Online Projects, and Assignment, review the material in the following Chapter Outline, then complete the Chapter Objectives, Review Exercises, and Key Words and Phrases. When these are mastered, complete the Online Projects, Additional Research, Quiz, and the Alternate Assignments.

CHAPTER OUTLINE

I. Jurisdiction Is the Authority of a Court to Render an Enforceable Judgment.

A. The court having jurisdiction is a proper forum for the case.

1. Several courts may have jurisdiction over a case.

B. One forum may be more advantageous than another.

C. There also may be a choice between federal and state court.

II. Substantive versus Procedural Laws

A. Substantive law defines the rights and obligations, and any remedies available to redress breaches of the law.

B. Procedural law defines the process to obtain the remedies established by substantive laws.

III. Federal Courts in California

A. Federal courts derive their power to render and enforce judgments from the U.S. Constitution and from laws passed by Congress and the people.

B. Article III of the U.S. Constitution vests the judicial power of the United States in the U.S. Supreme Court, and authorizes Congress to establish "inferior" courts.

1. Inferior courts are the U.S. district courts and the U.S. district courts of "appeals".

2. The U.S. district courts are the trial courts. Decisions made by the district courts are appealed to the courts of "appeals" and the Supreme Court.

3. The U.S. Supreme Court is the highest court in the federal system and the final authority on all federal law.

C. There are more than 90 federal judicial districts in the United States.

D. The federal trial court is the U.S. district court.

1. California has four federal judicial districts.
   a. Central District—Los Angeles
   b. Northern District—San Francisco
   c. Southern District—San Diego
   d. Eastern District—Sacramento

E. District courts also have original jurisdiction over civil actions

1. that involve federal law (including the Constitution).

2. that involve the United States as a party.

3. where there is complete diversity of citizenship and the amount in controversy exceeds $75,000.

F. The U.S. court of appeals is the intermediate court of appeal.

1. There are 12 circuit courts.

2. California is in the ninth circuit, along with Oregon, Washington, Nevada, Idaho, Arizona, Alaska, Hawaii, Guam, and the Northern Mariana Islands. This court is located in San Francisco.

G. The U.S. Supreme Court is the highest court in the United States.

1. It reviews decisions of the U.S. courts of appeals and the decisions of the state supreme courts involving federal questions.

2. It hears matters only by exercising its discretion.

H. Procedural rules for practice in the federal courts are

1. Federal Rules of Civil Procedure (FRCP).

2. local rules.

3. rules for conducting matters in each court, local local rules.

IV. California State Courts

A. The California Constitution authorizes various courts.

1. Superior courts
   a. Each county has a superior court.
   b. Superior courts have jurisdiction in all civil and criminal trial matters, juvenile, probate, and conciliation matters.
   c. Superior courts have jurisdiction over limited civil cases where the amount in controversy does not exceed $25,000.
      (i) Appeals go to superior court appellate department.

d. Superior courts have jurisdiction over all unlimited civil cases where the amount in controversy exceeds $25,000.
   (i) Appeals go to California courts of appeal.
e. Superior courts may order extraordinary writs, naturalization, and dissolution of corporations.
f. Superior courts also handle small claims matters involving less than $5,000 (corporate plaintiffs) and $7,500 (individual plaintiffs), and small claims appeals.
   (i) Attorneys may not represent small claims parties.

2. Courts of appeal
   a. Six districts handle all appeals in civil cases that originated in the superior courts, all criminal appeals except those where a death sentence has been rendered, and writs.

3. Supreme court
   a. is highest court in the state.
   b. issues writs and handles appeals from the death penalty.
   c. can transfer cases before the courts of appeal to itself for review.
   d. exercises discretionary review.

V. Administrative Courts

A. Nonjudicial courts to resolve disputes involving governmental agencies.

B. Paralegals may represent clients.

CHAPTER OBJECTIVES

1. Name all of the state courts that function in California and the jurisdictions of each.

____

____

____

____

2. Name all of the federal courts that have jurisdiction over qualifying cases from California, and their jurisdictions.

____

____

____

3. What is the difference between state courts and federal courts?

____

____

____

REVIEW EXERCISES

Fill in the Blanks:

1. Every court rendering an enforceable judgment in a matter has ____________________. More than one court may have ____________________, but a particular court may be more advantageous than another.

2. Rights and obligations are governed by ____________________ law, while the process to obtain remedies is the province of ____________________ law.

3. Federal courts are established by the ____________________ and by laws passed by ____________________ or ____________________.

4. The federal trial court is the ____________________.

5. The final authority for federal matters is the ____________________.

6. California is in the ____________________ federal district, or circuit.

7. California trial courts are the ____________________ courts.

8. California trial courts can hear ______________________ cases, with amounts in controversy over $25,000, and ______________________ cases, with amounts in controversy less than $25,000.

9. ______________________ hear appeals of state trial judgments of cases with amounts in controversy over $25,000; the ______________________ hears appeals of state trial judgments in cases with amounts in controversy less than $25,000.

10. ______________________ are trial courts where lawyers may not represent clients.

KEY WORDS AND PHRASES

Provide a Definition for Each of the Following:

Jurisdiction: ______________________

____

Forum: ______________________

____

Division: ______________________

____

Original jurisdiction: ______________________

____

Limited jurisdiction: ______________________

____

Unlimited jurisdiction: ______________________

____

Diversity of citizenship: ______________________

____

Circuit: ____________________

____

Courts of appeal: ____________________

____

Small claims court: ____________________

____

Depublish: ____________________

____

Superior court: ____________________

____

Superior court appellate department: ____________________

____

ONLINE PROJECTS

1. Access the Web site at **http://www.weblocator.com/**, and locate the *California Law Guide* and the essay on the California legal and judicial system, court system, and the process of a lawsuit. Using the essay, draft a time line of civil litigation, highlighting important terms.

2. Access the Web site at **http://www.weblocator.com/**, and locate the *California Law Guide* and the essay on constitutional law. What is the role of the U.S. Constitution? What is the role of the California Constitution? Which constitution provides the most protection for its citizens?

3. Access the official California courts Web site **(http://www.courtinfo.ca.gov/)**, and locate the California Supreme Court and appellate court home pages. What on-line resources are available for each?

4. Using the official California courts Web site **(http://www.courtinfo.ca.gov/)**, access and read carefully the court's opinion in *Hammell v. Superior Court* (1932) 217 C 5. What is the rule of the case relating to jurisdiction? Is it applicable to cases with single plaintiffs, or only to cases with multiple plaintiffs? From the clues in the text, what is a "chose in action"?

5. Using the Official California Legislative Information Web site **(http://www.leginfo.ca.gov/)**, locate Code of Civil Procedure sections 85–88. How do these sections define limited and unlimited civil cases? What do you have to know to decide whether a case is limited or unlimited?

ADDITIONAL RESEARCH

The following are cases accessible on the official California courts Web site **(http://www.courtinfo.ca.gov/)** on various topics of interest relating to this chapter.

Trafficschoolonline, Inc. v. Superior Court (2001) 89 CA4th 222 (state court unification)

City and County of San Francisco v. Small Claims Division Municipal Court (1983) 141 CA3d 470 (coordinated small claims filings)

Hammell v. Superior Court (1932) 217 C 5 (effect of joinder of separate claims of less than $25,000)

QUIZ

1. The state trial courts are the
   a. small claims and superior courts.
   b. unlimited superior courts.
   c. small claims and appellate courts.
   d. superior court appellate departments.

2. The federal trial courts are the
   a. small claims and superior courts.
   b. circuit courts.
   c. the district and circuit courts.
   d. the district courts.

3. The court which is the proper forum for the case has
   a. diversity jurisdiction.
   b. original jurisdiction.
   c. jurisdiction.
   d. diversity of citizenship.

4. Appeals from the small claims court are heard by the
   a. superior court.
   b. circuit court.
   c. superior court appellate department.
   d. court of appeal.

5. Appeals of judgments of unlimited civil cases are heard by the
   a. unlimited civil court.
   b. court of appeal.
   c. supreme court.
   d. ninth circuit court of appeal.

6. The state court with jurisdiction for matters over $150,000 is the
   a. unlimited civil court.
   b. superior court.
   c. court of appeal.
   d. supreme court.

7. A state court that can issue writs is the
   a. unlimited civil court.
   b. court of appeal court.
   c. superior court.
   d. small claims court.

8. The intermediate state courts of appeal are
   a. the unlimited civil courts.
   b. the superior court appellate departments and courts of appeal.
   c. the courts of appeal.
   d. the supreme courts.

9. California state courts are established by
   a. Congress.
   b. the legislature.
   c. the state constitution.
   d. the state supreme court.

10. Federal courts are established by
    a. Congress and the U.S. Supreme Court.
    b. the U.S. Constitution and Congress.
    c. the U.S. Supreme Court.
    d. Congress.

ALTERNATE ASSIGNMENTS

1. *Auntie Irma v. Rilling Enterprises:* What do you need to know about the Auntie Irma/Rilling Enterprises dispute to decide which court(s) can hear it?

2. *Whetstone v. Brian:* What do you need to know about the Whetstone/Brian dispute to decide which court(s) can hear it?

SUBJECT MATTER JURISDICTION

After completing the chapter reading, Discussion Questions, Online Projects, and Assignment, review the material in the following Chapter Outline, then complete the Chapter Objectives, Review Exercises, and Key Words and Phrases. When these are mastered, complete the Online Projects, Additional Research, Quiz, and the Alternate Assignments.

CHAPTER OUTLINE

I. Jurisdiction Is the Power and Authority of a Court to Decide a Particular Case or Controversy.

A. The court must have the power to act in the particular type of case (subject matter jurisdiction).

B. The court must acquire authority to act over the parties or the property involved in each specific case (personal jurisdiction).

C. Jurisdiction is initially the choice of the plaintiff at filing, but defendant may object.

II. Subject Matter Jurisdiction Is the Court's Power over the Particular Type of Case and the Ability to Render a Judgment for the Amount in Controversy.

A. Lack of subject matter jurisdiction means judgment is void.

B. Subject matter jurisdiction is determined in state court by

1. establishing the type of case.
2. the amount of money at issue in the case.

C. Subject matter jurisdiction in federal court is determined by

1. establishing the type of case.
2. the amount of money at issue in the case.
3. the citizenship of the parties.

III. Subject Matter Jurisdiction in Federal Courts Is Limited.

A. District courts have limited jurisdiction over

1. federal questions.
2. disputes between citizens of different states or countries, called diversity jurisdiction.

IV. Diversity Jurisdiction Is Jurisdiction over Civil Actions Where the Matter in Controversy Exceeds $75,000 and Is between Citizens of Different States, or Citizens of a State and Subjects of a Foreign State.

A. The purpose of diversity jurisdiction is to provide a neutral forum for citizens of different states or countries.

B. Diversity jurisdiction requires that all plaintiffs be of different citizenship than all defendants.

1. No plaintiff may be a citizen of the same state as any defendant.

C. A state court case qualified for diversity jurisdiction may be removed to federal court.

D. Unless a case is of a specific type that *must* be brought in federal court, the only way to bring a case in federal court is to qualify for federal court jurisdiction, either by involving a federal question or by having diversity jurisdiction.

V. Subject Matter Jurisdiction of California State Courts

A. Divided into limited and unlimited civil cases

1. Limited civil cases: the amount demanded or the value of the property involved does not exceed $25,000.
2. Unlimited civil cases: where amount involved exceeds $25,000.
3. The two types of cases have different procedural rules.
4. State courts must hear eminent domain proceedings, family law and probate matters, adoptions, guardianship and conservatorship proceedings, and corporate dissolutions.

B. May be challenged at any time

VI. Determining the Amount in Controversy

A. The amount in controversy determines subject matter jurisdiction and part of diversity jurisdiction in federal courts.

B. The amount in controversy is specified in the prayer, exclusive of interest, costs, or attorneys' fees.

C. Subject matter jurisdiction based on the amount of controversy attaches at time of filing based on allegation in the prayer.

D. Joinder of causes of action or of claims may defeat subject matter jurisdiction limitations.

E. Joinder of parties does not defeat subject matter jurisdiction limitations.

VII. Exclusive and Concurrent Jurisdiction between Federal and State Courts

A. Exclusive jurisdiction is when cases can only be brought in specific courts.

1. Federal courts have exclusive jurisdiction over admiralty and maritime claims, copyright disputes, cases where the United States is a party, and bankruptcy.

B. Concurrent jurisdiction is when cases may be brought in either federal or state courts.

1. Cases involving federal questions, such as civil rights and federal securities actions, may have jurisdiction in both the federal and California courts.

CHAPTER OBJECTIVES

1. What are the requirements for federal court subject matter jurisdiction?

____

____

____

____

2. What are the levels of California state trial court jurisdiction? What do you need to know to decide the proper level for a specific case?

____

____

____

3. Why might one court be preferable to another in a particular case?

____

____

____

REVIEW EXERCISES

Fill in the Blanks:

1. A court that has the power to act on a particular type of case has

____________________ over that case.

2. A court that has power over particular people or property has

______________________________ over them.

3. If the court does not have the proper type of power or authority, its judgments

are ______________________________.

4. What three things do you need to know to determine whether a federal court has

power over a specific case?

a. ______________________________

b. ______________________________

c. ______________________________

5. Federal courts have power over the following two types of cases:

a. ______________________________

b. ______________________________

6. An unlimited civil case is ______________________________; a limited civil case is

______________________________.

7. When does one determine the amount in controversy?

____

8. Joinder of causes of action may defeat ______________________________, but

joinder of parties does not defeat ______________________________.

9. Examples of cases that have ______________________________ (i.e., may only be

brought in federal court) include

a. ______________________________.

b. ____.

c. ____.

10. Examples of cases that have ____________________ jurisdiction (i.e., may be brought in either state or federal court) include

a. ____.

b. ____.

KEY WORDS AND PHRASES

Provide a Definition for Each of the Following:

Subject matter jurisdiction: ____

Personal jurisdiction: ____

Federal questions: ____

Attach: ____

Diversity jurisdiction: ____

Amount in controversy: ____

Complaint: ____

Prayer: ____

Joinder: ______________________________

____

Cause of action: ______________________________

____

Cross-claim: ______________________________

____

Exclusive jurisdiction: ______________________________

____

Concurrent jurisdiction: ______________________________

____

ONLINE PROJECTS

1. Using the official California courts Web site **(http://www.courtinfo.ca.gov/)**, access and read carefully the court's opinion in *Engebretson & Company, Inc. v. Harrison* (1981) 125 CA3d 436. Subject matter jurisdiction has changed since this opinion was decided. Is it still good law? Why or why not?

2. Using the Web site at **http://www.findlaw.com/**, locate 28 USC section 1332. What does this statute provide for? Where does it apply to California?

3. Using the official California courts Web site **(http://www.courtinfo.ca.gov/)**, access and read carefully the court's opinions in *People v. National Automobile and Casualty Insurance Co.* (2000) 82 CA4th 120 and *Ash v. Hertz* (1997) 53 CA4th 1107. What is the theme of these decisions relating to jurisdiction? The latter case concerns municipal courts, which no longer exist; is the decision still good law? Why or why not? Why is the question of jurisdiction so basic to the process of litigation?

ADDITIONAL RESEARCH

The following are cases accessible on the official California courts Web site **(http://www.courtinfo.ca.gov/)** on various topics of interest relating to this chapter.

Crowell v. Downey Community Hospital (2002) 95 CA4th 730 (parties cannot confer subject matter jurisdiction by agreement)

Chromy v. Lawrence (1991) 233 CA3d 1521 (who may challenge subject matter jurisdiction)

Greener v. Workers' Compensation Appeals Board (1993) 6 C4th 1028 (how to challenge subject matter jurisdiction)

QUIZ

1. To have the power to render an enforceable judgment, a court must have
   a. subject matter jurisdiction over the amount in controversy.
   b. subject matter jurisdiction and personal jurisdiction.
   c. personal jurisdiction over the amount in controversy.
   d. personal jurisdiction over the diversity of citizenship.

2. District courts are courts of
   a. limited, or residual, jurisdiction.
   b. limited, or general, jurisdiction.
   c. limited jurisdiction.
   d. residual jurisdiction.

3. Superior courts are courts for
   a. limited civil cases only.
   b. limited and unlimited cases only.
   c. limited, unlimited, and small claims cases only.
   d. limited, unlimited, and small claims cases; and appellate division appeals.

4. District courts have jurisdiction over cases presenting
   a. either federal questions or diversity of citizenship.
   b. both federal questions and diversity of citizenship.
   c. only federal questions.
   d. only diversity of citizenship.

5. For diversity jurisdiction
   a. all plaintiffs must be of one state.
   b. all defendants must be of one state.
   c. all plaintiffs must be of different states from all defendants.
   d. most of the parties must be from a state other than the forum state.

6. For state courts, subject matter jurisdiction is a question of
   a. which state the case must be brought in.
   b. which level of superior court case it is.
   c. the best court for the case to be brought in.
   d. the ability of the court to render authority over real property.

7. To determine the amount in controversy,
   a. the case must be removed to federal court.
   b. all claims for the case are added together.
   c. all claims on each side are added together.
   d. all claims for each side plus costs and interest are added together.

8. For jurisdictional purposes, the amount in controversy is determined
   a. based only on the complaint.
   b. based on the prayers of each of the parties.
   c. by the court.
   d. by the defendant.

9. Courts that have exclusive jurisdiction over some matters are
   a. superior courts and federal district courts.
   b. limited civil courts, superior courts, and federal district courts.
   c. small claims courts, superior courts, and federal district courts.
   d. courts of appeal.

10. Superior courts have subject matter jurisdiction over unlimited civil cases with
   a. joinder only.
   b. personal jurisdiction.
   c. diversity.
   d. over $25,000 in controversy.

ALTERNATE ASSIGNMENTS

1. *Auntie Irma v. Rilling Enterprises:* What do you need to know about the Auntie Irma/Rilling Enterprises dispute to decide which court(s) has subject matter jurisdiction?

2. *Whetstone v. Brian:* What do you need to know about the Whetstone/Brian dispute to decide which court(s) has subject matter jurisdiction?

CHAPTER 6

PERSONAL JURISDICTION

After completing the chapter reading, Discussion Questions, Online Projects, and Assignments, review the material in the following Chapter Outline, then complete the Chapter Objectives, Review Exercises, and Key Words and Phrases. When these are mastered, complete the Online Projects, Additional Research, Quiz, and the Alternate Assignments.

CHAPTER OUTLINE

I. Personal Jurisdiction Is the Ability to Render a Judgment over the Person and Property Involved in the Dispute.

A. Authority of the court extends to the border of the state in which it is located.

B. Personal jurisdiction can be waived by the person against whom it is asserted by

1. consent through participation in the litigation.
2. mistake or intention.
3. contract.

II. Types of Personal Jurisdiction

A. In personam jurisdiction is the jurisdiction of the court over a particular defendant.

B. In rem jurisdiction is the jurisdiction over the property at issue.

C. Quasi in rem jurisdiction is the jurisdiction over the property of the defendant.

III. Asserting Personal Jurisdiction over Property

A. In rem and quasi in rem jurisdiction are asserted over the property by obtaining a writ of attachment against the property.

IV. Asserting Jurisdiction over an Out-of-State Defendant

A. Long-arm statutes authorize personal jurisdiction outside borders of the state.

B. Defendant can consent to personal jurisdiction by presence within the state or activity within the state.

1. Defendant can consent by general appearance in the litigation.

C. In personam jurisdiction over out-of-state defendant can be general or limited.

1. General jurisdiction results from substantial activity justifying jurisdiction over acts in the forum state unrelated to the activity.
   a. Activity must be "substantial, continuous and systematic" to justify general jurisdiction.

2. Limited jurisdiction results from limited activity restricting jurisdiction to that over the facts out of which the case arose.
   a. Even a single contact may justify in personam jurisdiction if the facts of the case arose out of that contact.

V. Challenging in Personam Jurisdiction

A. Defendant can challenge in personam jurisdiction by making a special appearance.

1. Court must determine whether minimum contacts with the forum state justify jurisdiction.

B. Defendant has choice if his challenge is unsuccessful.

1. Defendant can refuse to defend himself and lose by default, hoping to challenge the judgment when it is asserted against him in his home state.

2. Defendant can defend on the merits.

VI. Nonjurisdictional Issues Concerning the Best Location of the Action

A. Forum non conveniens can be invoked to relocate the case because the forum is seriously inconvenient for the defendant.

1. Where more than one forum has jurisdiction, the California court may decline jurisdiction if California is inconvenient for the defendant.
   a. Courts usually stay the matter until it is brought in the alternative forum.

B. Venue is the best location for the action.

1. Venue is usually, the best superior court within the state to hear the matter.

2. Local actions concerning real property or issues with special connections with the community are brought in that jurisdiction.

3. Transitory actions are unrelated to the community and could have occurred anywhere, so venue is proper where
   a. the personal injury or wrongful death occurred.
   b. the injury to personal property occurred.
   c. the contract was entered into or was to be performed.

4. Where the defendant is a corporation, venue is proper in the county where
   a. its principal office is located.
   b. the obligation or liability arose.
   c. the contract was made or to be performed.

CHAPTER OBJECTIVES

1. What are the three types of personal jurisdiction?

____

____

____

2. How is personal jurisdiction asserted over out-of-state defendants?

____

____

____

3. How is personal jurisdiction challenged?

____

____

____

REVIEW EXERCISES

Fill in the Blanks:

1. The authority of a court extends as far as its _______________.

2. Personal jurisdiction can be waived by

a. _______________.

b. _______________.

c. _______________.

3. The purpose of a writ of attachment is to assert jurisdiction over

_______________.

4. Jurisdiction over an out-of-state defendant is authorized by __________________________, which require minimum __________________________ with the state asserting jurisdiction, known as the __________________________ state.

5. A defendant who wishes to challenge personal jurisdiction may make a __________________________.

6. A defendant who objects to the court chosen for the case on the grounds of serious inconvenience may challenge location on the grounds of __________________________.

7. If more than one court has jurisdiction, and the defendant challenges the location of the case, the court will determine the best __________________________.

8. An action concerning real property is properly brought __________________________.

9. An action against a natural person with no special connection to a location in the state is called a __________________________, and can properly be located

a. ____.

b. ____.

c. ____.

10. An action against a corporation is properly brought

a. ____.

b. ____.

c. ____.

KEY WORDS AND PHRASES

Provide a Definition for Each of the Following:

Forum state: ______________________________

____

Foreign state: ______________________________

____

In personam jurisdiction: ______________________________

____

In rem jurisdiction: ______________________________

____

Quasi in rem jurisdiction: ______________________________

____

Full faith and credit: ______________________________

____

Long-arm statute: ______________________________

____

Waive: ______________________________

____

General appearance: ______________________________

____

Special appearance: ______________________________

____

Minimum contacts: ______________________________

____

General personal jurisdiction: ______________________________

____

Limited personal jurisdiction: ______

______

Default: ______

______

Summons: ______

______

Motion to quash service of summons: ______

______

Inconvenient forum: ______

______

Forum non conveniens: ______

______

Stay: ______

______

Venue: ______

______

Local actions: ______

______

Transitory actions: ______

______

Writ of attachment: ______

______

ONLINE PROJECTS

1. One of the most important cases concerning personal jurisdiction is *International Shoe v. State of Washington* (1945) 326 U.S. 310, located at **http://www.findlaw.com/**. Read the case carefully, and outline the court's ruling.

   a. If while in Washington, the International Shoe salesman had hit a pedestrian with his car, and the case were about those injuries, would the court's decision be the same?

b. If there had been a car accident, but the case were about payment of workers' compensation payments, would the answer have been the same?
c. What if the company sent a pair of defective shoes into the state that caused injury?
d. How does the court's rationale assist in answering these questions, or does it?

2. Using the official California courts Web site **(http://www.courtinfo.ca.gov/)**, access and read carefully the court's opinion in *DeYoung v. DeYoung* (1946) 27 C2d 521. What is the difference between domicile and residence? Why is this distinction important in deciding issues of personal jurisdiction?

3. Using the Official California Legislative Information Web site **(http://www.leginfo.ca.gov/)**, locate Code of Civil Procedure sections 410.30 and 392–6. Read these sections carefully, and determine to what jurisdictional issues each refers, and the power of the superior court with respect to transferring cases.

ADDITIONAL RESEARCH

The following are cases accessible on the official California courts Web site **(http://www.courtinfo.ca.gov/)** on various topics of interest relating to this chapter.

Nobel Floral, Inc. v. Pasero (2003) 106 CA4th 654 (personal jurisdiction over plaintiffs as cross-defendants)

Cal-State Business Products & Services Inc. v. Ricoh (1993) 12 CA4th 1666 (reasonableness of contract forum selection clauses)

Stangvik v. Shiley, Inc. (1991) 54 C3d 744 (forum non conveniens)

Barquis v. Merchants Collections Association (1972) 7 C3d 94 (venue)

QUIZ

1. Personal jurisdiction is really a question of the jurisdiction of the court over
   a. the out-of-state defendant.
   b. the amount in controversy.
   c. the diversity of citizenship.
   d. the "res."

2. The determination of personal jurisdiction is made by
   a. the plaintiff.
   b. the defendant.
   c. the court in the forum state.
   d. the court in the foreign state.

3. The three types of personal jurisdiction are
   a. in personam, in res, and quasi in rem.
   b. in personam, in rem, and quasi in rem.
   c. in personam, local, and transitory.
   d. in personam, personal, and quasi in rem.

4. The purpose of achieving personal jurisdiction over the out-of-state defendant is to achieve
   a. a writ of attachment over his property within the forum state.
   b. minimum contacts.
   c. venue.
   d. the full faith and credit of other state courts.

5. A court may assert jurisdiction over an out-of-state defendant because it has
   a. minimum contacts.
   b. full faith and credit.
   c. a long-arm statute.
   d. venue.

6. The state court has jurisdiction over an out-of-state defendant with a single contact with the forum state if
   a. he makes a special appearance.
   b. he makes a general appearance.
   c. the action arose out of that contact.
   d. b and c.

7. An out-of-state defendant who wishes to challenge the personal jurisdiction of the court may
   a. make a motion to quash service of summons.
   b. default and test the judgment in his home state.
   c. seek full faith and credit of his home state.
   d. a and b.

8. Grounds for challenging the location of the action are
   a. minimum contacts and full faith and credit.
   b. venue and full faith and credit.
   c. forum non conveniens and minimum contacts.
   d. a, b, and c.

9. A transitory action is one which
   a. has a relationship to the county in which it is brought.
   b. has no relationship to the county in which it is brought.
   c. has minimum contacts to the county.
   d. is brought only where the corporation has its principal office.

10. A court orders a stay after a motion based on forum non conveniens because
    a. it assures the action can resume if the other court refuses it.
    b. it has minimum contacts.
    c. it wants full faith and credit.
    d. it wants to avoid a default.

ALTERNATE ASSIGNMENTS

1. *Auntie Irma v. Rilling Enterprises:* For this assignment, analyze the following fact pattern solely from Rilling Enterprises' point of view, and write a memorandum discussing briefly each factor you think is important, indicating whether additional information is required, and giving your conclusion.

Auntie Irma's Cookie Company has threatened Rilling Enterprises, an Illinois corporation, with a lawsuit if Rilling fails to cease operating its own cookie store in Fremont County, account for sales of the Lacy Irma, and pay all of Auntie Irma's attorneys' fees incurred in connection with the dispute. Rilling Enterprises is looking for other potential defendants who may be liable for various aspects of the dispute.

Rilling records indicate that the license agreement for its rights to market and sell the Lacy Irma was negotiated by a business broker headquartered in Florida, Judy Roberts. Roberts contacted Rilling Enterprises by telephone, and told Alice Rilling that Roberts could obtain the license for Rilling. Roberts negotiated the license agreement between Rilling and Auntie Irma's entirely by telephone. The only written records of the negotiations are notes taken by Alice Rilling during conversations with Roberts. Roberts has negotiated many other agreements for other companies within California by telephone, fax, and mail, although she has never been in the state herself.

When Auntie Irma first threatened suit, Rilling contacted Roberts, who said that the Lacy Irma license agreement was drafted by attorney Helen Herschel in Washington, D.C., to Roberts's specifications. Rilling believes that the license agreement itself is flawed, and that Herschel should have advised Rilling of the risks it undertook when it agreed to the contract. Herschel is licensed to practice law in California, although she has never had an office in the state and has never represented anyone in California. Rilling had no knowledge of Herschel's work, and was only aware that the drafting of the license was part of the services offered by Roberts.

Rilling also believes that it may have failed to pay royalties on sales of the Lacy Irma because the outside accounting firm that reviews its books, Mary Hurst and Sons, failed to notify Rilling that payment had not been made. Mary Hurst and Sons has a single office in Waverly, Illinois, and has no clients in or connected with California. It has never had any contact with Auntie Irma's, Lucille Fitzhugh, or any other individual associated with Auntie Irma's. It reviewed the books of the Rilling Enterprise store located in Fremont County, which were provided to it by the Illinois headquarters of Rilling Enterprises; it has never had direct communication with the store.

Rilling also says that a California attorney located in Fremont, Fern Mayhew, helped negotiate the lease for the store premises in Fremont. Rilling claims that Mayhew should have advised Rilling to qualify to do business in the state before entering into any agreements there; Rilling failed to qualify to do business, which may adversely affect its ability to defend itself in any suit by Auntie Irma's.

Rilling says that if it is sued by Auntie Irma's, it wants to name all of these potential defendants in a cross-complaint.

Can any of the four be sued in California? Why or why not?

2. *Whetstone v. Brian:* For purposes of this assignment only, assume that you work for the firm that represents Whetstone. You have heard a rumor that Brian has moved from California to Nevada and is setting up a brokerage/property management company near Las Vegas.

How does this affect Whetstone's desire to sue Brian i[illegible] Sea[illegible]de [illegible]nty, California? Is it likely that she can be sued in Seaside? Why or [illegible] Draft a memorandum addressing these questions.

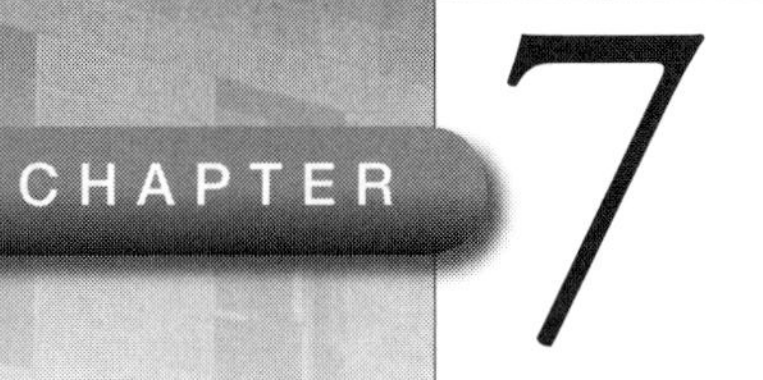

CHAPTER 7

INTRODUCTION TO PLEADINGS

After completing the chapter reading, Discussion Questions, Online Projects, and Assignments, review the material in the following Chapter Outline, then complete the Chapter Objectives, Review Exercises, and Key Words and Phrases. When these are mastered, complete the Online Projects, Additional Research, Quiz, and the Alternate Assignments.

CHAPTER OUTLINE

I. Pleadings Define the Dispute and the Remedy Sought for Presentation to the Court for Determination.

A. The plaintiff states the facts of the dispute and the remedy he seeks.

B. By denying some or all of the facts pled by plaintiff, defendant puts them in dispute.

C. The contradictory claims will be presented for determination at trial.

II. The Purposes of Pleadings

A. Pleadings define the issues.

1. The defendant admits or denies the plaintiff's allegations, defining what is disputed.
2. Only evidence required to decide the disputed facts will be presented at trial.

B. Pleadings serve as a permanent record of the issues.

1. Discovery is limited to disputed facts set forth in the pleadings.
2. The trial is limited to the evidence relating to the pleadings, and the type and amount of recovery available.
3. Pleadings guide the appellate court to the relevant issues.

C. Pleadings satisfy due process requirements of notice to the defendant.

III. Causes of Action

A. Causes of action communicate the affirmative claims against the opposing parties.

1. Federal causes of action are claims or counts.

B. Causes of action are legal theories applied to the facts of each case entitling the plaintiff to relief.

1. Causes of action are composed of essential elements.
    a. A missing element is a fatal defect preventing the court from providing relief.

IV. Types of Pleadings

A. The complaint contains the plaintiff's allegations and prayer for relief.

B. The defendant's answer admits or denies the plaintiff's allegations.

C. The defendant can also file challenges to the complaint, called

1. demurrers in state court practice.
2. motions to dismiss in federal court practice.

V. Affirmative Claims for Relief by Defendants

A. The defendant may assert affirmative claims against the plaintiff or third parties.

1. The pleading asserting causes of action against the plaintiff is a cross-complaint in California state court.
2. The pleading asserting causes of action against the plaintiff is a counterclaim in federal practice.
3. The pleading asserting causes of action against codefendants is a cross-complaint in federal practice.
4. The pleading asserting causes of action against a new, third party to the action by a defendant is a third-party complaint in federal practice.
5. The defendant asserting affirmative claims is either a cross-complainant (state court) or a counterclaimant (federal practice).
6. The plaintiff is either a cross-defendant (state court) or a counterdefendant (federal court).

VI. Real Parties in Interest

A. The real party in interest is the person who has the right to sue under substantive law.

B. The real party in interest has standing to sue, which cannot be transferred to another person.

1. Debt collections, employment disputes, and insurance matters may be transferred from one party to another.

VII. Capacity

A. Plaintiff and defendant must have the capacity to sue and defend.

B. Lack of capacity means that

1. a plaintiff cannot sue.
2. a defendant cannot defend and will default.

C. All natural persons have the capacity to sue, except the following, who must be represented by guardians:

1. minors.
2. incompetent persons.

D. Corporations are statutory persons which do not have capacity to sue or defend if they are improperly formed.

1. Corporations must be certified and pay taxes to have capacity.
2. Out-of-state corporations must qualify to do business and pay taxes to have capacity.

VIII. Joinder

A. Some parties must be joined in the action or any right to recover from them is lost, which is compulsory joinder. Joinder is compulsory if

1. relief cannot be obtained without (him), and
2. lack of joinder exposes the parties to further litigation.

B. Some parties may be joined with the court's permission or sued in a separate action, called permissive joinder. Additional plaintiffs and defendants may be joined if

1. the right to relief arises out of the same transaction or series of transactions.
2. the right to relief is asserted by or against them jointly, severally, or in the alternative.
3. there is at least one question of law or fact common to all the parties.

CHAPTER OBJECTIVES

1. What is a cause of action?

____

____

2. What are the types of pleadings in state court?

____

____

3. What are the types of pleadings in federal court?

____

____

____

4. Name the types of parties in state court practice and their relationships to each other.

____

____

____

5. Name the types of parties in federal court practice and their relationships to each other.

____

____

____

REVIEW EXERCISES

Fill in the Blanks:

1. In her pleadings, the plaintiff sets forth her

a. ______________________________

b. ______________________________

2. In response to the plaintiff's pleading, the defendant may either

a. ______________________________

b. ______________________________

c. ______________________________

3. Pleadings are important to the trial of the case because

____

____

4. Claims or counts are ____________________.

5. Why is it important to have a permanent record of the claims in a case?

____

____

6. Causes of action and counts are made up of ____________________ that are stated as ____________________.

7. ____________________ are those who own causes of action.

8. To successfully sue or defend, the parties must have both ____________________ and ____________________.

9. California corporations must be properly formed and have paid their taxes to have the ____________________ to defend; an out-of-state corporation must also have ____________________ to successfully sue or defend.

10. If relief cannot be obtained without him, a party must be ____________________ in the action.

KEY WORDS AND PHRASES

Provide a Definition for Each of the Following:

Causes of action: ____

____

Allegations: ______________________________

____

Claims or counts: ______________________________

____

Answer: ______________________________

____

Demurrer: ______________________________

____

Motion to dismiss: ______________________________

____

Cross-complaint: ______________________________

____

Counterclaim: ______________________________

____

Cross-defendant: ______________________________

____

Counterdefendant: ______________________________

____

Third-party complaint: ______________________________

____

Cross-complainant: ______________________________

____

Real party in interest: ______________________________

____

Standing: ______________________________

____

Capacity: ______________________________

____

Statutory persons: ______________________________

____

Qualify to do business: ______________________________

____

Compulsory joinder: ______________________________

____

Permissive joinder: ______________________________

____

ONLINE PROJECTS

1. Using the official California courts Web site **(http://www.courtinfo.ca.gov/)**, access and read carefully the court's opinion in *Bank of California v. Superior Court* (1940) 16 C2d 516. If you were one of the persons joined in the case, what does the court's opinion indicate you could do to enforce your rights? Is there a specific standard for joinder of necessary parties, and if so, what is it? What should the court consider when deciding if a party is necessary to the action?

2. Access the Federal Rules of Civil Procedure **(http://www.law.cornell.edu/)** and review rules 7, 17, and 18. What does the FRCP say with respect to capacity and joinder?

3. Access the Federal Rules of Civil Procedure **(http://www.law.cornell.edu/)** and review rules 13 and 14. When and how does a federal defendant plead against other parties? Against third parties?

4. Using the Official California Legislative Information Web site **(http://www.leginfo.ca.gov/)**, locate Code of Civil Procedure sections 426.10 through 428.80. Prepare a list of rules about who and what may be joined in a state case.

5. Using the Official California Legislative Information Web site **(http://www.leginfo.ca.gov/)**, locate Code of Civil Procedure section 425.10. Locate Federal Rule of Civil Procedure rule 8(e)(1) at **http://www.law.cornell.edu/**. Compare the two; how are they different? How will these differences affect pleadings?

6. Using the official California courts Web site **(http://www.courtinfo.ca.gov/)**, compare the Judicial Council of California pleading forms and those in the appendix of the Federal Rules of Civil Procedure **(http://www.law.cornell.edu/)**. How are they different? Which are more useful?

ADDITIONAL RESEARCH

The following are cases accessible on the official California courts Web site **(http://www.courtinfo.ca.gov/)** on various topics of interest relating to this chapter.

Barrington v. A. H. Robins Co. (1985) 39 C3d 146 (liberality in pleading)

Tokyo Marine & Fire Insurance Corporation v. Western Pacific Roofing Corporation (1999) 75 CA4th 110 (failure to prove pleading)

Carlson v. State of California Department of Fish and Game (1998) 68 CA4th 1268 (effect of violation of local rule on pleading)

Stevens v. Superior Court (1999) 75 CA4th 594 (complaints liberally construed)

QUIZ

1. The complaint sets forth the plaintiff's accusations against the defendant, called
   a. the prayer.
   b. the demurrer.
   c. the allegations.
   d. capacity.

2. The relief sought is in
   a. the prayer.
   b. the demurrer.
   c. the allegations.
   d. the standing.

3. A defendant may respond to a federal court complaint with
   a. an answer.
   b. a counterclaim.
   c. a motion to dismiss.
   d. a or c.

4. A corporation does not have standing if it does not have
   a. an answer.
   b. a counterclaim.
   c. a motion to dismiss.
   d. capacity.

5. All affirmative allegations must be answered before a case is
   a. at issue.
   b. in discovery.
   c. joined.
   d. qualified to do business.

6. Causes of action consist of
   a. elements.
   b. parties.
   c. claims and counterclaims.
   d. compulsory joinder.

7. One who is not the real party in interest
   a. has a right to sue but not defend.
   b. has capacity.
   c. has standing.
   d. has no right to sue.

8. Compulsory joinder occurs when
   a. complete relief cannot be granted without the new parties.
   b. the parties already in the suit cannot otherwise be free from further litigation.
   c. the defendant wishes to sue the plaintiff on unrelated causes of action.
   d. a and b.

9. The three purposes of pleading are to
   a. define the issues, record the issues, and guide the appeals court.
   b. define the issues, record the issues, and meet due process requirements.
   c. define the issues, meet due process requirements, and join unrelated issues in one case.
   d. define the scope of the appeal, record the prayer, and join related issues.

10. A cross-complaint in federal practice is
    a. a complaint filed by the defendant against the plaintiff.
    b. a complaint filed by the defendant against codefendants.
    c. a complaint filed by new parties against the plaintiff.
    d. a complaint filed by new parties against the defendant.

ALTERNATE ASSIGNMENTS

1. *Auntie Irma's v. Rilling Enterprises:* Assume that Rilling Enterprises, Inc. names all of the potential parties described in the Alternate Assignment for Chapter 6. Draft a memo discussing which courts have jurisdiction over the case for each party.

2. *Whetstone v. Brian:* Assume that Brian believes that her psychotherapist Masters had not been treating her properly for stress prior to the altercation with Gregory. She wants to sue both Masters and Whetstone for malpractice in the same action in response to the complaint filed by Whetstone. Can she do it? Assuming that she can do it, how are each of the pleadings described in state court? Federal court? How are each of the parties described in state court? Federal court? Draft a memo presenting your analysis and answers.

COMPLAINTS AND CROSS-COMPLAINTS

After completing the chapter reading, Discussion Questions, Online Projects, and Assignments, review the material in the following Chapter Outline, then complete the Chapter Objectives, Review Exercises, and Key Words and Phrases. When these are mastered, complete the Online Projects, Additional Research, Quiz, and the Alternate Assignments.

CHAPTER OUTLINE

I. Drafting the State Court Complaint

A. The complaint, filed and served by the plaintiff, initiates the lawsuit.

B. The complaint is drafted on pleading paper.

C. Failure to comply with applicable rules, including local rules, may prevent the complaint from being filed.

D. The caption is the identification of the drafting attorney, the names of the parties, and the title of the document.

1. The attorney filing the complaint must place his name (with state bar number), address, and telephone number, and identify himself as the "Attorney for Plaintiff" starting at line "1."
   a. If there are several plaintiffs, the designation should specify the party or parties represented.
2. The court name begins on line "8."
3. A box containing the names of all the parties, categorized as plaintiffs or defendants, begins under the court name.
   a. The identities of all parties must be used in the complaint.
   b. Corporations must be identified as such.

4. The case number, provided by the clerk upon filing, is placed opposite the box.
    a. The case number is the name of the case for court purposes, and must be on every document filed with the court.
5. The title of the document appears below the case number.

II. Naming the Defendant

A. Individual defendants can be identified through investigation of tax rolls, telephone books, Internet, and so on.

B. Corporate defendants can be identified through inquiry with the secretary of state.

1. The secretary of state can also indicate whether the corporation is properly formed and qualified to do business, which is important to determine whether the potential defendant has capacity to defend.

C. The plaintiff may identify unknown defendants as "Does."

1. Identification must be supported by two essential allegations.
    a. The plaintiff is unaware of the identities of the "Doe" defendants at the time of filing.
    b. The "Does" are responsible in some manner for the damages claimed.
2. "Does" are universally used in state practice, to permit filing an action before the expiration of the statute of limitations when defendants may be unknown.
3. An amendment identifying the "Does" after the expiration of the statute will relate back if
    a. the plaintiff was ignorant of their names at the time of filing.
    b. the original complaint alleged that the "Does" were responsible for the injury claimed.
    c. the original complaint contained a valid cause of action against the "Does."
    d. the amendment inserting the names of the "Does" is based on the same general facts as the original.

III. The Allegations

A. Allegations are statements of the facts constituting the cause of action in ordinary and concise language.

1. Fact pleading informs the defendant of the basis of suit.

B. The allegations begin with "Plaintiffs allege."

C. Each cause of action is numbered and headed, with a title giving the nature of the allegations and the parties to whom they apply.

D. Allegations are drafted in paragraphs consecutively numbered with Arabic numerals.

1. Any subparts are lettered.

E. Allegations usually introduce parties and facts in succeeding paragraphs as necessary to tell the story.

IV. Drafting Allegations

A. Know the elements of the cause of action to be pleaded.

B. Know the parties and their relationships.

1. Add the two essential "Doe" allegations.

C. Know the facts of the case.

D. Divide the information into paragraphs corresponding to the elements of the causes of action, and relate the facts objectively rather than argumentatively.

1. Conclusory allegations are improper.

V. The Four Pleading Devices

A. Inconsistent allegations allow pleading on every possible theory and every version of the facts as long as

1. the inconsistencies are in different causes of action.
2. the pleading is not verified.
   a. Inconsistent theories may be pleaded in verified pleadings.

B. Incorporation by reference permits incorporation of earlier allegations from other causes of action but presents two dangers:

1. Inconsistent allegations may be made in unverified complaints, but the facts of each cause of action must be internally consistent.
2. Incorporation by reference may result in inconsistent facts pleaded within the same cause of action, or omission of an essential element.

C. Alleging "on or about" permits pleading dates generally.

D. Alleging on "information and belief" is the ability to plead that the alleged facts are believed true and accurate, without the absolute knowledge of their truth and accuracy.

1. This is most valuable for verified complaints.

VI. Pleading with Particularity

A. This is required for some allegations posing a greater danger to the defendant, such as fraud, malice, and breach of fiduciary relationships.

VII. The Prayer

A. The complaint ends with a prayer for relief, which specifies what remedy is sought and establishes the amount in controversy.

B. Personal injury complaints may not state a dollar amount of damages.

1. A statement of damages served after filing specifies the damages.

C. Includes requests for fees and costs.

VIII. Subscription and Verification

A. The complaint is signed by the attorney or the plaintiff.

B. The complaint may be verified by the plaintiff.

1. The attorney never signs the verification.
2. The corporate plaintiff verifies through an officer or director having personal knowledge of the facts alleged.

IX. The Summons

A. Statutes and local rules require service of the complaint within a specific period of time.

1. Prompt service is required within 30 to 60 days of filing, depending on the local rules.

B. The clerk issues and files the original summons at the time of filing the complaint, and provides copies to the filing party.

C. Each defendant is served with copies of the complaint and the summons.

D. Process server must be over 18 years old and not a party to the action.

E. Service informs the defendant of the suit.

1. If served in California, establishes the basis of personal jurisdiction.
2. Service outside California is notice but does not establish jurisdiction.
   a. Contacts with state establish jurisdiction.
3. If served on a defendant who was a "Doe," that fact must be stated on the summons.

F. Individuals may be served by personally delivering the summons and complaint to the person or someone authorized to accept service on his behalf.

1. Minor children are served by serving their guardians.
2. A child over 12 must be served in addition to his guardian.

G. Corporations are personally served

1. by service on agents designated for service of process.
2. by, after reasonable diligence, the secretary of state.

H. Unincorporated business entities are served by

1. serving any general partner, general manager, designated agent.
2. the secretary of state.

I. Local public entities are served by serving

1. any clerk, secretary.
2. head of the governing body.

J. The state is served through the attorney general.

X. The Four Methods of Service

A. Personal service: the process server personally delivers the summons and complaint to the individual qualified to accept service.

1. The defendant must respond within 30 days from the date of delivery.

B. Substituted service: may be made after diligent attempts to personally serve.

1. The summons and complaint is left at the house or business of the individual to be served, with a competent member of the household or person in charge of business.
2. After delivery to the home or business, a second copy of the summons and complaint must be mailed to the same place the first copy was left.
3. Service is complete 10 days after mailing the second copy; after 10 days the 30-day response period begins to run.

C. Acknowledgment and receipt: one copy of the summons and complaint is sent to the defendant, with two copies of a notice and acknowledgment form and a self-addressed, stamped envelope.

1. Service is complete on the date that the defendant signs the notice, which is then returned in the envelope to the server.

D. Publication: after due diligence, a court may allow the plaintiff to serve the defendant by publishing a legal notice in a newspaper, generally once a week for four successive weeks.

1. Service is complete on the last day of publication, after which the defendant has 30 days to respond.

E. Once service is complete, the defendant must respond within 30 days or default.

XI. Cross-Complaints

A. The defendant may, as a matter of right, initiate his own action against the plaintiff by filing a cross-complaint with his answer.

1. The defendant also may file a cross-complaint later with the court's permission.

B. Cross-complaints are independent actions filed by any party to the action against any other party, using the same case number.

1. Cross-complaints may be compulsory or permissive. (See Chapter 6.)

C. An additional box is appended to the bottom of the original caption box. The new box names the parties to the cross-complaint.

1. This becomes the new caption for the entire action.

D. Cross-complaints are served on existing parties with a proof of service; summons and cross-complaint must be served on new parties to the action.

XII. Official Form Pleading

A. Forms comply with all format requirements, such as size and type of paper, layout, and caption style.

XIII. Pleading in Federal Courts

A. FRCP require notice pleading rather than fact pleading as required in state court.

B. FRCP provide an appendix with sample forms.

C. The rules of joinder are generally the same as those in superior court except that

1. the court must have jurisdiction over each third party and additional claim.
2. venue must be proper.

D. There are three types of pleadings for affirmative claims by the defendant.

1. The counterclaim is filed against an opposing party, such as claims by a defendant against a plaintiff.
2. The cross-complaint contains claims by a party against a coparty, such as claims by a defendant against a codefendant.
3. Third-party complaints are against third parties who are new to the original action.

E. Venue is proper where personal jurisdiction is established.

XIV. Drafting Pleadings in Federal Court

A. Federal pleadings contain captions, allegations, prayers, and subscriptions/verifications just as superior court pleadings do.

1. Causes of action are called counts.
2. Facts establishing jurisdiction must be included.
3. *"Doe" pleadings are prohibited*.

B. Local rules provide detailed, explicit, and demanding requirements that will be strictly enforced.

CHAPTER OBJECTIVES

1. Name the three main parts of a complaint and their functions.

a. ______________________________

b. ______________________________

c. ______________________________

2. What are judicial council pleading forms, and when are they used?

____

____

____

3. Name the four types of service of a complaint.

a. ______________________________

b. ______________________________

c. ______________________________

d. ______________________________

REVIEW EXERCISES

Fill in the Blanks:

1. A drafted complaint is prepared on ______________ paper, and begins with the ______________, which identifies the attorney and the party the attorney represents. In order, it then identifies the ______________ (which is placed on line "8") and the ______________ (which appear to the left of center of the first page).

2. The case number is left blank because ______________; it must be placed on all subsequent court documents because ______________.

3. Below the case number, the document's ______________ appears.

4. Information about corporations can be obtained from sources such as:

a. ______________________________

b. ______________________________

5. In state court pleadings, persons who are unknown to the pleader may be named as ______________, which will serve to hold their places in the litigation if the pleader also alleges that

a. ______________________________

b. ______________________________

6. What is the form of a cause of action in a drafted complaint?

____

____

7. What is the content of a cause of action in a drafted complaint?

____

____

8. What is the form of a cause of action in a form complaint?

____

____

9. What is the content of a cause of action in a form complaint?

____

____

10. All pleadings in California state court require ____________________ pleading.

11. All pleadings in federal court require ____________________ pleading.

12. What are the four pleading devices, and what is the function of each?

a. ____

____

b. ____

____

c. ____

____

d. ____

____

13. Prayers for personal injury cases do not contain a dollar amount of damages sought because ____________________.

14. The attorney usually signs the ____________________, but the client should always sign the ____________________.

15. When a federal complaint is filed, the clerk issues a ____________________, which must be served along with the complaint for proper service.

16. Corporations may be served through their ____________________ or, after reasonable diligence, ____________________.

17. Why is a notice of acknowledgment an inefficient means of service?

____

____

18. The parties named in a cross-complaint are listed in the ____________________ as well as in the body of the document.

19. Name the three types of affirmative pleadings a defendant may have in a federal case and the parties against whom they are alleged.

a. ____

____

b. ______________________________

____

c. ______________________________

____

20. Pleading in federal courts is similar to that in state court except that

a. ______________________________

____

b. ______________________________

____

c. ______________________________

____

KEY WORDS AND PHRASES

Provide a Definition for Each of the Following:

Caption: ______________________________

____

Pleading paper: ______________________________

____

Et al.: ______________________________

____

Case number: ______________________________

____

"Doe" defendants: ______________________________

____

Statute of limitations: ______________________________

____

Relate back: ______________________________

____

Notice pleading: ______________________________

____

Verified: ______________________________

____

Statement of damages: ______________________________

____

Subscription: ______________________________

____

Verification: ______________________________

____

Personal service: ______________________________

____

Substituted service: ______________________________

____

Acknowledgment and receipt: ______________________________

____

Publication: ______________________________

____

Proof of service: ______________________________

____

Compulsory cross-complaint: ______________________________

____

Permissive cross-complaint: ______________________________

____

Form files: ____

____

ONLINE PROJECTS

1. Using the official California courts Web site **(http://www.courtinfo.ca.gov/)**, access and read carefully the court's opinion in *Perkins v. Superior Court* (1981) 117 CA3d 1. Do you think that the termination of the home telephone service was intentional? Does it matter to the court's determination on the validity of the pleadings? Why or why not? How could the pleading be drafted to avoid this challenge?

2. Using the official California courts Web site **(http://www.courtinfo.ca.gov/)**, access and read carefully the court's opinion in *Orr v. Byers* (1988) 198 CA3d 666. How did the problem arise? Could it have been avoided? What is the doctrine of indem sonans? Do you think it will continue to be viable in the age of electronic information?

3. Using the official California courts Web site **(http://www.courtinfo.ca.gov/)**, access and read carefully the court's opinion in *Mannesmann v. Demag* (1985) 172 CA3rd 1118. How did the problem arise? What do you need to know to determine whether it could have been avoided? What types of internal office policies could have assisted the plaintiff in avoiding the result?

4. Access the Federal Rules of Civil Procedure **(http://www.law.cornell.edu/)**, and review rules 4 and 4.1. How is a federal summons different from a state court summons? How is service different? Why do you think service is different?

5. Access the Federal Rules of Civil Procedure **(http://www.law.cornell.edu/)**, and review rules 10 and 11. What do these rules tell you about differences between federal and state pleadings?

6. Using the Official California Legislative Information Web site **(http://www.leginfo.ca.gov/)**, locate Code of Civil Procedure section 474. Under what circumstances can a default be taken against a "Doe" defendant?

7. Using the Official California Legislative Information Web site **(http://www.leginfo.ca.gov/)**, locate Code of Civil Procedure sections 415.10–415.95. Prepare a chart of the various methods of service and the additional requirements for proper service in various situations.

8. Review the judicial council pleading forms at **http://www.courtinfo.ca.gov/**. Are the forms in the text current? What other pleading forms are available?

ADDITIONAL RESEARCH

The following are cases accessible on the official California courts Web site **(http://www.courtinfo.ca.gov/)** on various topics of interest relating to this chapter.

> *People ex rel. Department of Transportation v. Superior Court* (1992) 5 CA4th 1480 (fact pleading in official forms)

Careau v. Security Pacific Business Credit (1990) 222 CA3d 1371 (effect of improper fact pleading)

Committee on Children's Television Inc. v. General Foods Corporation (1983) 35 C3d 197 (pleading fraud with particularity)

DeCamp v. First Kensington Corporation (1978) 83 CA3d 268 (permissible attorney verification)

Woo v. Superior Court (1999) 75 CA 4th 169 ("Doe" pleading)

City of Santa Cruz v. Municipal Court (1989) 49 C3d 74 (pleading on information and belief)

Kajima Engineering & Construction, Inc. v. City of Los Angeles (2002) 95 CA4th 921 (incorporation by reference)

Childs v. State of California (1983) 144 CA3d 166 ("on or about" allegations)

QUIZ

1. A defendant serves his cross-complaint on the plaintiff by
   a. notice and acknowledgment.
   b. substituted service.
   c. service of process.
   d. service by mail or hand delivery on the plaintiff or his attorney.

2. Types of service of process which add time to the defendant's 30-day response period are
   a. personal service.
   b. substituted service.
   c. service by publication.
   d. b and c but not a.

3. The following permit the pleader to assert information about which he is unsure:
   a. on or about, incorporation by reference, "Doe."
   b. on or about, information and belief, verification.
   c. on or about, "Doe."
   d. subscription.

4. State court requires
   a. verification.
   b. pleading with particularity.
   c. fact pleading.
   d. notice pleading.

5. A statement of damages
   a. is alleged before the prayer.
   b. provides an amount of damages in personal injury cases.
   c. is required in federal court pleading.
   d. relates back before the expiration of the statute of limitations.

6. Naming "Doe" defendants will relate back if
   a. it is accompanied by two essential allegations.
   b. the pleading is verified.
   c. the pleading is subscribed.
   d. they are identified in the statement of damages served after their identities are discovered.

7. The following must be pleaded with particularity:
   a. fraud, malice, and damages.
   b. fraud, malice, and breach of fiduciary relationships.
   c. fraud, malice, and jurisdiction.
   d. fraud but not malice.

8. Whether a case is at law or equity is determined by
   a. the prayer for relief.
   b. the verification.
   c. service.
   d. the statement of damages.

9. "Cross-complaint" is a term used
   a. in state court only.
   b. in federal court only.
   c. in state and federal court.
   d. only against new parties to the action.

10. Official forms
   a. are desirable because they meet all format requirements.
   b. may be desirable because they meet format requirements, but they still require notice pleading.
   c. may be desirable because they meet format requirements, but they still require fact pleading.
   d. may be desirable because they eliminate the need for fact pleading.

ALTERNATE ASSIGNMENTS

1. *AUNTIE IRMA'S COOKIE COMPANY v. RILLING ENTERPRISES, INC.*:
In the real sequence of events, Auntie Irma's would file a complaint against Rilling Enterprises and Alice Rilling, and Rilling Enterprises and Alice Rilling would respond with either a motion to dismiss or an answer, along with an affirmative pleading against Auntie Irma's and Lucille Fitzhugh. Auntie Irma's and Fitzhugh would then move to dismiss or answer the pleadings against them. In this assignment, the two phases will be completed simultaneously. For this assignment, Auntie Irma and Rilling Enterprises will prepare complaints, counterclaims, and/or third-party complaints on pleading paper. The next assignment will require responses—either motions to dismiss or answers.

Pretend that you are a sole practitioner working at 1234 Main Street in Seaside City; use your actual phone number where appropriate. If you are representing Auntie Irma's, prepare a complaint; if you represent Rilling enterprises, prepare a cross-complaint and/or a counterclaim. The action will be filed in the Western District of the United States district court located in Seaside. Each pleading should contain two counts for breach of contract.

The elements of a contract cause of action are: existence of a valid contract, performance, breach, injury, and damages. The elements of professional negligence are a professional relationship resulting in a duty to the client, and a breach of duty proximately causing injury and damages.

IF YOU REPRESENT AUNTIE IRMA'S COOKIE COMPANY: Lucille Fitzhugh says she and Alice Rilling discussed the Fremont County license agreement for several months before executing the agreement itself. In fact, Fitzhugh attended the Rilling Roll Licensee School before entering into the agreement. At the school, she learned how to make the Rilling Roll secret recipe, and obtained a copy of the Rilling Roll operations manual and several old editions of the Rilling Enterprises Newsletter, sent to all active licensees. Both the manual and the newsletters contain statements that Rilling Enterprises believed that the best and only viable marketing approach was to insist on direct sales to the public only through the licensees, and that Rilling had never attempted to sell directly to the public. Fitzhugh says that Rilling assured her personally that Rilling would not attempt to market or sell cookies in Fremont County; as Fitzhugh points out, she never would have entered into the exclusive and permanent license agreement if she knew that Rilling would compete against her in Fremont County.

Fitzhugh also says that three years into the Rilling Enterprises license agreement, Rilling expressed interest in adding the Lacy Irma to its cookie repertoire. Rilling promised to sublicense the recipe for the Lacy Irma to all of its Rilling Roll licensees, provide a nondisclosure agreement from each sublicensee so that the Lacy. Irma recipe would be protected, account to Auntie Irma's for all sales, and pay all royalties for all of the sublicensees to Auntie Irma's. Fitzhugh says that Rilling never provided any nondisclosure agreements with sublicensees, never accounted for any sales of the Lacy Irma, and never made any royalty payments to Auntie Irma's. Fitzhugh has notified Rilling that the Lacy Irma license is terminated.

IF YOU REPRESENT RILLING ENTERPRISES: Alice Rilling says that Lucille Fitzhugh contacted her a little over five years ago, when Fitzhugh wanted to negotiate a special permanent license agreement for the Rilling Roll for Fremont County, California. Instead of paying a percentage royalty on gross sales, Fitzhugh wanted to pay a very high license fee which would permit her to make and sell the Rilling Roll forever. Rilling Enterprises needed cash at the time, so agreed to the deal. It collected the five $50,000 annual payments. After the last payment, a routine accounting review of the sales for the license revealed that sales of the Rilling Roll in Fremont County had diminished dramatically. As the standard license provides, the licensor was permitted to open another store in the same area, to keep a presence in the marketplace for the Rilling Roll. Rilling Enterprises opened a store, consistent with its policy concerning all licensees failing to meet minimum standards, and began to market and sell to the public.

Rilling also says that about two years ago she wanted to add the Lacy Irma to the list of cookies sold by her licensees. She negotiated a master license with Fitzhugh which permits Rilling Enterprises to sublicense the recipe to all of its licensees, in return for a royalty. However, she and Fitzhugh orally agreed that Auntie Irma's would provide new flavors of the Lacy Irma every year. Auntie Irma failed to provide the new flavors. Rilling Enterprises has received the termination notice for the Lacy Irma license, but it continues to sell the Lacy Irma through its sublicensees.

2. *WHETSTONE v. BRIAN:* In the real sequence of events, Whetstone would file a complaint against Brian, and Brian would either demurrer to the complaint or file an answer and a cross-complaint. For this assignment, Whetstone and Brian will prepare complaints and cross-complaints on pleading paper. The next assignment will require responses—either demurrers, motions to strike, or answers.

Pretend that you are a sole practitioner working at 1234 Main Street in Seaside City; use your actual phone number where appropriate. If you are representing Whetstone, prepare a complaint against Brian for breach of contract for failure to pay fees for legal services totaling $55,000 plus interest at 18 percent. (Assume no requirements for fee arbitration apply.) If you represent Brian, prepare a cross-complaint against Whetstone for professional negligence (malpractice) on behalf of Brian and her real estate brokerage, Brian International.

The elements of a contract cause of action are existence of a valid contract, performance, breach, injury, and damages. The elements of professional negligence are a professional relationship resulting in a duty to the client, and a breach of duty proximately causing injury and damages.

IF YOU REPRESENT WHETSTONE: Thomas Whetstone tells you that he had known Megan Brian for years and had advised her on any number of relatively minor real estate transactions. He had never had a written fee agreement with her, and just sent her a bill at the conclusion of each matter. Sometimes she argued about the amount, and sometimes she paid late, but she always paid him and always paid the 18 percent interest he charged for late payment. She never complained about the quality of his services or the outcome of any matter before. She had been a little erratic in her dealings with him—and with her real estate clients, as far as he could tell—but nothing serious.

Brian called Whetstone a year ago asking for his help in suing Gregory James for assault and battery. Brian had been showing an apartment building in Seaside a few days before when, she said, James had jumped her on the stairs and tried to strangle her and throw her down the stairs. She went to the emergency room, was treated for cuts and bruises, and then released. She had been seeing her psychotherapist Minnie Masters and had not been able to sleep or return to work since the incident.

Brian implored Whetstone to sue James, refusing to see any other attorney. While Whetstone had not done any personal injury cases for a decade, he agreed to represent her, since she was such a good client. He also reasoned that the matter was pretty straightforward and did not require a substantial amount of personal injury expertise.

He represented her and ended up going through a jury trial three months ago. Mel Witnig, a gardener on the property whom Whetstone had interviewed early on in his investigation, had told Whetstone that he had seen nothing; at trial Witnig changed his testimony and said he now recalled that James had been talking to Brian on the stairs when she turned and fell down the stairs—and James had never touched her. The jury believed Witnig, did not believe Brian's testimony, and found against her.

As usual, Whetstone sent her a bill at the end of the matter at his customary rate. The total was more than $55,000. She refused to pay, and he wants to recover the total sum, plus the 18 percent interest that has accrued.

IF YOU REPRESENT BRIAN: Megan Brian tells you she had known Thomas Whetstone for 15 years when she first called him about a small fender bender. She thought that accident had given her whiplash, but after their appointment, the pain went away in three days on its own. Since then Whetstone had advised her on any number of relatively minor real estate transactions. He had never had a written fee agreement with her and just sent her a bill at the conclusion of each matter. Sometimes she argued about the amount, but she always paid him. From time to time she thought his advice was not as sharp as it could be, but his office was in a convenient location near her hairdresser, and he charged $25 an hour less than the other fellow in town, so she stuck with him. She never complained to him about the quality of his services or the outcome of any matter.

Brian called Whetstone about a year ago to tell him that Gregory James, her biggest competitor, had tried to strangle her and throw her down the stairs of an apartment building she was showing at the time. No one had seen the fight, and she was left with serious cuts and bruises, continuing mental distress, and emotional trauma. She called Whetstone about a week after the incident and demanded that he do something to stop James from coming near her, to get James to pay for her injuries, and also to keep him from selling the apartment building to his client, since she wanted it for her own.

Brian recalls that Whetstone had wanted her to come to his office to be interviewed and that he wanted copies of her medical records. However, she was far too distraught to leave her home and insisted that he file something right away so that James knew she was serious. Brian and Whetstone never discussed financial arrangements, although Brian assumed Whetstone would take the matter on contingency, as she understood all personal injury cases were done. During the entire case she insisted that he do everything possible to pursue her case vigorously, and she refused to consider the $45,000 settlement offered by James's insurance company before trial.

She was embarrassed and humiliated when the jury did not believe her account of James's attack. She was outraged by Witnig's testimony and believed that Whetstone should have realized that he would testify as he did before the case was even filed. She was even more outraged when she received Whetstone's bill for services.

Brian believes that Whetstone did not properly prepare the matter for trial and that he should have told her to accept the settlement offer. She is also upset that his bill included $250 for a "paralegal" to chronologize documents for 10 hours at $25 an hour, especially since she knows the "paralegal" is a local high school student.

Brian wants to sue Whetstone for professional negligence.

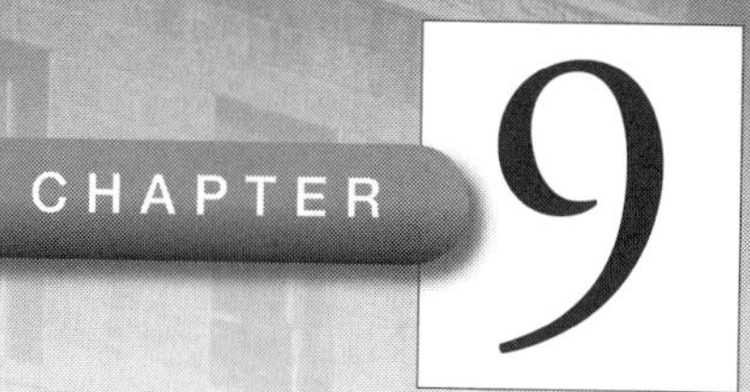

ANSWERING THE COMPLAINT

After completing the chapter reading, Discussion Questions, Online Projects, and Assignments, review the material in the following Chapter Outline, then complete the Chapter Objectives, Review Exercises, and Key Words and Phrases. When these are mastered, complete the Online Projects, Additional Research, Quiz, and the Alternate Assignment.

CHAPTER OUTLINE

I. Answering a State Court Complaint

A. The defendant has 30 days to attack the complaint or answer.

1. If there is no attack or the attack is unsuccessful, the defendant must answer.

B. The answer is the defendant's denial of the allegations in the complaint, not a request for affirmative relief.

1. Affirmative claims are made in cross-complaints.
2. The defendant may assert affirmative defenses in his answer in addition to denials.

C. An answer may result in admitting some facts.

D. Any allegation which is not denied is deemed admitted.

II. Two Types of Denials to State Court Complaints

A. A general denial

1. generally denies all the allegations of the complaint.
2. may be used to respond to any unverified complaint.
3. can deny true allegations since it is not verified.

B. A specific denial

1. admits or denies each allegation.
2. must be used to respond to a verified complaint.
3. must also be verified if it responds to a verified complaint.

III. Denying Allegations

A. Allegations can be denied on information and belief if the defendant is unsure of the facts.

B. Denials of conjunctive allegations can result in negative pregnants.

IV. Affirmative Defenses

A. In addition to the denials, a defendant may assert affirmative defenses, which are based on substantive law.

1. Common affirmative defenses for tort actions include comparative negligence, assumption of risk, and release.
2. Common affirmative defenses for contract actions include statute of frauds, fraud in the inducement, and estoppel.

B. Good sources for additional affirmative defenses are *Summary of California Law* by Witkin and *California Forms of Pleading and Practice.*

V. Plea in Abatement

A. Objects to the facts alleged in the complaint.

1. Claims that
   a. facts not pleaded by the plaintiff would establish that the complaint is defective.
   b. since the defect does not appear on the face of the complaint, it must be asserted in the answer as an affirmative defense.
2. An example of a plea in abatement is that plaintiff lacks capacity to sue.

VI. Drafted and Form Answers in State Court

A. A general denial may be made on an official form or a drafted pleading.

B. The specific denial is usually a drafted pleading.

C. A drafted pleading has a caption, case number, and title.

1. The paragraphs are numbered consecutively with Arabic numbers.
2. Several allegations can be denied in a single statement.
3. An allegation may be admitted in part and denied in part.

D. The affirmative defenses appear after the denials, whether general or special, whether form or drafted.

1. The defenses are listed (e.g., "The Fourth Affirmative Defense: Statute of Limitations").

E. The prayer appears after the defenses.

1. The prayer seeks judgment for defendant.
2. The only relief sought is the expense of defending the suit.

F. The answer is subscribed in the same manner as a complaint, and, if required, verified.

G. The answer is served by mail or by hand, with a proof of service.

H. No response to the answer is necessary.

VII. Answering a Federal Court Complaint

A. The answer serves the same purposes as in state court practice.

B. General denials are not permitted except where the answering party actually denies each material allegation of the complaint, including allegations of jurisdiction.

C. The answer usually must be filed within 20 days of service.

CHAPTER OBJECTIVES

1. What is the sentence used in a general denial?

____

____

____

2. What are the three types of statements used in a specially drafted answer?

a. ____

b. ____

c. ____

3. What are the circumstances when a general denial is an appropriate response?

____

A specially drafted answer?

____

REVIEW EXERCISES

Fill in the Blanks:

1. A state court complaint must be answered within ______________________ days of service; a federal court complaint must be answered within ______________________ days of service.

2. Any allegation that is not denied in an answer is ______________________.

3. A verified state court complaint requires that the answer be ______________________ and signed ______________________, called a ______________________.

4. Denying a conjunctive allegation can result in creating a ______________________.

5. ______________________ are statements that shield the defendant from liability in the event the allegations of the complaint are found to impose liability.

6. Estoppel and assumption of risk are examples of ______________________.

7. That the plaintiff lacks capacity to sue is an example of a ______________________.

8. The three main parts of an answer are

a. ______________________

b. ______________________

c. ______________________

9. Answers are served by ______________________ or ______________________, with a ______________________ because ______________________.

10. In federal court practice, general denials are ______________________.

KEY WORDS AND PHRASES

Provide a Definition for Each of the Following:

General denial: ______________________

Specific denial: ______________________

Negative pregnant: ______________________

Affirmative defenses: ______________________

Admission: ______________________

Plea in abatement: ______________________

Insufficient information: ______________________

Information and belief: ______________________

ONLINE PROJECTS

1. Using the official California courts Web site **(http://www.courtinfo.ca.gov/)**, access and read carefully the court's opinion in *Conley v. Lieber* (1979) 97 CA3d 646. How could the answer have been phrased to avoid the claim that it contained

a negative pregnant? Why did the plaintiff refrain from providing evidence to prove the issues which it claimed were not denied by the negative pregnant?

2. Using the official California courts Web site **(http://www.courtinfo.ca.gov/)**, access and read carefully the court's opinion in *Hulsey v. Koehler* (1990) 218 CA3d 1150. What is the doctrine of res judicata? When must it be specifically denied? Why?

3. Access the Federal Rules of Civil Procedure **(http://www.law.cornell.edu/)**, and review rule 12. How is a federal answer presented? What are the various rules of time to respond?

4. Using the Official California Legislative Information Web site **(http://www.leginfo.ca.gov/)**, locate Code of Civil Procedure sections 431.10 through 431.40. Are there times when a general denial may be filed in an action when the complaint was verified?

5. Using the Official California Legislative Information Web site **(http://www.leginfo.ca.gov/)**, locate Code of Civil Procedure sections 415.10–415.95. Prepare a chart of the various methods of service and the additional requirements of the code for proper service in various situations.

6. Review the judicial council pleading forms at **http://www.courtinfo.ca.gov/**. Are the forms in the text current? What other forms for responses are available?

ADDITIONAL RESEARCH

The following are cases accessible on the official California courts Web site **(http://www.courtinfo.ca.gov/)** on various topics of interest relating to this chapter.

FPI Development, Inc. v. Nakashima (1991) 231 CA3d 367 (nature of pleading in answer)

Walsh v. West Valley Mission Community College District (1998) 66 CA4th 1532 (effect of general denial)

California Academy of Sciences v. County of Fresno (1987) 192 CA3d 1436 (pleading affirmative defenses)

Styne v. Stevens (2001) 26 C4th 42 (effect of statutes of limitations on affirmative defenses)

DeCamp v. First Kensington Corporation (1978) 83 CA3d 268 (attorney verification of answer discouraged)

QUIZ

1. Every allegation of the complaint must be admitted or denied because
   a. every allegation not denied is deemed admitted.
   b. otherwise the plaintiff will demurrer.
   c. otherwise the answer is defective.
   d. otherwise the answer will not be filed.

2. One pleading error for the defendant is
   a. a demurrer.
   b. a negative pregnant.
   c. a denial.
   d. at issue.

3. An answer to a federal complaint is usually due in
   a. 10 days.
   b. 20 days.
   c. 30 days.
   d. 40 days.

4. Common affirmative defenses are
   a. fraud, malice, and fiduciary relationships.
   b. pleaded with particularity.
   c. estoppel and statutes of frauds.
   d. admissions.

5. Affirmative defenses follow the
   a. denials.
   b. specific denials.
   c. plea in abatement.
   d. prayer.

6. A plea in abatement asserts that
   a. the complaint is defective.
   b. the complaint has omitted relevant facts which would reveal defects.
   c. there are admissions in the complaint.
   d. the prayer in the complaint is defective.

7. Affirmative defenses
   a. are excuses for the actions alleged in the complaint.
   b. seek attorneys fees and costs.
   c. seek other appropriate relief.
   d. seek affirmative relief.

8. A federal court answer cannot be a general denial if
   a. the complaint is unverified.
   b. even one allegation of the complaint is true.
   c. it contains a negative pregnant.
   d. local rules require a specific answer.

9. A defendant may file a motion to dismiss if
   a. he challenges a federal court complaint.
   b. he challenges a federal court plea in abatement.
   c. he challenges a superior court plea in abatement.
   d. the complaint contains a negative pregnant.

10. A defendant in superior court must file a specific denial
    a. in response to a verified complaint.
    b. in response to an unverified complaint.
    c. in response to a plea in abatement.
    d. to avoid a demurrer.

ALTERNATE ASSIGNMENT

1. Draft an answer to the affirmative pleading served by your opposing party in *Auntie Irma's v. Rilling Enterprises* and/or *Whetstone v. Brian*.

CHAPTER 10

ATTACKING THE PLEADINGS

After completing the chapter reading, Discussion Questions, Online Projects, and Assignment, review the material in the following Chapter Outline, then complete the Chapter Objectives, Review Exercises, and Key Words and Phrases. When these are mastered, complete the Online Projects, Additional Research, Quiz, and the Alternate Assignments.

CHAPTER OUTLINE

I. Attacking the Pleadings in State Court

A. There are three substantive reasons to attack the complaint.

1. An attack can narrow the issues.
2. Attacking the pleadings will clarify the legal issues at the outset.
3. An attack on the pleadings may be necessary to remove extraneous claims that do not belong in the complaint.

B. There are three strategic reasons to attack the pleadings.

1. Attacking the pleadings sets the tone for the litigation.
2. Issues over the validity of a cause of action will be resolved, saving time and money.
3. Attacking the pleadings may shorten the trial and save money.

C. Attacking the complaint is not automatic because

1. it can be expensive.
2. the plaintiff is usually allowed to correct any defect in his pleading, resulting in only a short delay.

II. Demurrers and Motions for Judgment on the Pleadings

A. The demurrer tests the legal sufficiency of the complaint filed in superior court.

1. The demurrer assumes that all of the allegations on the face of the complaint are true, and asserts only that what has been pleaded, even if true, is defective.

2. A demurrer is a pleading, but unlike a complaint, cross-complaint, and answer, it is made as a motion and requests a judicial determination.

3. It cannot refer to matters outside the face of the complaint, except to bring matters subject to judicial notice to the court's attention.

B. General demurrers

1. General demurrers claim that the court lacks jurisdiction to handle the matter, usually because
   a. the complaint fails to state facts sufficient to constitute a cause of action or
   b. the court lacks jurisdiction over the matter.

2. Because there is no jurisdiction, failure to demur does not waive the defect, which can be brought at any time in the litigation, including trial and appeal.
   a. Later attacks on these grounds are made in motions for summary judgment, or for judgment on the pleadings.

3. General demurrers are useful only when they will resolve the litigation.

C. Special demurrers

1. Special demurrers are only brought in unlimited civil cases on five specific grounds.
   a. lack of capacity
   b. another action pending
   c. defective joinder
   d. uncertainty in the allegations
   e. failure to allege that a contract was oral or written

2. If not raised, special demurrers are waived.

3. The special demurrer should only be brought if it will dispose of the action.

D. A demurrer also is rarely made to answers that fail to state sufficient facts to constitute a defense, are uncertain, or fail to specify a written or oral contract (if the existence of a contract is asserted as a defense).

III. Demurrer Procedures

A. A demurrer must be filed within 30 days from service of the complaint; a demurrer to an answer must be filed within 10 days of service of the answer.

B. The hearing must be set within 35 days from the date of filing the demurrer or as soon thereafter as the court's calendar permits.

C. A party filing a demurrer is not required to file an answer until his demurrer is overruled.

D. The demurrer may dispose of the entire action or attack only one of several causes of action; a partial demurrer delays an answer on the entire complaint.

E. A demurrer is a short pleading stating the grounds of the demurrer, a notice of motion that tells the other parties where and when the hearing will be held, and a memorandum of points and authorities that outlines the substantive law supporting the demurrer.

F. If the demurrer is sustained, the court will usually permit an amendment, and if so, it is usually due within 10 days.

   1. If amendment is not possible, the pleading will be dismissed and the case is over.

G. If the demurrer is overruled, the demurring party is ordered to answer, usually within 10 days.

IV. Motions to Strike

A. A motion to strike requests that the court strike a pleading that

   1. has been filed or drafted in conflict with the CRC, CCP, or
   2. is in violation of a direct order of the court, or
   3. contains false, irrelevant, or improper matter.

B. It is usually filed with a demurrer.

C. A motion to strike is a motion, but since it is not a pleading, it does not require a separate pleading document.

D. A motion to strike is a general appearance.

V. Two Types of Pleading Attacks in Federal Court

A. Motions challenging the pleadings themselves are motions to dismiss.

   1. An order granting the motion does not dismiss the *action*, just the pleading at issue in the motion.

B. Motions challenging jurisdiction and venue are also motions to dismiss, and must be brought or waived for the following grounds:

   1. lack of personal jurisdiction
   2. improper venue
   3. defective service of process

C. Nonwaivable grounds permitting challenge at any time are

   1. lack of subject matter jurisdiction.
   2. failure to join an indispensable party.
   3. failure to state a claim upon which relief can be granted.

CHAPTER OBJECTIVES

1. What is the function of a demurrer?

____

____

____

2. What are the two types of demurrer, and when is each properly imposed?

a. ______

b. ______

3. What are the parts of a demurrer, and what does each contain?

______

______

______

REVIEW EXERCISES

Fill in the Blanks:

1. Why demurrer?

a. ______

b. ______

c. ______

d. ______

e. ______

f. ______

2. What are the disadvantages of demurring?

a. ______

b. ______

3. When does one move for judgment on the pleadings?

______

4. Why is the demurrer called the "so what?" motion?

____

____

5. Demurrers rely on what is shown on the face of the complaint or answer, or what can be ____________________.

6. A demurrer is different from other pleadings because ____________________.

7. Challenges to the complaint for ____________________, called ____________________ demurrers, can be made at any time in the litigation.

8. Uncertainty is a ground for a ____________________ demurrer.

9. Demurrers must be filed within ____________________ days of service.

10. Hearings on demurrers must be held within ____________________ or, if there is court congestion, ____________________.

11. ____________________ can only be asserted against complaints in ____________________ civil actions.

12. What happens if the demurrer is sustained with leave to amend?

____

____

____

13. What happens if the demurrer is sustained without leave to amend?

____

____

____

14. What happens if the demurrer is overruled?

____

____

____

15. What are the three main parts of a demurrer?

a. ______________________________

b. ______________________________

c. ______________________________

16. A ______________________ challenges a state court pleading, but it is not a pleading.

17. A ______________________ challenges a federal court pleading, but is not a pleading.

18. A ______________________ challenges the jurisdiction of a federal court over a pleading.

19. Failure to name an indispensable party is grounds for a ______________________.

20. Failure to state a claim upon which relief can be granted is grounds for a ______________________ in state court, and a ______________________ in federal court.

KEY WORDS AND PHRASES

Provide a Definition for Each of the Following:

Motion to strike: ______________________

____

Motion for judgment on the pleadings: ______________________

____

General demurrer: ______________________

____

Special demurrer: ______________________

____

Sustained: ______________________

____

Overruled: ______________________

____

ONLINE PROJECTS

1. Using the official California courts Web site **(http://www.courtinfo.ca.gov/)**, access and read carefully the court's opinion in *Department of Transportation v. Superior Court* (1992) 5 CA4th 1480. If judicial council forms are subject to demurrer, of what benefit are they? How could the forms have been drafted in this case to avoid the challenge of the demurrer?

2. Using the official California courts Web site **(http://www.courtinfo.ca.gov/)**, access and read carefully the court's opinion in *Blank v. Kirwan* (1985) 39 C3d 311. What are the "long settled rules" concerning demurrers? What does this opinion suggest about the art of pleading complaints?

3. Using the official California courts Web site **(http://www.courtinfo.ca.gov/)**, access and read carefully the court's opinion in *Guardian North Bay, Inc. v. Superior Court* (2001) 94 CA4th 963. Were these demurrers brought on technical

grounds, or were they testing new law? What would have happened had they not been brought?

4. Using the Official California Legislative Information Web site **(http://www.leginfo.ca.gov/)**, locate Code of Civil Procedure section 425.16. This code section authorizes a motion to strike SLAPP suits. What is a SLAPP suit? Why is such a procedure necessary? Outline the procedure involved in a motion to strike under this code section.

5. Access the Federal Rules of Civil Procedure **(http://www.law.cornell.edu/)**, and review rule 12. What is another means of challenging a federal complaint for uncertainty?

6. Using the Official California Legislative Information Web site **(http://www.leginfo.ca.gov/)**, locate Code of Civil Procedure sections 435 and 436, access the Federal Rules of Civil Procedure **(http://www.law.cornell.edu/)**, and review rule 12. How are the rules for moving to strike a state court complaint different from the federal rules for motions to dismiss?

7. Using the Official California Legislative Information Web site **(http://www.leginfo.ca.gov/)**, locate Code of Civil Procedure section 430.80. What does this code section suggest about the decision to demurrer?

8. Using the Official California Legislative Information Web site **(http://www.leginfo.ca.gov/)**, locate Evidence Code sections 451 and 452. What do these sections communicate is judicially noticeable material that could be considered by demurrer? Develop a list of 10 examples of judicially noticeable matter.

ADDITIONAL RESEARCH

The following are cases accessible on the official California courts Web site **(http://www.courtinfo.ca.gov/)** on various topics of interest relating to this chapter.

Hamilton v. Asbestos Corporation, Ltd. (2000) 22 CA4th 1127 (demurrer as general appearance and pleading)

Rains v. Superior Court (1984) 150 CA3d 933 (demurrer as motion)

Guardian North Bay, Inc. v. Superior Court (2001) 94 CA4th 963 (demurrer challenging defects appearing on face of complaint)

Del E. Webb Corporation v. Structural Materials Company (1981) 123 CA3d 593 (demurrer must treat even unlikely allegations as true)

Angie M. v. Superior Court (1995) 37 CA4th 1217 (leave to amend liberally given)

QUIZ

1. Reasons to attack a state court complaint include
   a. narrowing the issues.
   b. setting the tone for the litigation.
   c. moving the case to law and motion court.
   d. a and b but not c.

2. Reasons to attack a federal court complaint
   a. are the same as those in state court.
   b. are the same as those in state court except they do not include attempts to strike offensive matter.

c. are the same as those in state court except they do not include attempts to challenge jurisdiction and venue.
d. are not the same as those in state court.

3. A demurrer must assume that
   a. the complaint can be amended.
   b. all of the allegations in the complaint are true.
   c. the court will automatically review its jurisdiction.
   d. the expense and delay justify the motion.

4. A general demurrer may assert that
   a. the offensive matter in the complaint must be stricken.
   b. the plaintiff lacks capacity.
   c. the court lacks jurisdiction.
   d. venue is improper.

5. A special demurrer may assert
   a. lack of capacity, defective joinder, and uncertainty.
   b. lack of capacity, defective joinder, and improper venue.
   c. lack of capacity, improper venue, and uncertainty.
   d. lack of capacity.

6. A defendant demurring to part of the complaint
   a. must answer the rest within the 30 days permitted to respond.
   b. will be overruled since partial demurrers are not permitted.
   c. need not answer the remainder of the complaint.
   d. must always file a special demurrer.

7. If a complaint is not challenged within the time to respond,
   a. venue is waived.
   b. the demurrer can be brought later if it is based on jurisdictional grounds.
   c. the defects sometimes can be challenged by other motions later.
   d. the defects must be challenged by a summary judgment motion.

8. In federal court, special and general demurrers are replaced by
   a. law and motion.
   b. motions for judgment on the pleadings.
   c. motions to strike.
   d. motions to dismiss.

9. If a special demurrer is not brought within the time to respond,
   a. it can be brought later in a motion for summary judgment.
   b. it can be brought later in a motion for judgment on the pleadings.
   c. it can be brought later as a motion to dismiss.
   d. it is waived forever.

10. If the federal court agrees with the challenge to the complaint,
    a. the action is over.
    b. the complaint is dismissed.
    c. the plaintiff can usually amend.
    d. b and c but not a.

ALTERNATE ASSIGNMENTS

1. *Auntie Irma's v. Rilling Enterprises:* Prepare an answer or demurrer to the pleading you received in *Auntie Irma's v. Rilling Enterprises*. If you can move to strike, do so, even though you might choose not to in real life for economic reasons. Consider the following facts obtained from your client, as well as all of the facts provided in previous alternate assignments.

AUNTIE IRMA'S knows that Rilling Enterprises is not qualified to do business in California. It has had the Fremont County store for several months but has not even notified the secretary of state that it is doing business in California. Nor has it obtained a business license for Fremont County. It is doing business under the name "Lucille's Rilling Rolls" but has failed to file a "doing business as" application in the county.

Fitzhugh has also learned that Rilling Enterprises has sublicensed the Lacy Irma to more than a hundred cookie shops all over the country, and should have paid royalties of at least $150,000—maybe twice that—to Auntie Irma's over the last two years. It has also failed to obtain nondisclosure agreements from the sublicensees, so that the Lacy Irma recipe is not protected. Rilling Enterprises has also bragged to many sublicensees that it developed the Lacy Irma.

Fitzhugh remembers discussing her intention to add new Lacy Irma flavors each year with Rilling, but it was never part of any contract. Since flavors are hard to add, and depend on expensive market research and food engineering, it would have been foolhardy to promise new flavors as part of a contract.

Fitzhugh acknowledges that sales of the Rilling Roll by her shop have fallen below the minimum required of Rilling Roll licensees, but points out that since she doesn't pay a royalty based on sales, and has already paid all of the fees connected with the license, the amount of sales is irrelevant to Auntie Irma's. In fact, she intended to get the Rilling Roll license mostly to control the cookie's availability in Fremont County while developing and marketing the Lacy Irma.

RILLING ENTERPRISES now realizes that it is not qualified to do business in California and needs to get a business license and a "dba" for the name of the shop in Fremont County, "Lucille's Rilling Rolls." It will take about two weeks to qualify and get the business license; it will take about five weeks to get the "dba" published. The response is due next week.

Rilling says that it has sublicensed the Lacy Irma to dozens of shops throughout the country, including two in Southern California. It did not get a separate nondisclosure agreement from each sublicensee because the license agreement from Rilling Enterprises to each licensee provides for nondisclosure of any recipe provided to the individual cookie shop licensees; Rilling claims that another nondisclosure agreement is unnecessary. Rilling also claims that before signing the master license agreement for the Lacy Irma, Lucille Fitzhugh orally promised that Auntie Irma's would add a new flavor cookie to the Lacy Irma line every year; it has failed to do so. This failure is the reason she gives for Rilling Enterprises' refusal to pay royalties for the Lacy Irma.

Rilling says that its standard license agreement permits Rilling Enterprises to take over shops which have failed to meet minimum sales standards. It reasons that if the shop does poorly, it reflects badly on the entire company and all of the other licensees. It has taken over several shops in other states, and has opened its own stores in two states when it felt that the location of the licensee's store was a reason for poor performance.

Rilling also says that at the time it sold the license to Auntie Irma's, it intended to open its own shops and market directly to the public. She acknowledges that prior to that time the operations manual and newsletters implied that Rilling Enterprises would not open its own shops. Rilling also strenuously questions whether the federal district court has jurisdiction over Rilling Enterprises, since it is headquartered in Illinois and has few contacts with California.

2. *Whetstone v. Brian:* Prepare an answer or motion to dismiss the pleading you received in *Whetstone v. Brian*. If you can move to strike, do so, even though you might choose not to in real life for economic reasons. Consider the following facts obtained from your client, as well as all of the facts provided in previous alternate assignments.

WHETSTONE knows that Megan Brian's real estate license had expired by the time of the alleged James attack and has not been renewed. In addition, he knows that Brian International's dba expired several years ago and has not been renewed.

Brian also told Whetstone for the first time during the trial that she was in dire financial straights and did not know if she could survive if she did not win big with James.

Brian says that since she never had a written fee agreement with Whetstone, he cannot sue her for fees.

CHAPTER 11

AMENDING THE PLEADINGS

After completing the chapter reading, Discussion Questions, Online Projects, and Assignments, review the material in the following Chapter Outline, then complete the Chapter Objectives, Review Exercises, and Key Words and Phrases. When these are mastered, complete the Online Projects, Additional Research, Quiz, and the Alternate Assignments.

CHAPTER OUTLINE

I. Amending State Court Pleadings

A. An amended pleading replaces the previous pleading, so must be a complete statement of all allegations.

B. An amendment is a supplementary allegation augmenting the original pleading.

II. Amending by Right in State Court

A. Complaints and cross-complaints may be amended once as a matter of right before

1. service of the answer.
2. filing a demurrer.
3. the demurrer hearing.

B. An answer may be amended once before the hearing of the demurrer to the answer.

C. Any new matter within the statute of limitations may be pleaded, against existing or new parties.

1. Amendments barred by the statute of limitations must be based on the same general set of facts already pleaded.

III. Amending by Leave of State Court

A. Any amendment after the answer must be by order of court obtained by a motion for leave to amend a cross-complaint.

1. Some requests for leave to amend may be ex parte.
    a. Ex parte applications for leave to amend include amendments substituting defendant's true name for a "Doe" defendant, and correcting a misspelled name.

B. Material changes must be made by noticed motion, which includes a copy of the proposed amended pleading.

1. If the motion is granted, the pleading may be filed and served by mail on the parties who have appeared.
2. The responding parties have the statutory time to respond, unless shortened by the court in its order.

C. Courts liberally grant leave

1. to encourage the parties to have the case decided on the merits rather than on technicalities.
2. for judicial economy.

D. The court does not review the amendment for validity but will consider

1. the proximity to trial.
2. prejudice to other parties.

IV. Relation Back Doctrine

A. A complaint must be filed within the statute of limitations.

B. Once filed, the complaint tolls the statute of limitations.

C. When a party wishes to amend his pleading to add claims against existing parties to the action which would have run except for the filing of the complaint, the claims may relate back if

1. the amended pleading is based on the same general set of facts as the original,
2. it seeks damages for the same injuries, AND
3. it refers to the same occurrence.

D. When a party wishes to amend his pleading to add claims against new parties to the action which would have run except for the filing of the complaint, the claims may relate back if

1. the original pleading named sufficient "Doe" defendants,
2. the original pleading stated a cause of action against the "Does,"
3. the pleader was genuinely ignorant of the identity of the "Does" at the time of filing the original pleading, and
4. it meets the three requirements applicable to new claims against existing parties.

V. Amending Pleadings in Federal Court

A. An amendment or amended pleading in federal court changes allegations concerning matters occurring before the original pleading was filed.

B. A supplemental pleading refers to matters occurring after the filing of the original pleading.

C. Federal pleadings may be amended once as a matter of right after filing but before response; thereafter, leave of court is required.

D. Federal courts consider the same factors as superior courts do in granting leave; federal courts also liberally grant leave.

CHAPTER OBJECTIVES

1. What is the difference between an amended pleading and an amendment?

____

____

____

2. When may a party serve an amended pleading by right?

____

____

3. When—and how—is leave of court obtained to amend a pleading?

____

____

____

____

REVIEW EXERCISES

Fill in the Blanks:

1. An ____________________ completely replaces the previous pleading.

2. A complaint may be amended once by right, either

a. ______________________________

b. ______________________________

c. ______________________________

3. A cross-complaint may be amended once by right, either

a. ______________________________

b. ______________________________

c. ______________________________

4. Answers may be amended once by right before ______________________________.

5. Amendment by leave of court requires ______________________________.

6. Requests to make pleading changes that are not material can be presented to the court in ______________________________.

7. Why do courts liberally grant requests to amend pleadings?

a. ______________________________ and

b. ______________________________

8. What is the relation back doctrine?

____

____

____

9. What are the three requirements for amending a pleading to name "Doe" defendants?

a. ______________________________

____

b. ______________________________

____

c. ______________________________

10. When asked to amend a pleading, federal courts consider

a. ______________________________ and

b. ______________________________;

state courts consider

c. ______________________________ and

d. ______________________________.

KEY WORDS AND PHRASES

Provide a Definition for Each of the Following:

Amended pleading: ______________________________

____

Amendment: ______________________________

____

Leave of court: ______________________________

____

Ex parte: ______________________________

____

Tolling the statute of limitations: ______________________________

____

Supplemental pleading: ______________________________

____

ONLINE PROJECTS

1. Using the official California courts Web site (**http://www.courtinfo.ca.gov/**), access and read carefully the court's opinion in *Parker v. McKee* (1992) 3 CA4th 512. Is this case about the relation back doctrine? Why or why not? What does it tell you about dismissing parties?

2. Using the official California courts Web site (**http://www.courtinfo.ca.gov/**), access and read carefully the court's opinion in *Herrera v. Superior Court* (1984) 158 CA3d 255. Why might a party seeking leave to amend a complaint cite this case? How did the trial court err in denying Herrera's motion? What is the result in the case concerning amending the pleadings?

3. Access the Federal Rules of Civil Procedure (**http://www.law.cornell.edu/**) and review rule 15. What is the federal relation back doctrine? How and why is it different from California's? What is the difference between an amendment and a supplemental pleading?

4. Using the Official California Legislative Information Web site (**http://www.leginfo.ca.gov/**), locate Code of Civil Procedure sections 471, 472, and 472b. What do these tell you about amending a complaint following a successful demurrer? What do these tell you about the response time for amended pleadings?

5. Using the Official California Legislative Information Web site (**http://www.leginfo.ca.gov/**), locate Code of Civil Procedure section 474. When and how are "Doe" defendants properly named?

ADDITIONAL RESEARCH

The following are cases accessible on the Official California Legislative Information Web site (**http://www.courtinfo.ca.gov/**) on various topics of interest relating to this chapter.

Angie M. v. Superior Court (1995) 37 CA4th 1217 (leave to amend liberally given)

Morgan v. Superior Court (1959) 172 CA2d 527 (denial of leave to amend rarely justified)

People v. Clausen (1967) 248 CA2d 770 (limits on amending following demurrer)

Woo v. Superior Court (1999) 75 CA4th 169 (right to amend)

Ryan G. v. Department of Transportation (1986) 180 CA3d 1102 (amendments permitted)

Austin v. Massachusetts Bonding and Insurance Company (1961) 56 C2d 596 (effect of amending after statute of limitations expired)

QUIZ

1. A state court pleading which changes the original pleading by adding a single allegation is
   a. an amended pleading.
   b. an amendment.
   c. a supplemental pleading.
   d. by leave of court.

2. A state court pleading which replaces the original pleading is
   a. an amended pleading.
   b. an amendment.
   c. a supplemental pleading.
   d. by leave of court.

3. A federal pleading referring to matters occurring before the original pleading was filed is
   a. an amended pleading.
   b. an amendment.
   c. a supplemental pleading.
   d. by leave of court.

4. A federal pleading referring to matters occurring after the filing of the original pleading is
   a. an amended pleading.
   b. an amendment.
   c. a supplemental pleading.
   d. by leave of court.

5. An order of the court permitting the filing of a new allegation or changing an existing pleading is
   a. an amended pleading.
   b. an amendment.
   c. a supplemental pleading.
   d. by leave of court.

6. An amended pleading that asserts new claims against existing parties and refers to matters against which the statute of limitations has expired will relate back if
   a. it is based on the same facts, asserts the same injuries, and has tolled the statute of limitations.
   b. it is based on the same facts, asserts the same injuries, and refers to the same occurrence.
   c. it is based on the same facts, asserts the same injuries, and has enough "Doe" allegations.
   d. it is based on the same facts and asserts the same injuries.

7. An amended pleading that asserts new claims against new parties and refers to matters against which the statute of limitations has expired will relate back if
   a. it is based on the same facts, asserts the same injuries, and has tolled the statute of limitations.
   b. it is based on the same facts, asserts the same injuries, and refers to the same occurrence.
   c. the pleader was previously ignorant of the parties' identities, previously alleged a cause of action against them, and named sufficient "Does."
   d. b and c.

8. The superior court's consideration of leave to file
   a. occurs before the response is filed to the original pleading.
   b. is based on the validity of the new allegations.

c. is always ex parte.
d. is based on whether the opposing parties will be prejudiced, and the proximity to trial.

9. The federal court's consideration of leave to file
a. occurs before the response is filed to the original pleading.
b. is based on the validity of the new allegations.
c. is always ex parte.
d. is based on whether the opposing parties will be prejudiced, and the proximity to trial.

10. A motion for leave
a. attaches the proposed pleading for the court to review for validity.
b. attaches the proposed pleading for the opposing parties and the court to review for validity.
c. is a demurrer.
d. is always ex parte.

ALTERNATE ASSIGNMENTS

1. *Auntie Irma's v. Rilling Enterprises:* Both Auntie Irma's and Rilling Enterprises have decided to amend their pleadings. They will both add a cause of action for fraud.

Prepare the amended pleading for your client. If the Appendix to the Federal Rules of Civil Procedure forms (**http://www.law.cornell.edu/**) are suitable, use them to amend your pleading.

2. *Whetstone v. Brian:* Whetstone has learned from a business acquaintance that Brian told several people weeks before the James trial that she did not intend to pay Whetstone a dime after the trial, even if she won. She figured that he had made a lot of money from her and her referrals to him over the years, and this was his payback to her. He wants to amend his complaint adding a cause of action for fraud.

Brian claims that when she was leaving the parking lot of Whetstone's offices on her way to the hairdresser the day after the jury verdict, she twisted her ankle on an unobtrusive pothole. That must be the cause of her persistent ankle pain. She has seen a chiropractor and a masseuse, and has been taking over-the-counter pain medication. Since she has not been able to go back to work since the trial due to her emotional injury, there has been no additional loss of income from this injury. She wants to amend her complaint to include a cause of action for premises liability.

Amend the pleading for your client using official forms.

CHAPTER 12

CALENDARING PLEADINGS

After completing the chapter reading, Discussion Questions, Online Projects, and Assignments, review the material in the following Chapter Outline, then complete the Chapter Objectives, Review Exercises, and Key Words and Phrases. When these are mastered, complete the Online Projects, Additional Research, Quiz, and the Alternate Assignments.

CHAPTER OUTLINE

I. Calendaring Is Calculating and Recording the Days on Which Codes and Court Rules Require Performance.

A. The firm's master calendar contains all pertinent dates.

1. Entries usually
   a. are by client and matter name.
   b. show the nature of the event calendared.
   c. show the responsible attorney.

B. Most attorneys have their own calendars also.

C. Calendaring requires adding new dates daily

1. from the incoming mail.
2. to reflect changes as they are made throughout the day.

D. Calendaring is done for the firm's performance, as well as that of opposing parties, to determine when they have not complied with required dates.

E. Calendars may be traditional diary types, or computerized.

II. Basic Calendar Rules

A. In state court,

1. to compute the time in which any act provided by law is to be done, exclude the first day and include the last, unless the last day is a holiday, and then exclude it.

2. if the last day for performance of any act provided or required by law to be performed within a specific period of time shall be a holiday, then such period is hereby extended to and including the next day which is not a holiday. The term "holiday" means all day on Sundays and all holidays.

B. In federal court, rules make the same provisions

1. for the inception of calendaring.
2. for the exclusion of holidays and weekends.

III. Calendaring in State Court

A. Complaints and cross-complaints must be filed before the expiration of their statutes of limitations.

1. Examples of statutes of limitations are four years (actions on written contract), three years (actions for fraud, trespass, or injury to real property), two years (actions on oral contract and personal injury), one year (actions for many intentional torts such as libel, slander, assault, and battery).
2. The statute of limitations may be tolled by
   a. the defendant's absence from the jurisdiction.
   b. the minority of the plaintiff.
   c. the lack of knowledge of the cause of action.

B. Dismissal statutes define the dates by which matters must be served.

1. The CCP requires dismissal where the defendant has not been served within three years of filing the action.
2. Local rules may require dismissal for failure to serve within 30 to 60 days of filing.

C. Responses to pleadings must be filed within 30 days of the effective service of summons.

1. Note the difference between delivery of the summons and complaint and the effective date of service.
   a. Service is effective on the date the summons and complaint are personally served.
   b. Substituted service is complete 10 days after mailing the copies of the summons and complaint to the defendant's address.
   c. Service by notice and acknowledgment is perfected the date the defendant signs the notice and acknowledgment.
   d. Service by publication is complete on the last day of publication.

D. Demurrers must be filed with a motion requesting resolution by the court.

1. Demurrers require a minimum of 16 days' notice if the notice is served by hand, or 21 days' notice if served by mail.
   a. Notice for out-of-state addresses and addresses outside the country are extended.
   b. A proof of service must be filed five days before the hearing.
2. The date for hearing can be no later than 35 days after filing the demurrer.

3. Opposition to demurrers must be filed and served 10 days before the hearing, and replies by the 5th day before the hearing.
4. A demurrer to an answer must be filed and served by the 10th day after service of the answer.

E. Motions to quash service of summons must be filed during the time available for the defendant to answer, and automatically extend the defendant's right to plead to 15 days after service of notice that the motion has been denied.

IV. Calendaring in Federal Court

A. Matters may be dismissed by the court for failure to prosecute, which usually means failure to serve the complaint.

1. There is no specific limit for service.
2. There is little practical danger in California since cases are monitored by the trial judge from the time of filing.

B. An answer to a complaint must be filed and served within 20 days of service of the summons and complaint on the defendant.

1. The court will specify the time for response for an out-of-state defendant.

C. An answer to a counterclaim or cross-complaint must be filed and served within 20 days of service on the counterdefendant or the cross-defendant.

D. Motions to dismiss, to strike, for a more definite statement, and for judgment on the pleadings also must be filed and served within 20 days of service of the summons and complaint.

CHAPTER OBJECTIVES

1. Where are pleading calendaring rules for state and federal cases located?

____

____

____

____

2. What is the most basic rule of calendaring?

____

____

____

____

3. What do you need to know to determine when a response to a complaint must be filed?

____

____

____

4. What do you need to know to determine when a demurrer hearing must be held?

____

____

____

____

REVIEW EXERCISES

Fill in the Blanks:

1. What is calendaring?

____

____

____

2. Someone within the firm enters ______________ in the master calendar, usually by ______________, including ______________ and ______________.

3. How are days counted for calendaring purposes?

____

____

____

4. Why must complaints and cross-complaints be filed before their statutes of limitations?

____

____

____

5. What is the "tolling" of a statute of limitations, and how does it occur?

____

____

____

6. Provide the effective date of service for state court complaints served in the following ways:

a. Personal service ______________________________

b. Substitute service ______________________________

c. Notice and acknowledgment ______________________________

d. Publication ______________________________

7. Demurrers must provide ______________ days' notice to the date of the hearing if the notice is served by hand, ______________ if served by mail.

8. Motions to quash must be filed within ______________ days of service of the complaint.

9. Responses to federal court complaints, cross-complaints, counterclaims, and third-party complaints must be within ______________ days of service.

10. Motions to dismiss must be filed within ______________________ days of service of the pleading.

KEY WORDS AND PHRASES

Provide a Definition for Each of the Following:

Calendaring: ______________________

____

Master calendar: ______________________

____

Dismissal statutes: ______________________

____

Failure to prosecute: ______________________

____

Five-year statute: ______________________

____

Direct calendar system: ______________________

____

Master calendar system: ______________________

____

Service of summons: ______________________

____

ONLINE PROJECTS

1. Using the official California courts Web site (**http://www.courtinfo.ca.gov/**), access and read carefully the court's opinion in *Robbins v. Los Angeles Unified School District* (1992) 3 CA4th 313. Could the plaintiffs' problems have been avoided by careful calendaring? What does this case tell you about calendaring court orders? How did this court respond to nonlawyers?

2. Using the official California courts Web site (**http://www.courtinfo.ca.gov/**), access and read carefully the court's opinion in *Billings v. Health Plan of America*

(1990) 225 CA3d 250. How many mistakes did plaintiff's lawyer make? How could they have been avoided? What is the ruling in this case? What do you think will happen next?

3. Access the Federal Rules of Civil Procedure (**http://www.law.cornell.edu/**) and review rule 6. Using the Official California Legislative Information Web site (**http: www.leginfo.ca.gov/**), locate Code of Civil Procedure section 12. Are they the same, or do they have the same effect?

4. Using the Official California Legislative Information Web site (**http://www.leginfo.ca.gov/**), locate Code of Civil Procedure sections 10, 12, 12a, and 12b. What are court "holidays"? How does a party handle a situation when on the last day to file his document the courthouse is closed because of natural disaster?

ADDITIONAL RESEARCH

The following are cases accessible on the official California courts Web site (**http://www.courtinfo.ca.gov/**) on various topics of interest relating to this chapter.

Trujillo v. Trujillo (1945) 71 CA2d 257 (service of summons—failure to accept)

Watts v. Crawford (1995) 10 CA4th 743 (date service by publication complete)

Ginns v. Schumate (1977) 65 CA3d 802 (effective date of service by substitution)

Johnson & Johnson v. Superior Court (1985) 38 C3d 243 (effective date of service on out-of-state defendant)

QUIZ

1. Most malpractice carriers require
   a. a master calendar and direct calendar system.
   b. at least two calendar systems.
   c. preference in calendaring.
   d. calendaring only of statute of limitations.

2. To calendar a date an answer served by personal service is due,
   a. start counting the day after receipt of summons, for 30 days.
   b. start counting the day after receipt of the proof of service, for 30 days.
   c. start counting the day after service of summons.
   d. always count 30 days after the return of service.

3. In counting days,
   a. all holidays are skipped.
   b. holidays are skipped if they are the days that performance is due.
   c. holidays are skipped if service was on a holiday.
   d. count only holidays that are on Sunday.

4. Statutes of limitations
   a. are tolled after the filing of the complaint.
   b. for personal injury are two years.
   c. may commence on the date of discovery or of occurrence.
   d. a, b, and c.

5. State dismissal statutes may be irrelevant
   a. because the summons requires service within 60 days of filing.
   b. preference may give the case priority.
   c. failure to prosecute has a three-year statute of limitations.
   d. local rules require action in the case before the time period expires for a dismissal.

6. "Service" refers to
   a. either service of process or service of summons.
   b. either service by proof of service or service of summons.
   c. only service of summons.
   d. only service by proof of service.

7. A demurrer
   a. must be filed within 15 days of service.
   b. must be heard within 30 days of effective service of the complaint.
   c. must be filed within 30 days of effective service of the complaint.
   d. must be heard within 15 days after the time to file an answer.

8. Motions to quash
   a. must be filed within 15 days of service.
   b. must be heard within 30 days of effective service of the complaint.
   c. must be filed within 30 days of effective service of the complaint.
   d. must be heard within 15 days after the time to file an answer.

9. The service of federal complaints
   a. must be within 30 days of filing.
   b. is subject to the same limitations as service of state court complaints.
   c. must be within a reasonable time of filing.
   d. a and b.

10. All superior courts must have
    a. a direct calendar system.
    b. a direct calendar system or a master calendar system.
    c. a combination of the direct calendar system and master calendar system.
    d. b and c.

ALTERNATE ASSIGNMENTS

1. *Red v. Green:* Recalculate the responses to the sample problems in the text, with personal service on November 14.

2. *Blue v. Yellow:* Recalculate the responses in the previous question with personal service on November 25.

3. *Pink v. Aqua:* A complaint is filed in federal court and personally served on a California resident defendant on November 26.

   a. Use the sample calendar that follows and calculate the last day for defendant to serve and file his answer.
   b. Use the sample calendar that follows and calculate the last day for defendant to serve and file his motion to dismiss.
   c. Are the answers the same if the defendant is out of California?

4. *Orange v. Brown:* Recalculate the responses in the previous question with personal service on November 25.

5. *Mauve v. Lavender:* Using the same calendar, calculate the date for response to a superior court complaint served by substituted service. The summons and complaint were delivered to the defendant's office on November 21; copies were mailed to the same office on November 23 and received on November 25.

6. *Grey v. Gray:* Calculate the date of response to a complaint served by notice and acknowledgment, where the notice is mailed to defendant on November 28, received by defendant on November 29, signed by the defendant on November 30, and mailed to plaintiff on December 1.

7. *Black v. White:* Two years ago, a client of the firm was injured in a car accident at 11:30 P.M., December 31. On what day does his statute of limitations run?

   a. What if the actual injury was suffered after midnight?
   b. What if the complaint will contain causes of action for breach of written contract and personal injury?
   c. Does it make any difference if the case is in state court or federal court?

8. *Rose v. Cream:* A complaint was filed by the firm on December 12, 2005, with causes of action for wrongful death and breach of oral contract. By what date must it be served on the defendant?

9. Create a hard copy diary or computerized calendar for all of the dates in the previous eight questions.

SAMPLE CALENDAR

November

S	M	T	W	T	F	S
						1
2	3	4	5	6	7	8
9	10	11	12	13	14	15
16	17	18	19	20	21	22
23	24	25	26	**27**	28	29
30						

January

S	M	T	W	T	F	S
				1	2	3
4	5	6	7	8	9	10
11	12	13	14	15	16	17
18	19	20	21	22	23	24
25	26	27	28	29	30	31

December

S	M	T	W	T	F	S
	1	2	3	4	5	6
7	8	9	10	11	12	13
14	15	16	17	18	19	20
21	22	23	24	**25**	26	27
28	29	30	31			

February

S	M	T	W	T	F	S
1	2	3	4	5	6	7
8	9	10	11	12	13	14
15	**16**	17	18	19	20	21
22	23	24	25	26	27	28

CHAPTER 13

DISCOVERY OVERVIEW

After completing the chapter reading, Discussion Questions, Online Projects, and Assignments, review the material in the following Chapter Outline, then complete the Chapter Objectives, Review Exercises, and Key Words and Phrases. When these are mastered, complete the Online Projects, Additional Research, Quiz, and the Alternate Assignments.

CHAPTER OUTLINE

I. Discovery Permits Inquiry into the Legal Contentions and Facts Supporting the Opposition's Position, and the Knowledge and Evidence Available to Third Parties.

A. Discovery is used at almost every stage of litigation.

II. The Three Purposes of Discovery

A. Improving presentation of trial evidence

1. Information and evidence means that cases can be decided on the merits.
2. Discovery also improves efficiency for the parties and the courts.

B. Focusing on issues

1. Discovery clarifies the legal issues and narrows the legal issues.
2. Discovery preserves evidence that might otherwise be lost before trial.
3. Discovery promotes settlements.

C. Eliminating surprise at trial

1. Knowing the issues saves time and money in trial preparation.
2. Knowing the issues results in better presentation of evidence, leading to decisions on the merits.
3. Information means better logistical preparation for presenting evidence at trial.

III. The Disadvantages of Discovery

A. Expense of discovery can exceed trial costs.

1. Discretion must be exercised to decide
   a. what type of discovery to implement.
   b. how much time and money should be spent given the probable recovery for the plaintiff or potential exposure for the defendant.
2. Discovery is expensive for the propounding party as well as the responding party.
3. Discovery expenses are a primary reason for the development of the paralegal profession.
   a. Discovery is primarily factual, not substantive law, and it is more efficient and less expensive for paralegals to propound discovery and analyze the results.

B. Disputes arise over discovery that are also expensive and time consuming.

1. The disputes are usually over observance of discovery rules.
2. Discovery disputes add to the court's burden and delay the case.

C. Seeking discovery can educate the opposition about the propounder's theories and strategy.

IV. The Six Discovery Tools

A. Interrogatories are written questions propounded from one party to another, answered under oath by the responding party within 30 days.

1. Interrogatories can obtain basic facts such as names, dates, and places. They are also useful for obtaining confirmation of, and facts supporting, legal contentions.
2. Interrogatories are limited to 35 per unlimited civil case, unless good cause exists for additional interrogatories.

B. Depositions are oral questions propounded by counsel to the opposing party or third parties.

1. The answers given under oath have the same importance as the sworn testimony at trial, and are subject to the same rules and objections as at trial.

C. Document requests are used to obtain any type of physical, tangible evidence, as well as access to land or structures.

1. Business and personal files of documents are routinely produced for inspection and copying.
2. Access to physical evidence allows the parties to evaluate the oral and written accounts of events, and measure, survey, test, and analyze physical properties of the evidence.

D. Requests for admissions are statements of fact or legal conclusions propounded to the opposition, requesting that the opposition admit or deny them under oath.

1. Requests for admissions are more of a tactic than a discovery tool, but they can effectively commit the opposition to a particular theory or approach and eliminate issues or facts that are not in dispute.

E. Independent medical examinations are medical examinations of the party claiming the physical or mental injury.

F. Expert discovery is subject to a whole set of rules and procedures to assure that expert discovery is fair and efficient.

V. Discovery Plans Outline What Will Be Sought from Whom, When, and How.

A. The three purposes of a discovery plan

1. The plan outlines the essential elements of each cause of action, using the pleadings as a guide, to show what must be proven and what evidence is available.
   a. The pleadings are the foundation of a discovery plan.
2. Devising the plan helps figure out the facts and theories upon which the opposition will rely.
   a. The litigant finds out where he should spend his time and money in locating and controverting evidence.
   b. The litigant commits the opposition to a particular approach.
3. The plan provides a blueprint for the entire discovery process.
   a. The litigant can decide which discovery tool is more likely to provide needed information.
   b. Counsel also can decide the order in which the desirable discovery methods should be used.

VI. Limits to Discovery

A. The basic limitation on discovery is scope.

1. The permissible scope of discovery is that which reasonably assists a party in evaluating the case, preparing for trial, and negotiating for settlement.
2. Anything reasonably expected to lead to discovery of admissible evidence is discoverable.
3. Both state and federal courts apply the discovery standard liberally, favoring discovery in disputed cases.

B. Privileges protect some information from discovery.

1. Privileged information, protected by virtue of a special relationship, is not discoverable even if relevant.
   a. Privileges established by California law govern not only state court proceedings but those in the federal courts located in California.
   b. Privileges established by state law include:
      (i) attorney-client.
      (ii) spousal.

(iii) physician-patient.
(iv) clergyman-penitent.

c. Privileges encourage participants in special relationships to be open and honest with each other, by keeping communications private.

2. The attorney-client privilege exists as long as the communications are made between the client and his counsel, without "unnecessary" third parties, with the purpose of seeking or rendering legal advice.
   a. Communications between the client and the attorney's employees and agents, such as paralegals, are also protected, as long as the communications are necessary to the attorney's work.
   b. Care must be taken to keep client communications confidential and to caution the client to keep his discussions with counsel and his employees confidential.
   c. The attorney-client privilege can be claimed by either the client or the attorney speaking for the client, and waived by either.
   d. The attorney-client privilege can be waived if either party sues the other.

3. Attorney-workproduct privilege protects from discovery all written "mental impressions" of the attorney, and all oral communications between members of the firm.
   a. The attorney-workproduct privilege includes reports from the attorney's agents, such as investigators, expert consultants, and paralegals.
   b. The workproduct privilege belongs to the attorney alone, since it reflects his mental processes.

VII. Limitations on the Timing and Quantity of Discovery in State Court

A. Discovery statutes prohibit discovery by the plaintiff before the 10th day after service of summons.

1. The 10 days after service are intended to give the defendant time to analyze the case just served on him.

2. Exceptions include situations where a witness is leaving the state and will not be available for deposition later in the process, or where a party is near death and may not survive until the trial.

B. No discovery except expert discovery is permitted after the 30th day before trial.

1. The 30-day cutoff before trial requires that all discovery be completed on or before the 30th day before trial.

2. Once the 30-day cutoff has occurred with the first trial setting date, discovery does not reopen.

3. If served without agreement or court order, it need not be answered.

4. The 30-day pretrial period is intended to allow for trial preparation rather than adversarial proceedings.

C. Absent an agreement or court order, discovery may not be served during these periods.

D. Limitations on amounts of discovery

1. For unlimited civil cases, parties are restricted to a total of 35 interrogatories and 35 requests for admission that may be served without a declaration of necessity.

2. For limited civil cases, an aggregate total of 35 interrogatories, requests for admission and for production, and depositions can be served without stipulation or order of the court.
   a. Only one deposition per side is permitted.

VIII. Limitations on the Timing and Quantity of Discovery in Federal Court

A. There is no "hold" on written discovery by the plaintiff immediately after serving the summons and complaint, but there is no discovery until after initial discovery conference.

B. Trial judges assigned to each case at the time of filing will specify a discovery cutoff date for each case.

C. The parties cannot extend the discovery deadline without a court order.

IX. Limitations on Quantity of Discovery

A. Rule of 35 limits discovery to 35 special interrogatories (exclusive of form interrogatories) and 35 requests for admissions in unlimited civil cases.

B. Rule of 35 limits discovery to a total of 35 written discovery tools, including form interrogatories in limited civil cases.

C. The federal courts have similar limitations in their local rules.

X. Discovery Sanctions

A. Counsel and parties must be sanctioned by the court for bad faith violations of discovery rules.

CHAPTER OBJECTIVES

1. Name and define the six main discovery tools.

   a. ______________________________

   b. ______________________________

   c. ______________________________

   d. ______________________________

   e. ______________________________

   f. ______________________________

2. What is a discovery plan, and how is one drafted?

   ____

   ____

____

____

3. What are discovery privileges, and how do they operate?

____

____

____

____

REVIEW EXERCISES

Fill in the Blanks:

1. What are the three main purposes of discovery?

a. ______________________________

b. ______________________________

c. ______________________________

2. What are the three main disadvantages of discovery?

a. ______________________________

b. ______________________________

c. ______________________________

3. For unlimited civil cases, the "rule of 35" means ______________________________, while for limited civil cases, the "rule of 35" means ______________________________.

4. Interrogatories are useful for obtaining ______________________________ and ______________________________, while document requests are useful for obtaining access to any type of ______________________________ evidence.

5. The three purposes of a discovery plan are

a. ____

b. ____

c. ____

6. The scope of discovery is

____

____

____

7. Privileges are intended to

____

____

____

____

8. Two types of privileges concern attorneys. The ______________________ privilege belongs to the client and can be asserted by the attorney. The ______________________ privilege belongs to the attorney.

9. State court discovery cannot be served before the ______________________ or after the ______________________.

10. All discovery except expert discovery must be concluded by the 30th day before trial, known as the ______________________.

KEY WORDS AND PHRASES

Provide a Definition for Each of the Following:

Merits: ______

Interrogatories: ______

Depositions: ______

Document requests: ______

Third party: ______

Requests for admissions: ______

Independent medical examination (IME): ______

Expert discovery: ______

Discovery plan: ______

Relevancy: ______

Privilege: ______

Attorney-client privilege: ______

Attorney-workproduct privilege: ______________________________

____

30-day cut off: ______________________________

____

Rule of 35: ______________________________

____

Reset: ______________________________

____

Adjudicate: ______________________________

____

ONLINE PROJECTS

1. Using the official California courts Web site **(http://www.courtinfo.ca.gov/)**, access and read carefully the court's opinion in *Greyhound Corporation v. Superior Court* (1961) 56 C2d 355. This is one of the most important discovery opinions, rendered prior to the discovery acts of 1986 and 2005, when most of the rules we use today were adopted and revised. Why is it important? To what extent is it still good law?

2. Using the official California courts Web site **(http://www.courtinfo.ca.gov/)**, access and read carefully the court's opinion in *West Pico Furniture Co. v. Superior Court* (1961) 56 C2d 407. This opinion is found in the same volume as *Greyhound Corporation v. Superior Court* and was also rendered prior to the Discovery Act of 1986. Why do you think the state's supreme court decided to take these two cases? How do they complement each other?

3. Locate the discovery essay at **http://www.lawschoolhelp.com/**, the essay on discovery techniques at **http://www.dicarlolaw.com/**, and the discovery information at **http://californiadiscovery.findlaw.com/**. Compare and contrast the three sites and the information they provide.

4. Access the Federal Rules of Civil Procedure **(http://www.law.cornell.edu/)**, and review rules 4 and 4.1. How is a federal summons different from a state court summons? How is service different? Why do you think service is different?

5. Access the Federal Rules of Civil Procedure **(http://www.law.cornell.edu/)**, and review rule 26. What does this rule tell you about the federal court's approach to discovery? What is the duty of disclosure in federal court? How is it different from state court?

6. Access the Federal Rules of Civil Procedure **(http://www.law.cornell.edu/)**, and review rule 37. What does this rule tell you about the federal court's

approach to discovery? What is a discovery plan in the nomenclature of federal court? When and how is a federal court discovery plan prepared? What is its purpose?

7. Using the Official California Legislative Information Web site **(http://www.leginfo.ca.gov/)**, locate Code of Civil Procedure sections 2017.010 and 2018.020. What is the scope of discovery? What privileges are specifically defined in these two rules?

8. Using the Official California Legislative Information Web site **(http://www.leginfo.ca.gov/)**, locate Code of Civil Procedure section 2019.010. What types of discovery does this section authorize? What is the purpose of this section? Why do you think it was adopted?

ADDITIONAL RESEARCH

The following are cases accessible on the official California courts Web site **(http://www.courtinfo.ca.gov/)** on various topics of interest relating to this chapter.

Emerson Electric Company v. Superior Court (1997) 16 C4th 1101 (purposes of discovery)

Kravitz v. Superior Court (2001) 91 CA4th 1015 (risks in discovery)

Pullin v. Superior Court (2000) 81 CA4th 1161 (informal discovery not subject to discovery limitations)

Bridgestone/Firestone Inc. v. Superior Court (1992) 7 CA4th 1384 (scope of discovery)

Rittenhouse v. Superior Court (1991) 235 CA3d 1584 (extent of protection of privileged communications)

Mitchell v. Superior Court (1984) 37 C3d 591 (attorney-client privilege)

People v. Hayes (1999) 21 C4th 1211 (disclosure as waiver of privilege)

QUIZ

1. Written discovery tools are
   a. IMEs, interrogatories, and requests for admissions.
   b. document requests, interrogatories, and expert discovery.
   c. interrogatories and expert discovery.
   d. interrogatories.

2. Discovery tools which may be used to obtain information from third parties are
   a. depositions.
   b. document requests.
   c. requests for admission.
   d. interrogatories.

3. The purposes of discovery include
   a. encouraging settlements and resolutions on the merits.
   b. forcing economic attrition of the weaker party and eliminating surprise at trial.
   c. eliminating surprise at trial and educating the opposition.
   d. eliminating surprise at trial and increasing costs.

4. The disadvantages of discovery include
   a. causing expense and disputes.
   b. eliminating surprise at trial and cost.
   c. causing discovery disputes and eliminating surprise at trial.
   d. encouraging settlements and resolutions on the merits.

5. Educating the opposition
   a. is bad because then the opposition knows the issues and strategy.
   b. is good because then the issues are narrowed.
   c. occurs in all discovery.
   d. a and c.

6. Discovery plans are advisable because
   a. discovery tools must be used in a specific order.
   b. they serve as a blueprint for the discovery process.
   c. they can help control expenses and focus effort.
   d. b and c.

7. Limits to discovery include
   a. cost and delay.
   b. scope of discovery.
   c. privilege.
   d. b and c.

8. Counsel's ideas and mental impressions are protected from discovery by
   a. the attorney-workproduct privilege.
   b. the attorney-client privilege.
   c. law and motion court.
   d. a and b.

9. In the absence of an order of the superior court or a stipulation of counsel, written discovery by the plaintiff generally does not occur
   a. in the first 10 days after service of summons and the 15 days before trial.
   b. in the first 10 days after service of summons and the 30 days before trial.
   c. in the first 15 days after service of summons and the 15 days before trial.
   d. only in the pretrial cutoff.

10. In federal court, the plaintiff generally cannot engage in written discovery
   a. in the first 10 days after service of summons and the 15 days before trial.
   b. in the first 10 days after service of summons and the 30 days before trial.
   c. in the first 15 days after service of summons and the 15 days before trial.
   d. until after the initial discovery conference.

ALTERNATE ASSIGNMENTS

1. Prepare a discovery plan for your side of the *Auntie Irma's v. Rilling Enterprises* and/or *Whetstone v. Brian litigation*.

To show that you understand the issues of the case, outline your client's claims and defenses and those of the opponent. Then, list the discovery tools you plan to use, in the order you intend to use them, discussing how each will provide proof for your case and pin down your opponent. Remember that to prevail on your case you must prove each element of your case and disprove each defense of the opposition. To defend yourself against your opponent, you must disprove at least one element of each cause of action alleged against you or prove at least one affirmative defense.

2. Draft a memo describing what discovery you believe your opposition in the *Auntie Irma's v. Rilling Enterprises* and/or *Whetstone v. Brian* litigation will undertake—a type of defensive discovery plan—using the same approach as in Alternate Assignment 1 outlined previously.

CHAPTER 14

INTERROGATORIES

After completing the chapter reading, Discussion Questions, Online Projects, and Assignments, review the material in the following Chapter Outline, then complete the Chapter Objectives, Review Exercises, and Key Words and Phrases. When these are mastered, complete the Online Projects, Additional Research, Quiz, and the Alternate Assignments.

CHAPTER OUTLINE

I. Interrogatories Are Written Questions Propounded by One Party to Another Party.

A. Responses are in writing and given under oath.

B. State court practice prohibits serving interrogatories until 10 days after service of the summons and complaint and requiring responses during the 30-day pretrial cutoff.

C. Federal court rules prohibit interrogatories until after the initial discovery conference and just before trial, as specified by the trial judge.

II. The Five Advantages of Interrogatories

A. They are inexpensive.

1. Interrogatories are typewritten questions on pleading paper, served by mail or by hand.

B. They obtain all evidence within the knowledge of the respondent and all information "available" to him.

1. Thus, if information is within the knowledge of someone associated with the respondent, it must be provided in response to relevant interrogatories.

C. They are a stronghold for paralegals, some of whom can spend their entire careers propounding and responding to interrogatories.

D. They do not depend upon the respondent's spontaneous memory, allowing time to research details, consult his written records, and obtain information.

E. Interrogatories are one of the few methods of determining the legal contentions of the respondent.

1. But since responses are usually drafted by counsel, the respondent has time to carefully draft them in language of his own choice.

III. The Four Disadvantages of Interrogatories

A. They are frequently reduced to a game of objection and evasion.

B. Since responses are not spontaneous, they do not allow for any evaluation of the respondent's credibility and presentation as a witness.

C. They allow for artful drafting of responses, which avoids providing any real information.

D. Interrogatories can only be propounded to parties to the action, not third parties.

IV. Interrogatories for State Court Practice

A. The caption for interrogatories is that for the most recent pleading, which may be the complaint, an amended complaint, or a cross-complaint.

1. The case number is at the right-hand side of the box containing the names of the parties.
2. The document is entitled "Interrogatories."
3. Immediately below the document title appears
   a. the name of the propounding party.
   b. the set number, since several sets can be propounded during the litigation.
   c. the identity of each party who is to respond to the interrogatories, to alert each party to his obligation to respond.

B. Interrogatories must be consecutively numbered from set to set.

C. No spaces are required for the answers.

D. Interrogatories cannot be combined with other discovery, such as requests for admission.

1. Discovery tools can be served together and refer to each other, however.

V. Form of Interrogatory Questions

A. Each question must be "full and complete in and of itself" and "separately set forth."

B. No preface or instructions may be included.

1. Official form interrogatories include instructions and definitions.

C. Any definition must be typed in capital letters in each interrogatory in which it is used.

D. Questions that are "compound, conjunctive, or disjunctive" are also prohibited.

E. Subparts are prohibited.

1. Any interrogatory containing subparts need not be answered if the responding party objects on that ground.

VI. Limitations on Numbers of Interrogatories

A. A party in an unlimited civil case is limited to a total of 35 drafted interrogatories propounded to each other party for the entire litigation.

1. A party may propound an unlimited number of official form interrogatories.

2. A party may propound the 35 drafted interrogatories in as many sets as desirable.
   a. Interrogatories may be coordinated with requests for admissions, or rationed in small sets for the duration of the litigation, for maximum effectiveness.
3. Any interrogatory that exceeds this limit need not be answered if the responding party states an objection to it on that ground.

B. The five means to exceed the unlimited civil case rule of 35 include:

1. Supplemental interrogatories may be propounded up to three times, each of which may be in addition to the 35 allowed under the statute.
   a. Supplemental sets may be propounded twice before the date on which a trial is set and once after each trial setting.
2. Interrogatories exceeding the 35 limit may be propounded if counsel attaches a declaration of necessity.
   a. The declaration states that the declarant is familiar with the issues, has examined each question, that the information sought is necessary for proper presentation of the case, that the number of interrogatories is reasonable, and "none of the questions is propounded for any improper purpose" such as harassment of the respondent, delay in the action, or to increase the cost of litigation.
   b. The main purpose of the declaration is to provide the court with a vehicle to sanction the attorney who signed the declaration if it appears later that the statement of necessity was false.
3. The propounding party can use as many official form interrogatories as he likes.
4. The parties may stipulate to exceed the 35 permitted by statute.
5. The court may order additional discovery upon a showing of good cause.

C. In a limited civil case, a party cannot exceed an aggregate total of 35 discovery tools, including form interrogatories.

1. Leave of court must be obtained to exceed 35, with the same types of considerations as in unlimited civil cases.

VII. Subscription and Service

A. The interrogatories are signed by the propounder's attorney and served with a proof of service.

B. They must be served on all parties to the action, even those not required to respond.

1. Interrogatories are not filed with the court.
2. The propounder retains the original, and he will be served the original responses.

VIII. Interrogatories for Federal Court Practice

A. Federal rules governing discovery tools like interrogatories are almost identical to those in state court.

B. The major difference is that, while the FRCP generally authorizes interrogatories, it is the local rules that specify limitations.

C. A court order is required to exceed the maximum number for that district.

D. There are no limitations on instructions or definitions.

IX. Types of Interrogatories

A. Contention interrogatories should focus on the heart of the case.

1. Contention interrogatories ask for information which the respondent contends support his allegations or defenses.

B. Fact interrogatories can be used to obtain simple, factual information.

1. They should focus on the objective facts necessary to prove the propounder's case.

C. Interrogatories can identify documents as required for a request for production of documents.

X. Drafting Interrogatories

A. Outline the information the interrogatories are designed to obtain.

B. Consider the limits to the scope of discovery.

XI. Three Approaches to Responding to Interrogatories

A. A party can seek a protective order to excuse him from responding.

B. A party may respond to interrogatories.

1. Unless excused by protective order, the responding party must respond to each question separately, under oath, and within 30 days of service.
   a. If the interrogatories are served by mail, the respondent gets an additional five days in superior court cases, an additional three in federal court cases.
   b. The time limit may be extended by court order upon noticed motion or by stipulation of the propounder and the respondent.

C. The respondent can fail to respond.

1. A failure to respond during the time allowed waives all objections to the interrogatories.
   a. Relief may be obtained from waiver upon noticed motion.

XII. Analyzing Responses to Interrogatories

A. "Response" includes answers and an election to allow inspection and photocopying of records instead of a summary of their contents.

B. The response follows the same format as the interrogatories and is entitled "Responses to Interrogatories."

C. Responses are numbered consecutively to correspond to the interrogatories.

D. In federal court practice, the interrogatory must be repeated, with the response to each interrogatory inserted.

E. Responding to objectionable interrogatories

1. Identify objectionable interrogatories.
2. State objections separately.
3. Proper objections
   a. call for privileged information (seek the substance of communications between a party and his attorney).
   b. exceed the scope of discovery (seek information not relevant to the subject matter or reasonably calculated to lead to the discovery of admissible evidence).
   c. seek information about the contents of documents (only the identity and location of documents is obtainable by interrogatory).
   d. are burdensome and oppressive (seek extraordinary effort of the respondent so great as to be unjust).
   e. violate format requirements, such as interrogatories that contain subparts; instructions; improperly stated definitions; incorporations by reference; compound, conjunctive, or disjunctive phrases; or exceed 35.
4. Improper objections
   a. include calls for hearsay, opinion or conclusion, facts not in evidence, and confidential (as opposed to privileged) information.
   b. are ambiguous, confusing, or overbroad—the respondent must respond as best he can in good faith.

F. Answers

1. Answers must be "as complete and straightforward as the information reasonably available to the responding party permits. If an interrogatory cannot be answered completely, it shall be answered to the extent possible."
2. Answers may not reference other documents, incorporate previous responses by reference, or deliberately evade clear interrogatories.
3. Read the interrogatories as literally as possible and provide the narrowest possible answer.
4. The respondent also must make a good-faith effort to obtain information sought unless it is equally available to the propounder.
5. If an interrogatory requires compilation or summarization of the contents of documents, the respondent has the option of making the documents available to the propounder for inspection and copying.

G. The responses to interrogatories are verified, by the signature of the respondent under oath.

1. Verification by the attorney is improper, unless the attorney is the authorized agent for the party, such as corporate counsel.
2. Unverified responses are no responses: the respondent has waived all objections and the propounder may make a motion to compel.

H. Responses are served on all parties, with the originals to the propounder.

XIII. Challenges to Responses to Interrogatories

A. Inadequate answers or improper objections are subject to a motion to compel further answers to interrogatories.

1. Counsel must meet and confer to try to work out the dispute before bringing the motion.
2. State rules require that the motion be noticed within 45 days of service of the responses by hand, 50 if by mail, or any right to relief is waived.
3. There is no time limit for the motion in federal court.

B. A motion to compel answers may be brought at any time if no response is made to the interrogatories.

1. No meeting is required prior to making the motion.

CHAPTER OBJECTIVES

1. How are form interrogatories used?

____

____

____

2. What are the rules for drafting interrogatories?

____

____

____

3. How are responses to interrogatories prepared?

____

____

____

REVIEW EXERCISES

Fill in the Blanks:

1. Interrogatories are written questions propounded by

______________________ to ______________________.

2. The five advantages of interrogatories are

a. ______________________

b. ______________________

c. ______________________

d. ______________________

e. ______________________

3. The four disadvantages of interrogatories are

a. ______________________

b. ______________________

c. ______________________

d. ______________________

4. What information is provided in the caption of drafted interrogatories in state court actions that is different from the information provided in the pleadings?

____

____

5. Interrogatories ______________________ be combined with other discovery in the same document.

6. A party in an unlimited civil case can propound more than 35 drafted interrogatories if

a. ______________________________ or

b. ______________________________.

7. Upon receipt of interrogatories, a respondent can either

a. ______________________________,

b. ______________________________, or

c. ______________________________.

8. How is the form of interrogatory responses in federal court different from the form of interrogatory responses in state court?

____

____

____

9. Proper objections include

a. ______________________________

b. ______________________________

c. ______________________________

d. ______________________________

10. The responding party, not counsel, must ______________ the responses.

KEY WORDS AND PHRASES

Provide a Definition for Each of the Following:

Propound: ______________________________

____

Declaration of necessity: ______________________________

____

Protective order: ______________________________

____

Meet and confer: ______________________________

____

Motion to compel further responses: ______________________________

____

Motion to compel answers: ______________________________

____

ONLINE PROJECTS

1. Using the official California courts Web site **(http://www.courtinfo.ca.gov/)**, access and read carefully the court's opinion in *Deyo v. Kilbourne* (1979) 84 CA3d 771. Is there a specific guideline for "oppression"? What guidance does the court give litigants? What would be the best response to an interrogatory seeking excessive information from business records?

2. Using the official California courts Web site **(http://www.courtinfo.ca.gov/)**, access and read carefully the court's opinion in *Demyer v. Costa Mesa Mobile Home Estates* (1995) 36 CA4th 393. What does this opinion suggest about an efficient way to use interrogatories in multiparty cases? How could the number of interrogatories effectively be expanded?

3. Using the official California courts Web site **(http://www.courtinfo.ca.gov/)**, access and read carefully the court's opinion in *Scheiding v. Dinwiddie Construction Company* (1999) 69 CA4th 64. What is the responding party's duty? What is the standard that must be met? How could this dispute have been avoided?

4. Using the official California courts Web site **(http://www.courtinfo.ca.gov/)**, access and read carefully the court's opinion in *Catanese v. Superior Court* (1996) 46 CA4th 1159. What types of interrogatories are objected to in this case? What must a party objecting to excessive numbers of interrogatories do? Is an objection sufficient? Why or why not?

5. Access the Federal Rules of Civil Procedure **(http://www.law.cornell.edu/)**, and review rule 33. Using the Official California Legislative Information Web site **(http://www.leginfo.ca.gov/)**, locate Code of Civil Procedure section 2030. Compare the two statutes. How are they different? Why do you think they are different? Which one gives more guidance? Which one would you prefer to follow? Why?

ADDITIONAL RESEARCH

The following are cases accessible on the official California courts Web site **(http://www.courtinfo.ca.gov/)** on various topics of interest relating to this chapter.

Kalaba v. Gray (2002) 95 CA4th 1416 (scope of discovery for interrogatories)

Burke v. Superior Court (1969) 71 C2d 276 (contention interrogatories)

Leach v. Superior Court (1986) 180 CA3d 701 (effect of delay to respond)

Regency Health Services, Inc.v. Superior Court (1998) 64 CA4th 1496 (duty of responding party)

Appleton v. Superior Court (1988) 206 CA3d 632 (effect of unverified response)

QUIZ

1. Advantages of interrogatories are that they
   a. are the most common discovery tool.
   b. get the respondent to provide all responsive information available to him.
   c. elicit spontaneous responses.
   d. a and b.

2. The CCP requires that the introductory paragraph include
   a. the set number.
   b. the name of the respondent.
   c. the name of the propounder.
   d. a, b, and c.

3. In superior court, the basic rule on the maximum number of sets of interrogatories which may be propounded is
   a. limited to 35.
   b. limited to 15.
   c. unlimited, as long as they are judicial forms.
   d. unlimited.

4. In an unlimited civil case, the basic rule on the maximum number of interrogatories which may be propounded is
   a. generally limited to 35 drafted interrogatories.
   b. unlimited.
   c. generally unlimited, as long as they are judicial forms.
   d. a and c.

5. Federal court prohibits
   a. subparts.
   b. verification.
   c. instructions.
   d. a and c.

6. State court prohibits
   a. subparts.
   b. definitions.
   c. instructions.
   d. a and c.

7. A motion to compel further responses must be preceded by
   a. a meet and confer in both federal and state court cases.
   b. a meet and confer in federal cases only.
   c. a meet and confer in state court only.
   d. a 45-day waiting period in state court practice, to permit counsel to work out their dispute.

8. Answers to a motion to compel
   a. may be made at any time after the answers are due in state court.
   b. may be made at any time after the answers are due in federal court.
   c. require a meet and confer in state court only.
   d. a and b.

9. The responding party serves the
   a. original on the propounder, so it is available if a motion must be made.
   b. original on the propounder, because the propounder is required to file it with the court.
   c. original on the court, with a copy to all parties.
   d. original on the court, with a copy to the propounding party only.

10. The failure of the respondent to verify answers
    a. invalidates the answers.
    b. can be cured by a protective order.
    c. can be resolved by a meet and confer.
    d. can be avoided if the attorney verifies them.

ALTERNATE ASSIGNMENTS

1. *Auntie Irma's v. Rilling Enterprises:*

A. Prepare interrogatories to be propounded by your client in *Auntie Irma's v. Rilling Enterprises*, following the rules of the Federal Rules of Civil Procedure and the local rules of the Western District (which limit interrogatories to 10; require a footer; and prohibit subparts and conjunctive, disjunctive, and compound interrogatories).

B. If you are doing this assignment as part of a class assignment, exchange your interrogatories with your opponent and respond to his interrogatories, using the following information, as well as the information provided in previous assignments:

IF YOU REPRESENT AUNTIE IRMA'S: Your client tells you that its business address is 2468 Maple Avenue in Seaside City, California. It was incorporated in California in 1989. The telephone number is 555-1234. Lucille Fitzhugh assists you in drafting the answers, and owns 85 percent of the stock in the company. Her niece Robin owns the rest.

Fitzhugh remembers absolutely nothing about the oral promises she alleges were made by Rilling concerning the Rilling Enterprises policy of not competing with licensees by owning shops and marketing cookies to the public, except that the discussion took place sometime before Fitzhugh signed the license agreement. She doesn't remember where she was, what day it was, or even what time of day the agreement was made.

Rilling did tell Fitzhugh that she wanted new flavors for the Lacy Irma each year, and Fitzhugh agreed.

Fitzhugh remembers that Robin was present during this discussion. Another person, Ray Rouse, an employee of Rilling Enterprises who has since been terminated, was also present. Fitzhugh thought she was quite clever by failing to include any language concerning the new flavors in the written agreement. Fitzhugh also notes that she paid for a permanent license only to keep the Rilling Roll from competing with the Lacy Irma in Fremont County, and that she never had any intention of marketing it aggressively.

Fitzhugh has a copy of both license agreements, the operations manual, and the newsletters she obtained before entering into the Rilling Roll license. She once saw a letter written to another licensee at the same time she signed the Rilling Roll license agreement; the letter stated that the company policy had changed and Rilling Roll would compete with licensees. Fitzhugh saw the letter before she signed the license agreement but does not have a copy and does not remember to whom it was written.

After Rouse was terminated by Rilling Enterprises, Fitzhugh offered him a job at Auntie Irma's for double his salary at Rilling Enterprises. He politely refused, saying that he didn't want to be in the middle of the dispute. He told Fitzhugh that he remembers the discussion about flavors and clearly recalls that she promised to provide them, no matter what the agreement said.

Fitzhugh claims to have suffered at least $150,000 in damages for Rilling Enterprises' failure to pay royalties for the Lacy Irma, $250,000 in damages for the lack of nondisclosure agreements, and $50,000 for the damage to the business caused by the unfair competition from the Rilling Enterprises store in Fremont.

IF YOU REPRESENT RILLING ENTERPRISES: Your client tells you that its principal place of business is 324 Riverview Drive, Jacksonville, Illinois. It was incorporated in Illinois in 1973. It has thousands of shareholders and is publicly traded. It is now qualified to do business and has a local business license, but its "dba" has not yet been published. Alice Rilling assists you in drafting the responses.

Rilling says there was never any agreement with Auntie Irma's that Rilling Enterprises would not compete with Auntie Irma's. In fact, Rilling says she told Fitzhugh quite clearly that the policy had changed and that Rilling Enterprises intended to begin establishing its own shops. Ray Rouse, a Rilling Enterprises employee who was later fired, was present during this discussion. Rilling does not know how to contact him. There also was an agreement preventing competition with another licensee, signed at about the same time Auntie Irma's signed its license agreement. The copy of the letter has been lost.

Rilling told Fitzhugh that she wanted new flavors for the Lacy Irma each year, and this was a condition of the agreement. Fitzhugh agreed. There is no language concerning the new flavors in the written agreement.

Rilling believes other people were present during this discussion, but she does not remember who they were.

Rilling admits that royalties for the Lacy Irma sublicenses were "technically" due Auntie Irma's, but she refused to pay them, since she felt these obligations were offset by the lack of new flavors for the Lacy Irma.

Rilling has a copy of both license agreements, the operations manual, and the newsletters she obtained before entering into the Rilling Roll license.

Rilling confides that the real reason she terminated the license for the Rilling Roll is that she heard through industry sources that Auntie Irma's is about to be sold to

Monster Cookie Company, a huge conglomerate. She is afraid that Monster Cookie Co., through the license with Auntie Irma's, will market the Rilling Roll worldwide, since it would not have to pay a royalty to Rilling Enterprises. This would effectively put Rilling Enterprises and all of its licensees out of business. She had voiced these concerns to Ray Rouse a few days before he was fired. She fired him because she thought he was a spy from Monster Cookie Company. It appears now that he was not.

Rilling claims that Rilling Enterprises has suffered at least $150,000 in damages for the lack of new cookie flavors, and $150,000 in losses for the damage to Rilling Enterprises' reputation resulting from low sales at Auntie Irma's Fremont County shop.

2. *Whetstone v. Brian:*

A. Prepare interrogatories to be propounded by your client in *Whetstone v. Brian*, following the Code of Civil Procedure.
B. If you are doing this assignment as part of a class assignment, exchange your interrogatories with your opponent and respond to his interrogatories, using the following information as well as the information provided in previous assignments:

IF YOU REPRESENT WHETSTONE: Your client tells you that his business address is 2468 Maple Avenue in Seaside City, California. The telephone number is 555-1234. He has an unremarkable and uninteresting educational and personal background.

Whetstone admits that he did not have a written fee agreement with Brian but that they had an ongoing attorney-client relationship for almost 10 years. He had not changed his rates or changed his billing practices in all of that time. They never discussed any different billing arrangement at the time Brian demanded that he file an action against James.

Whetstone does use a high school student to do simple tasks around the office, especially in a situation like this when he can save the client money by not doing it himself. Although he charged $25 an hour for the student's time, he actually paid her $5 an hour, and she spent more than 50 hours doing the chronology, not 10.

As for the cross-complaint, Whetstone has notes from his initial interview with Mel Witnig, who insisted that he had not seen either Brian or James on the property the day of the alleged incident. Whetstone did not take a deposition of Witnig, but says there is no way he could have known that Witnig was lying to him. He can't explain the change in stories. He says the jury just didn't like Brian and believed Witnig.

IF YOU REPRESENT BRIAN: Your client tells you that her office is located at 1413 Shady Lane, Seaside. She now has a current real estate license, and her fictitious business name statement has been renewed.

Brian admits that there was never any discussion with Whetstone at any time of the fee for the James case. He made some remark halfway through his representation that she should be careful in demanding so many services in connection with the action because it could end up costing her more than she received, even if she won. Brian realized then that Whetstone probably intended to bill her at the end, but she couldn't afford to pay him, so she kept quiet.

Brian says she never would have agreed to allow a high school student to work on her matter, even to save money.

Brian says that Whetstone probably did not question Witnig at all before the trial and that his notes of the interview are fakes. She says he was sloppy and disorganized, and probably forgot to question Witnig, even though she reminded him many times.

Brian also says that she did know about the settlement offers from James's insurance company, but she thinks now that Whetstone should have been more pushy in demanding that she settle. She says Whetstone is somewhat soft-spoken, and she just didn't listen to him, but she would have if he had been more forceful.

Brian had seen the pothole in the Whetstone parking lot several times before the day she twisted her ankle. It was right near the only "reserved for visitors" parking place. The day she twisted her ankle, she was angry and upset because of the trial and was carrying a box of papers she had retrieved from Whetstone. She just didn't remember the pothole, and she didn't see it with her arms full of documents and her eyes full of tears.

She wore an elastic bandage for a week or so and elevates her leg most of the day now. She has seen a chiropractor seven times and paid $100 for each visit. She has also had 11 massages at $65 each. She also joined a health club to try swimming therapy, which was suggested by her internist for the ankle pain and insomnia. The initiation fee was $1,500, and monthly dues are $125; she joined just after the incident.

She has had a few expenses for medical care as a result of the attack by James. She continued to see her therapist, but every week instead of every other week. She has taken some herbal medicines she read about in a magazine at the chiropractor's office, which have helped her sleep; they cost her about $47. She is now sleeping better, although her ankle pain has forced her to give up tennis, and she is a little wakeful from lack of activity.

Her loss to James has caused her complete humiliation in the professional community and among her friends. Since the attack, she has not gotten a single listing and has not made a single sale. She had been considering a change of career since a year or so before the attack, since real estate had fallen off and she really didn't like it anymore. She is now taking a correspondence course from an accredited school for $3500, to learn how to become a paralegal.

CHAPTER 15

REQUESTS FOR ADMISSIONS

After completing the chapter reading, Discussion Questions, Online Projects, and Assignment, review the material in the following Chapter Outline, then complete the Chapter Objectives, Review Exercises, and Key Words and Phrases. When these are mastered, complete the Online Projects, Additional Research, Quiz, and the Alternate Assignments.

CHAPTER OUTLINE

I. Requests for Admissions Are Written Demands Made to Parties to Admit or Deny Written Statements of Fact or Contention.

A. The responses are under oath and can be used by any party against the respondent during the litigation and trial.

B. They are the only way to determine the opponent's position.

C. Requests can be followed by interrogatories seeking the facts supporting the responses.

D. Requests are inexpensive to prepare, conclusive, and binding.

II. Format for Requests for Admissions

A. Requests for admission are subject to the same timing limitations as other discovery devices.

1. In state court practice, the plaintiff must wait until at least 10 days after service of summons to serve requests; the defendant may serve his at any time.
2. In federal court, summons may not be served until after the initial discovery conference.
3. Requests must be completed before the pretrial discovery cutoff.

B. Responses

1. Responses are due 30 days after personal service.
2. An additional five days are allowed for mailing in state court actions, and an additional three days for mailing in federal court actions.

C. Requests may not be combined with other discovery, but they may be served with other discovery documents.

D. In state court the first paragraph below the document title tells the identity of the propounder, the respondent, and the set number.

1. This practice is customary but not required in federal practice.

E. The number of requests for admissions that can be propounded without a stipulation or court order is 35 in unlimited civil cases in state court, and 25 to 35 in federal court, depending on local rules.

1. A declaration of necessity may permit exceeding the limit in unlimited civil matters.
   a. In federal court, a court order is required to exceed the maximum number.
2. Litigants are limited to a total of 35 discovery tools in limited civil cases.

F. Each request must be an independent statement, separate and complete.

1. It may not incorporate other requests or other matter by reference.
2. Requests may not have subparts, instructions, or prefaces.
3. In state court, a request containing a definition must be recited in full in each request and typed in capital letters.
   a. There is no similar requirement in federal practice.

G. Requests may not be compound, conjunctive, or disjunctive.

1. This avoids the negative pregnant response.

H. Requests can ask about the "genuineness" of documents.

1. The documents must be attached and the originals made available for inspection before the responses are due.

III. Drafting Requests for Admissions

A. Requests may be propounded on any matter that is relevant to the subject matter of the action and not privileged, including genuineness of documents, factual matters, and the opinion of the respondent.

1. Proper subject matter for request for admissions does not include admissions of legal conclusions.

B. Drafting begins with a careful review of facts, opinions, and documents that might contribute to the case.

C. Special attention should be given to basic facts and documents and to details that are the source of dispute and controversy.

1. Equivocal testimony, pleading, or discovery should be pinned down.

D. Requests should be simple sentences.

E. Each request should be examined to make sure that it will contribute to the case in general and not waste any of the limited numbers of requests.

1. In unlimited civil cases, a declaration should be drafted if there are more than 35 requests.

F. Requests are signed by counsel and served on all parties in the action who have appeared, with the original retained by the propounder.

IV. Responding to Requests for Admissions

A. A respondent may seek a protective order to avoid responding.

B. Unless a court grants a motion for protective order, the respondent must serve responses under oath

1. within 30 days (if they are served by hand), with
   a. five additional days (state court) or
   b. three additional days (federal court) for service by mail.

C. The first page of the responses has the same identification as the requests.

D. Responses are numbered consecutively, corresponding to the requests.

E. The requests need not be repeated in state court practice.

1. Federal local rules may require that the request be repeated before the response.

F. Proper objections include relevancy, privilege, and any violation of the format requirements.

G. The only acceptable responses are "admitted," "denied," or a statement claiming and explaining an inability to admit or deny.

1. The respondent must admit everything he does not intend to contest at trial.
2. If the respondent does not admit matter he does not contest, forcing the propounder to prepare proof for trial, the respondent can be required to pay the propounder's costs of proof.
3. Denials must be unequivocal.

H. Responses must be verified and served on all parties to the action who have appeared, and the original response is served on the propounder.

V. Failure to Respond Properly

A. In state court, the propounder must seek a court order deeming the requests admitted for all purposes in the litigation.

1. A motion to compel further responses must be filed within 45 days of service of the responses if the responses were personally served, with an additional five days if they were served by mail.
2. Late responses automatically waive objections.
3. If no responses are served, the propounder moves the court for an order establishing the admissions.
   a. If the respondent does not serve the responses before the motion, the court *must* levy monetary sanctions against him.

B. A failure to respond to a request for admission in federal court practice means that admission is *automatically admitted.*

CHAPTER OBJECTIVES

1. Describe the general rules for drafting requests for admissions.

____

____

____

2. How are official form requests for admissions used?

____

____

____

3. What are the possible responses to requests for admissions?

____

____

____

REVIEW EXERCISES

Fill in the Blanks:

1. A response to a request for admission may be either a(n) ______________ or a(n) ______________ or a(n) ______________.

2. One advantage of requests for admissions is that ______________.

3. One disadvantage of requests for admissions is that ______________.

4. Requests can seek admissions about facts, contentions, or ______________.

5. Each request must be ______________________________,

______________________________, and ______________________________.

6. Drafted requests may not be ______________________________,

______________________________, or ______________________________.

7. A respondent who does not want to respond to requests for admissions must

____

____.

8. Responses to requests for admissions are due within 30 days of service by hand, or the requests in state court are ______________________________ and in federal court are ______________________________.

9. The lack of a verification means that ______________________________.

10. The main format difference between federal and state requests is that federal court rules require that ______________________________.

KEY WORDS AND PHRASES

Provide a Definition for Each of the Following:

Genuineness of documents: ____

____

Legal conclusions: ____

____

Opinions: ____

____

Motion for protective order: ______________________________

____

ONLINE PROJECTS

1. Using the official California courts Web site **(http://www.courtinfo.ca.gov/)**, access and read carefully the court's opinion in *Appleton v. Superior Court* (1988) 206 CA3d 632. What could have been done in the moving papers to persuade the judge that the sanctions were mandatory? What does this case tell you about the importance of obtaining verifications of discovery responses?

2. Using the official California courts Web site **(http://www.courtinfo.ca.gov/)**, access and read carefully the court's opinion in *Garcia v. Hyster Co*. (1994) 28 CA4th 724. Does this case suggest why one might ask about the opposing party's legal conclusions? Are there any reasons one would not? Are requests for admissions the best way to obtain that information?

3. Access the Federal Rules of Civil Procedure **(http://www.law.cornell.edu/)**, and review rule 36. What does this rule and rule 37(c) tell you about reasons for inquiring into an opposing party's legal conclusions?

4. Using the Official California Legislative Information Web site **(http://www.leginfo.ca.gov/)**, locate Code of Civil Procedure sections 2033.210–240. What do these code sections say about the procedural requirements for responding to requests for admissions? What do they say about the substantive requirements for responding to requests for admissions?

ADDITIONAL RESEARCH

The following are cases accessible on the official California courts Web site **(http://www.courtinfo.ca.gov/)** on various topics of interest relating to this chapter.

Tobin v. Otis (1992) 3 CA4th 814 (responses by multiple parties)

Chodos v. Superior Court (1963) 215 CA2d 318 (duty of respondent)

Smith v. Circle P Ranch Company, Inc. (1978) 87 CA3d 267 (cost of proof sanctions)

Cembrook v. Superior Court (1961) 56 C2d 423 (proper objections)

Hillman v. Stults (1968) 263 CA2d 848 (improper objections)

St. Paul Fire & Marine Casualty Insurance Company v. Superior Court (1992) 2 CA4th 843 (relief for failure to respond)

QUIZ

1. Requests for admissions
   a. are written requests.
   b. are propounded to parties by parties.
   c. are the same for federal and state court.
   d. a and b.

2. Requests for admission can contain
   a. instructions.
   b. interrogatories.
   c. subparts.
   d. definitions.

3. If requests for admission ask about the genuineness of documents,
   a. the original documents must be attached.
   b. copies must be attached.
   c. the originals must be available for inspection.
   d. b and c.

4. Requests for admission can ask for admissions concerning
   a. factual matter.
   b. contents of documents.
   c. legal conclusions.
   d. a and b.

5. One thing a respondent should do is
   a. seek a protective order.
   b. fail to respond.
   c. offer affirmative explanations.
   d. indicate an inability to answer.

6. A failure to respond timely in state court
   a. waives all admissions.
   b. means the facts are deemed admitted.
   c. results in mandatory sanctions.
   d. justifies a motion to compel responses.

7. A failure to respond timely in federal court
   a. waives all objections.
   b. means the facts are deemed admitted.
   c. results in mandatory sanctions.
   d. justifies a motion to compel responses.

8. Requests which are admitted
   a. are admitted for all purposes.
   b. are used for impeachment only.
   c. are only admitted if they are relevant.
   d. must be deemed admitted by a court order.

9. Requests which are not admitted
   a. may result in payment of costs of proof if the respondent should have admitted them.
   b. need not be denied.
   c. are followed by a factual explanation of the reasons for the denial.
   d. are called opinion requests.

10. A motion to compel further responses
    a. can be made at any time in state court.
    b. can be made at any time in federal court.
    c. can be made in state court until 45 days after service of the responses by hand, 50 days if served by mail.
    d. b and c.

ALTERNATE ASSIGNMENT

Prepare a set of requests for admissions to propound to your opponent in *Auntie Irma's v. Rilling Enterprises* and/or *Whetstone v. Brian.*

CHAPTER 16

DEPOSITIONS

After completing the chapter reading, Discussion Questions, Online Projects, and Assignments, review the material in the following Chapter Outline, then complete the Chapter Objectives, Review Exercises, and Key Words and Phrases. When these are mastered, complete the Online Projects, Additional Research, Quiz, and the Alternate Assignments.

CHAPTER OUTLINE

I. Depositions Are Oral Testimony of a Party or Third Party Taken by an Attorney for a Party.

A. The testimony is under oath and subject to the cross-examination by counsel for the other parties.

B. The court reporter records the testimony and prepares a transcript.

II. The Five Advantages of Depositions

A. Depositions may be taken of *any* witness.

B. Depositions are the only method of obtaining spontaneous testimony.

C. Depositions can require the adverse deponent to commit himself to a particular story.

D. Testimony can be preserved for use at trial.

E. Depositions can ask about the content of documents, not just their location and identity.

III. Disadvantages of Depositions

A. Depositions can be expensive.

1. Depositions the court reporter takes can cost $500–$1,000, while those an attorney takes can cost $100–$300 an hour.
2. Third-party witnesses can demand payment for their time and travel.

B. There is no way to control the length of the deposition.

C. The witness can only be asked for his personal knowledge, so he can only provide all the information "available" to him, as in interrogatories.

IV. The Paralegal's Role in Depositions

A. Paralegals can notice, schedule, and prepare for the deposition by organizing documents and other types of exhibits, and at the deposition by keeping documents and exhibits in order and taking notes of the proceedings.

B. The paralegal also can follow up after the deposition by communicating with other counsel about the case, summarizing the deposition transcript, and incorporating any new discovery into the discovery and trial plans.

V. Basic Deposition Timing Rules

A. State court

1. The defendant may notice and take a deposition at any time after service of the summons and complaint.
2. The plaintiff cannot notice a deposition until 20 days after service of the summons.

B. The federal plaintiff cannot take a deposition until after the initial discovery conference.

C. Depositions are also subject to the pretrial discovery cutoff.

1. In state court practice, expert depositions may be taken up to 15 days before trial.

D. Leave to take depositions before the complaint is filed and after the cutoff must be obtained from the court by noticed motion.

VI. Deponents

A. Parties and nonparties, natural persons and business entities, nonprofit organizations, and governmental agencies can be deposed.

B. Deposition testimony is admissible at trial to impeach the deponent.

VII. The Six Types of Depositions

A. oral testimony of a party

B. oral testimony of a party combined with a production of documents at the deposition

C. oral testimony of a third-party witness

D. oral testimony of a third-party witness combined with a production of documents at the deposition

E. production of documents by a third party at a time and place specified, without oral testimony

F. In a deposition on written questions, the examination is presented to the deponent in writing, and the answers are taken down by a stenographer who transcribes them into written form.

1. This deposition is useful where the deponent is extremely ill or aged and cannot be examined in person.

VIII. Party Depositions in State Court

A. A notice of deposition compels attendance of a party or party-affiliated witness.

1. A party-affiliated witness is an employee, officer, or director of a party.
2. The notice contains the name, address, and telephone number of each deponent and the time and place of deposition.
3. The notice and proof of service is served at least 10 days before the deposition if served by hand, 15 days if by mail.
4. If noticed, the deposition may be tape-recorded, videotaped, or taken by remote electronic means.
5. Any documents to be produced must be specified with reasonable particularity in a description attached or included in the notice of deposition.
   a. The descriptions are narrowly drafted.
6. A notice to a corporation must describe the matters to be covered.
   a. The entity must produce the most qualified person on those subjects to testify on the entity's behalf.

B. One deposition of each natural person may be taken in the entire action.

1. There is no limit on entity deponents.
2. If depositions are taken before all the parties have appeared, the new parties may take additional depositions.

C. One deposition per side is permitted in limited civil actions.

D. Defects in the notice may be challenged by serving an objection by three days before the deposition, followed by a motion to quash notice of deposition.

E. If the deponent fails to appear, the deposing party may move the court for an order compelling attendance and for monetary sanctions.

F. Natural persons must be deposed within 75 miles of their residences or in the county where the action was filed at a place within 150 miles of the deponent's home.

1. Corporate party-deponents must be deposed within 75 miles of their principal offices or executives, or in the county in which the action was filed, within 150 miles of the designated offices or executives.

IX. Third-Party Depositions in State Court

A. The deposing party must serve a notice of deposition on parties and personally serve a subpoena on the deponent a reasonable time before the deposition.

B. The three types of deposition subpoenas require

1. the physical attendance of the witness at the time and place specified to provide oral testimony.
2. only the production of business records at the time and place specified, without oral testimony.
3. both oral testimony and production of business records.

C. The notice requirements and geographical limitations for third-party witnesses are the same as for parties.

D. A statement may be attached to the subpoena describing materials to require production of documents and things at the deposition.

   1. If the subpoena duces tecum does not require oral testimony, the responsive documents may be delivered to the offices of the counsel noticing the deposition.

E. A subpoenaed nonparty witness who fails to attend the deposition or to provide subpoenaed documents is subject to contempt upon the order of the court.

X. Party and Third-Party Depositions in Federal Court Differ in Notice Requirements and Subpoena Procedures.

A. There is no minimum notice period for party depositions.

B. Depositions with production of documents require 30 days' notice.

C. The federal court clerk for the jurisdiction in which the deposition will be taken must issue subpoenas in federal matters.

XI. Consumer Records

A. Protections apply to those of the consumer's physician, hospital, attorney, accountant, financial institution, insurance carrier, and telephone company.

   1. There is no counterpart to the consumer records subpoena in federal court.

B. The subpoena duces tecum must be issued at least 15 days before the date of production and include an affidavit stating the necessity and relevancy of the records to the issues of the case.

C. The subpoena and affidavit must be served on the consumer as well as the person or entity in control of the records.

D. The consumer may seek to block production by making a motion to quash subpoena with the court.

E. The consumer must be served 10 days before the date of production if served by hand, 15 days if by mail.

XII. Conduct of the Deposition

A. The party who has noticed the deposition schedules the court reporter, who administers the oath and reports the testimony.

B. Parties may attend, and, if the party is a business entity, it may be represented.

C. The deposition begins with the deponent's oath.

D. The deposition is limited to relevant matter that is not privileged.

E. A deponent must provide information within his personal knowledge, not "all information available" to him.

F. Objections may be made by counsel, just as they would be made at trial.

G. The court reporter transcribes the testimony and makes it available to the deponent.

1. The deponent may correct any errors in the transcript.
2. The transcript may be expedited.

XIII. Role of the Paralegal in Depositions

A. The paralegal can help notice depositions, schedule the facilities and court reporter, draft the notice, prepare the subpoenas for signature, and figure out what documents might be found and how they might be described.

B. The paralegal also can prepare documents and other evidence for use at the deposition as exhibits and assist during the deposition by keeping the exhibits organized.

C. Deposition outlines are prepared by reviewing pleadings, written discovery, and deposition transcripts of anyone else in the case, and by asking questions about the facts and theories of the case.

1. Depositions should create contradictory statements and force the deponent to make choices.

D. The paralegal can assist at the deposition by

1. taking notes of the proceedings.
2. advising the attorney of follow-up questions and items that should be clarified on the record.
3. reviewing documents produced to see that they comply with the subpoena or notice.

E. The paralegal can prepare the witness and give the witness some indication of the appropriate form and format of the responses.

1. The paralegal can assist in compiling the records sought.
2. After the deposition, the deponent's paralegal can review the deposition transcript for errors.

XIV. Deposition Summaries Are Accurate, Objective Abbreviations of the Transcript.

A. There are at least five basic types of summaries, which are useful for different purposes.

1. The table of contents summary proceeds through the deposition setting forth the page and line numbers of key statements.
2. The narrative summary is a memorandum.
3. The chronological summary reorganizes the testimony and page and line cites in the chronological order of the underlying facts.
4. The topic format rearranges the summary statements and cites into topics relevant to the issues.
5. The topic index summary has one- or two-word topics corresponding to page and line cites.

XV. Technology and Depositions

A. Computer technology affects how depositions are taken and how the transcripts are used.

B. Court reporters typically have computer files of deposition transcripts.

C. Software programs assist in summarizing and indexing transcripts.

CHAPTER OBJECTIVES

1. How and why do you serve a deposition notice?

____

____

____

____

2. How and why do you serve a deposition subpoena?

____

____

____

____

3. What would you tell a client to prepare her for her deposition?

____

____

____

____

4. What is the purpose of summarizing a deposition transcript?

____

____

____

REVIEW EXERCISES

Fill in the Blanks:

1. The main difference between depositions and interrogatories and requests for admissions is that depositions are ______________________.

2. Two advantages of depositions are

a. ____

b. ____

3. Two disadvantages of depositions are

a. ____

b. ____

4. The only part(s) of the deposition process that a paralegal working for the party noticing the deposition cannot do is (are) ______________________; the only part(s) of the deposition process that the paralegal working for the side responding to the deposition notice cannot do is (are) ______________________.

5. A party in a federal case cannot notice a deposition until after ______________________.

6. In state court, an expert's deposition may be taken up to ______________________ days before trial.

7. A party may be compelled to submit to a deposition by serving a ______________________.

8. A nonparty whose personal appearance is required at deposition is compelled to attend by service on him of a

____

____.

9. A nonparty whose business records are required to be produced can be compelled to perform by service on him of a ______________________

____.

10. The minimal notice required for a state court deposition is ______________________; federal rules require ______________________________ minimum notice.

11. A natural person can be deposed ______________________ time(s) in an action; an entity can be deposed ______________________ time(s) in an action.

12. The six types of depositions are

a. ____

b. ____

c. ____

d. ____

e. ____

f. ____

13. For each side in a state court limited civil case, ______________________ deposition(s) can be taken; in a state court unlimited civil case ______________________ deposition(s) can be taken.

14. Geographical rules require that the deposition be taken within 75 miles of the residence of a ______________________________, or the ______________________________ of a corporation.

15. A ______________________________ court subpoena may be issued by the court clerk or the attorney; a ______________________________ court subpoena can only be issued by the court clerk.

16. The role of the court reporter in the deposition is

____

____

____

17. Consumer records require additional time for notice because

____

____

____.

18. Who may attend a deposition?

____

____

____

19. A party may ______________________________ to a defective notice of deposition.

20. What is the purpose of a chronological deposition summary?

____

____

____

KEY WORDS AND PHRASES

Provide a Definition for Each of the Following:

Court reporter: ______________________________

____

Impeach: ______________________________

____

Deposition on written questions: ______________________________

____

Notice of deposition: ______________________________

____

Party-affiliated witness: ______________________________

____

Personal and consumer records: ______________________________

____

Off the record: ______________________________

____

Certify the question: ______________________________

____

Expedited copies: ______________________________

____

Table of contents summary: ______________________________

____

Narrative summary: ______________________________

____

Chronological summary: ______________________________

____

Topic summary: ______________________________

____

Index summary: ______________________________

____

ONLINE PROJECTS

1. Using the official California courts Web site **(http://www.courtinfo.ca.gov/)**, access and read carefully the court's opinion in *Willoughby v. Superior Court* (1985) 172 CA3d 890. What advice would you give to a potential plaintiff in a similar case, before the case is filed? Is there any way that this plaintiff can avoid or limit the scope of the deposition, given the decision of the court?

2. Using the official California courts Web site **(http://www.courtinfo.ca.gov/)**, access and read carefully the court's opinion in *Maldonado v. Superior Court* (2002) 94 CA4th 1390. Who are "party-affiliated" witnesses? When can they be deposed? What kinds of protections do they have and why?

3. Using the official California courts Web site **(http://www.courtinfo.ca.gov/)**, access and read carefully the court's opinion in *Lowy Development Corporation v. Superior Court* (1987) 190 CA3d 317. Who can attend a deposition? When might that rule not be applied by a court? What kind of analysis will the court make when the rule is questioned? Why?

4. Access the Federal Rules of Civil Procedure **(http://www.law.cornell.edu/)**, and review rules 30 and 31. Compare these two procedures, and make a list of three instances when one might be preferable to the other.

5. Using the Official California Legislative Information Web site **(http://www.leginfo.ca.gov/)**, locate Code of Civil Procedure section 2025.220. If documents are sought to be produced at a deposition, how are they described in the notice?

ADDITIONAL RESEARCH

The following are cases accessible on the official California courts Web site **(http://www.courtinfo.ca.gov/)** on various topics of interest relating to this chapter.

Lund v. Superior Court (1964) 61 C2d 698 (failure of nonparty witness to appear)

Rosemont v. Superior Court (1964) 60 C2d 709 (priority)

Green v. GTE California Inc. (1994) 29 CA4th 407 (who may be videotaped)

Emerson Electric v. Superior Court (1997) 16 CA4th 1101 (deponent asked to perform act)

Rifkin v. Superior Court (1994) 22 CA4th 1255 (objections to contention questions)

QUIZ

1. A CSR
   a. swears in the witness.
   b. records the deposition testimony.
   c. prepares the deposition transcript.
   d. a, b, and c.

2. A CSR
   a. is a consumer subpoena reporter.
   b. is a certified subpoena request.
   c. is a certified stenographic reporter.
   d. prepares only expedited copies of deposition testimony.

3. Advantages to depositions include
   a. cost, efficiency, and spontaneous testimony.
   b. impeachment, cost, and spontaneity.
   c. preservation of testimony, cost, and efficiency.
   d. preservation of testimony, efficiency, and spontaneous testimony.

4. At the beginning of the litigation
   a. a state court defendant can take a deposition at any time.
   b. a state court plaintiff must wait 10 days to take a deposition.
   c. a federal court plaintiff must wait 30 days to take a deposition.
   d. a and c.

5. A party who provides testimony at a deposition
   a. can be impeached at trial if he changes his testimony.
   b. can be cited by the CSR for failing to provide consumer records.
   c. can make a motion to strike to have his testimony corrected before trial.
   d. can require the questions to be recorded in writing in a deposition on written questions.

6. Depositions are limited to
   a. natural persons.
   b. parties.
   c. one per person.
   d. one per natural person.

7. A deposition notice must be served
   a. on all parties for every deposition.
   b. on parties for party depositions.
   c. only for party-affiliated depositions.
   d. only for consumer records depositions.

8. Third-party business records
   a. can be required by notice in lieu of deposition testimony.
   b. can be required by subpoena in lieu of deposition testimony.
   c. are only required from party-affiliated witnesses.
   d. are only required from corporations.

9. Notices of deposition
   a. must be served no less than 15 days before a state court deposition.
   b. must be served 10 days before a state court deposition if service is by hand, 15 if service is by mail.
   c. must be served 10 days before a federal court deposition if service is by hand, 15 if service is by mail.
   d. must be served a reasonable time before a party's deposition, 15 days before a nonparty's deposition.

10. Consumer records depositions requirements
   a. are prohibited in federal court.
   b. shorten timing requirements for deposition.
   c. exclude testimony of the document producer.
   d. require a notice to be served on the persons whose records are sought.

ALTERNATE ASSIGNMENTS

1. *Auntie Irma's v. Rilling Enterprises:*
   A. Prepare an outline for the deposition of your opponent party in *Auntie Irma's v. Rilling Enterprises.*
   B. Prepare a short memorandum outlining which other potential witnesses in *Auntie Irma's v. Rilling Enterprises* should be deposed and why.
   C. Summarize the deposition of Lucille Fitzhugh found in the Study Guide Appendix.
2. *Whetstone v. Brian:*
   A. Prepare an outline for the deposition of your opponent party in *Whetstone v. Brian.*
   B. Prepare an outline of possible questions from the opposition to prepare your client for his or her deposition in *Whetstone v. Brian.*

CHAPTER 17

OBTAINING AND USING TANGIBLE EVIDENCE

After completing the chapter reading, Discussion Questions, Online Projects, and Assignments, review the material in the following Chapter Outline, then complete the Chapter Objectives, Review Exercises, and Key Words and Phrases. When these are mastered, complete the Online Projects, Additional Research, Quiz, and the Alternate Assignment.

CHAPTER OUTLINE

I. Production of Tangible Evidence Can be Compelled from Parties and Nonparties.

A. Third-party witnesses and parties can be compelled to bring evidence to a deposition through a subpoena duces tecum.

1. For a records-only subpoena, no oral testimony is provided, but the requesting party is limited to business records.
2. Production of any other tangible evidence requires a subpoena duces tecum for records and testimony.

B. A demand for inspection compels a party or party-affiliated witness to permit inspection, copying, measurement, and testing of documents, records, tangible evidence, and entry to land or structures.

1. It cannot be served on nonparties.

II. Demand Format

A. A demand for inspection can be made at any time during the litigation except

1. in state court practice, the plaintiff cannot serve a demand until 10 days after the service of summons or the defendant's appearance.

2. discovery is prohibited in federal practice prior to initial discovery conference.

3. neither party may serve a demand that is not completed by the pretrial discovery cutoff.

B. There is no limit on the number of demands that may be made or on the number or volume of items sought.

C. The same introductory heading as that used in interrogatories and requests for admissions is usually set out.

D. The items sought must be described in separate categories, with reasonable particularity.

E. The time and place for inspection must be specified, and

1. any activities planned for the inspection must be specified, with the manner or method of execution.

F. The demand must be served on all parties who have appeared in the action.

1. The demanding party retains the original.

III. Timing Requests to Inspect

A. A request to inspect triggers

1. service of a written response.

2. the actual inspection itself.

B. In state court matters, the written response is due 30 days after service of the demand if by hand, or 35 days after if by mail.

1. The date for inspection can be no earlier than 30 days from the date of service of the demand if by hand, or 35 days from the date of service if by mail.

C. In federal court matters, the written response is due 30 days after service of the demand if by hand, or 33 days after if by mail.

1. The inspection can be any time after the last date for serving a written response.

IV. Response to Demand for Inspection

A. The respondent may seek protective orders to relieve him of his obligation or may object to all or part of the inspection.

B. If protective orders are not sought, the respondent must provide a written response within the time permitted.

1. The written response states whether the respondent agrees or objects to the inspection.

2. The failure to timely serve the written response waives all objections.
   a. In state court, a belated response "in substantial compliance" may result in relief from waiver if the respondent notices a motion for relief and provides evidence excusing his delay.

3. The written response is either an agreement to comply with the demand, objections to all or part of the demand, or an explanation of an inability to comply.
   a. An agreement to comply must confirm that the items described in the demand are in the respondent's custody and control and that the inspection will be permitted, subject to any objections.
   b. The respondent may not provide conditional agreement and attempt to limit the inspection unilaterally.
4. Objections may be made to any part or all of the demand.
   a. Objections may be made that the items sought are too fragile for inspection, testing, or other types of physical examination.
5. In state court practice, the written response is verified and served on all parties who have appeared.
6. In federal court practice, the written response need not be verified but is served on all parties who have appeared.
7. The demanding party is served the original.

V. Enforcing the Demand

A. The demanding party may make a motion to compel further responses to demand for inspection and for monetary sanctions.

1. In state court practice, the motion must be made within 45 days of service of the response if service was by hand, or within 50 days if service was by mail.
   a. If the motion is not noticed by that time, the demanding party waives his right to compel further responses.
2. There is no time limit for bringing the motion on federal practice.
3. The moving party must meet and confer with the respondent before making his motion.
   a. If no response is served, the motion to compel responses can be made at any time, even in state court matters, without the necessity of a conference.

VI. The Production

A. The evidence must be made available to the demanding party for the purpose demanded.

1. If the respondent refuses to make the evidence available after a proper written response, the demanding party must make a motion for compliance.
   a. There is no time limit on the motion and no conference requirement.

B. The responding party need not provide the evidence in any condition other than that in which it is normally kept.

C. The respondent cannot evade the demand by producing huge quantities of voluminous files and indicating merely that they include the requested documents.

D. The documents should be sorted into the categories requested.

E. If the demanding party has included photocopying in his request, the documents must be made available for photocopying at the demanding party's expense.

F. If the evidence includes forms of evidence such as computer data, microfilm, videotapes, or audiotapes, the respondent must provide a method of reviewing the information stored in the evidence at the expense of the demanding party.

G. Any party may send a representative to the production, whether he participated in the demand or not.

VII. Role of the Paralegal in Inspection Demands

A. The paralegal should assist counsel by determining what types of documents and tangible evidence should be obtained, from whom, and by what method.

B. Paralegals frequently go to the production.

  1. Evidence must be returned to the respondent in the same condition in which it was produced.

C. Paralegals often prepare the evidence for production.

  1. Irrelevant and privileged material must be removed.

VIII. Organizing and Analyzing Documentary Evidence

A. Documents that are obtained in discovery are usually marked with number or letter codes by either the respondent, the demanding party, or both.

  1. The most common method is often called a Bates stamp.
  2. These markings give each document a unique name.

B. It is also important to distinguish who produced the documents.

  1. This is particularly important in cases where the issues are who knew what, and when.

C. Usually a master copy of all documents is kept, so that there is a complete set of produced documents in the event one is lost or damaged in processing.

  1. Documents are usually organized by chronology, witness, and issue.
     a. The chronology is necessary to show what happened when, who knew what when, and how the events developed.
     b. The chronology may suggest additional witnesses and additional factual issues for discovery.
     c. Witness files are used in the deposition preparation phase for the accumulation of
        (i) all documents that reference the witness.
        (ii) all documents that the witness received or wrote.
     d. The witness files are an invaluable resource, not only for preparing for deposition examination.
     e. Issue files should collect documents relevant to issues.
  2. In preparing documentary evidence, cost comes not from the duplication of paper but in the handling of paper, because time is more expensive than paper.

D. Documents are indexed by making a written log of each document and the relevant features of that document.

1. The master index is usually made of the master file, since it is possible that seemingly unimportant documents may be initially discarded from the issue, witness, and chronological files.
2. The index may contain any number of variables that are suggested by the issues in the case.

E. Documents appearing in more than one index usually develop into the key documents of the litigation.

F. Computer document organization is conceptually the same as manual organization.

CHAPTER OBJECTIVES

1. Describe the process of formulating a list for a request for production of documents.

____

____

____

2. Describe proper responses to a request for production of documents.

____

____

____

3. Describe how documents are prepared for production.

____

____

____

4. Describe a document organization scheme for a simple case.

____

____

____

REVIEW EXERCISES

Fill in the Blanks:

1. What type of evidence is obtained by a request to produce?

____

____

____

2. Give three examples of types of evidence that the demanding party might request, and what might be done with respect to each type of evidence.

a. ____

b. ____

c. ____

3. Documents can be obtained from third parties by service of a(n) ____________________, which may also require personal appearance.

4. Party-affiliated witnesses may be compelled to produce documents by service of a(n) ____________________.

5. How does the rule of 35 apply to document requests in a state court unlimited civil case?

____

____

____

6. How are the documents sought described?

____

____

____

7. In federal court matters, the written response is due no later than

____________________________, and the production itself is due

____________________________.

8. What is contained in the written response?

____

____

____

9. If a party does not want to respond, he must ____________________________;

if a party does not want to produce the items sought, he must

____________________________.

10. In a production of documents, usually the first step for the demanding party is

____________________________, because ____________________________.

KEY WORDS AND PHRASES

Provide a Definition for Each of the Following:

Subpoena duces tecum: ____

____

Indexing: ____

____

Key documents: ____

____

Stipulate: ____

____

Bates stamp: ____

____

Databases: ______________________________

____

Chronology: ______________________________

____

Witness files: ______________________________

____

Issue files: ______________________________

____

Records-only subpoena: ______________________________

____

Privilege log: ______________________________

____

ONLINE PROJECTS

1. Using the official California courts Web site **(http://www.courtinfo.ca.gov/)**, access and read carefully the court's opinion in *Mead Reinsurance Company v. Superior Court* (1986) 188 CA3d 313. Could the requests at issue have been drafted more narrowly to avoid this result? Could the parties have avoided a decision by the court of appeal? The superior court?

2. Using the official California courts Web site **(http://www.courtinfo.ca.gov/)**, access and read carefully the court's opinion in *San Diego Unified Port District v. Douglas E. Barnhart* (2002) 95 CA4th 1400. Why is the testing requested in this case unusual? Under what conditions will a court allow it? Who will pay for it and why?

3. Using the official California courts Web site **(http://www.courtinfo.ca.gov/)**, access and read carefully the court's opinion in *Calcor Space Facility Inc. v. Superior Court* (1997) 53 CA4th 216. What is the rule this court sets forth for describing the documents sought? Why?

4. Using the official California courts Web site **(http://www.courtinfo.ca.gov/)**, access and read carefully the court's opinion in *Deeter v. Angus* (1986) 179 CA3d 241. What are the consequences of failing to produce documents? Why?

5. Access the Federal Rules of Civil Procedure **(http://www.law.cornell.edu/)**, and review rule 34. What do this rule and rule 45 tell you about the process for obtaining documents from third parties?

6. Using the Official California Legislative Information Web site **(http://www.leginfo.ca.gov/)**, locate Code of Civil Procedure sections 2031010–510.

Outline the code sections, paying particular attention to the requirements for both a written response as well as for production. What do they say about enforcement of the right to demand production? What do they say about sanctions?

ADDITIONAL RESEARCH

The following are cases accessible on the official California courts Web site **(http://www.courtinfo.ca.gov/)** on various topics of interest relating to this chapter.

R.S. Creative, Inc. v. Creative Cotton, Ltd. (1999) 75 CA4th 443 (electronic data)

Providian Credit Card Cases (2002) 96 CA4th 292 (protective orders for proprietary information)

Standon Company, Inc. v. Superior Court (1990) 225 CA3d 898 (improper objections and sanctions)

Carter v. Superior Court (1990) 218 CA3d 994 (alternative production at deposition)

QUIZ

1. Documents may be obtained from third parties by
   a. a subpoena duces tecum for business records only.
   b. a subpoena duces tecum for business records and testimony only.
   c. a subpoena duces tecum.
   d. a notice of deposition.

2. A plant specimen may be obtained from a third party by
   a. a subpoena duces tecum for business records only.
   b. a subpoena duces tecum for business records and testimony only.
   c. a subpoena duces tecum.
   d. a notice of deposition.

3. Documents may be obtained from party-affiliated witnesses by
   a. a subpoena duces tecum for business records only.
   b. a subpoena duces tecum for business records and testimony only.
   c. a subpoena duces tecum only.
   d. a request for production.

4. A deposition notice requiring document production must
   a. contain a heading including the name of the propounding party, the respondent, and the set number for the number of deposition sets propounded.
   b. set forth the categories of documents, described with reasonable particularity.
   c. be verified.
   d. a and b.

5. The timing requirements for written responses to requests to produce
   a. are the same in state and federal court.
   b. are 30 days if served by hand, 35 if by mail, in state court.
   c. are 30 days if served by hand, 35 if by mail, in federal court.
   d. are 30 days in federal court.

6. Before making a motion to compel further production
   a. a party must meet and confer in federal court matters.
   b. a party must meet and confer in state court matters.
   c. a state court party must wait 45 days from the date production was due.
   d. a and b.

7. The purpose of the written response is
   a. to confirm the organization of the evidence requested.
   b. to consent to the categorization of the documents requested.
   c. to agree or object to the production of the documents requested.
   d. to notify all parties of the conditions of production.

8. The purpose of Bates-stamping is
   a. to give each document a numerical category.
   b. to give each document a unique name.
   c. to confuse the opposing party about what documents were produced.
   d. to reduce the cost of production.

9. For small cases, documents are usually organized into
   a. chronologies, witness files, and issue files.
   b. indexes of key documents.
   c. complex electronic databases.
   d. a and c.

10. Document requests are
    a. very useful because they can permit inspection of all types of tangible evidence.
    b. are somewhat useful because they are limited to documents only.
    c. are somewhat useful because they are limited to business records only.
    d. are not useful because they do not permit testing and measurement of evidence.

ALTERNATE ASSIGNMENT

Draft a request to produce documents to be propounded on behalf of your client in *Auntie Irma's v. Rilling Enterprises* and/or *Whetstone v. Brian.*

CHAPTER 18

INDEPENDENT MEDICAL EXAMINATIONS

After completing the chapter reading, Discussion Questions, Online Projects, and Assignment, review the material in the following Chapter Outline, then complete the Chapter Objectives, Review Exercises, and Key Words and Phrases. When these are mastered, complete the Online Projects, Additional Research, Quiz, and the Alternate Assignments.

CHAPTER OUTLINE

I. State Court IMEs

A. A party may obtain a medical examination of a person whose mental or physical condition is at issue in a state court action.

B. The person examined is usually the plaintiff who claims to have suffered an injury caused by a defendant or cross-defendant.

C. One defense medical examination is allowed as a matter of right.

1. The medical examination of any other party or any additional examinations (by additional doctors) require court orders.

D. The examination is limited to the named parties.

E. The examination is relevant because by making the claim for damages resulting from his injuries, the plaintiff has put his physical and/or emotional condition in issue.

1. The IME may provide evidence on both liability and damages.

F. Disadvantages of the IME

1. Independent medical examinations are expensive.
2. The medical report may support the plaintiff's case!

II. The State Court Physical IME Demand

A. Each defendant in a personal injury case is entitled to one physical IME of the plaintiff by serving a demand on plaintiff's counsel.

B. Additional medical examinations and all mental examinations require a court order.

C. The demand may be made at any time after the defendant has been served.

1. There is no requirement that the examination take place before the 30-day cutoff before trial.

D. The demand is served on all parties who have appeared in the action.

1. It contains the date for the examination—no earlier than 30 days after service of the demand on the plaintiff if service is by hand, no earlier than 35 days after service if service is by mail.
2. The demand specifies the place—no farther than 75 miles from the plaintiff's residence.
3. The demand also must include the examiner's name and medical specialty and the manner, conditions, scope, and nature of the examination.
   a. The examination must be made or supervised by a licensed physician or other appropriately licensed health care practitioner.
   b. The demand is still valid when the physician orders X-ray and lab technicians and other health care professionals to examine the plaintiff as part of the physical examination.
   c. Examinations by podiatrists, dentists, and physical therapists may be appropriate, even without the supervision of a physician, since they are licensed health care professionals.
4. The demand should contain a description of the tests and procedures that the examiner anticipates.
   a. The defendant should review with the examiner all types of examination that he intends to perform and list them in the demand.

E. The defendant retains the original demand, and copies are served on all parties to the action who have appeared.

III. The State Court Physical IME Response

A. A written response is required within 20 days of the demand served by hand, within 25 days if served by mail.

1. The original is served on the demanding party, and copies are served on all other parties who have appeared.

B. The plaintiff may agree or object to the examination.

1. A refusal to attend or conditions on attendance subject the plaintiff to a motion to compel and to monetary sanctions.

C. The examination is conducted as any other medical examination.

1. The examiner will take a medical history and may comment upon any notations in the plaintiff's medical records.

2. The plaintiff may be accompanied by another person, such as counsel or a paralegal.
   a. The paralegal should carefully review the demand and other discovery to figure out the proper scope of the examination, and should take notes and ask questions during the examination.

IV. The State Court Physical IME Report

A. If the plaintiff demands the examiner's report, he must produce reports from his own experts.

1. These reports prepared by the plaintiff's doctor at the request of the plaintiff's lawyer may be covered by the workproduct privilege and be not otherwise discoverable.
2. Any reports by consultant doctors not designated as expert witnesses are therefore not otherwise discoverable.

B. Plaintiff's counsel cannot avoid disclosure of written reports by instructing consultants and doctors to make verbal reports.

1. Counsel must disclose the identities of all consultants who have not submitted written reports.
2. Counsel must disclose any future reports made for the plaintiff before trial.

C. If the plaintiff demands the examiner's report, the defendant must provide a detailed written report within 30 days of the demand if served by hand, within 35 days if served by mail.

1. In no event shall the exchange be later than 15 days before trial.
2. The written report must set out the history, examinations, and findings (including the results of all tests made, diagnoses, prognoses, and conclusions of the examiner), and must include a copy of all reports from earlier examinations of the examinee regarding the same condition, whether these examinations were made by the reporting examiner or any other examiner.
3. If the defendant fails to deliver the report, the plaintiff may make a motion to compel delivery after meeting and conferring.
   a. If the report is not provided, the examiner may not testify at trial.

D. The plaintiff who demands defendant's report must supply his own reports to the defendant.

1. If he does not, the defendant may make a motion to compel delivery and disclosure of the identities of the plaintiff's doctors.
2. The plaintiff's failure does not excuse performance by the defendant.
3. In addition to monetary sanctions, if plaintiff does not produce reports or identify doctors, plaintiff's doctors can be prevented from testifying at trial.

V. The State Court Mental IME

A. All mental examinations require leave of court because of the potential for harm to the plaintiff by invasion of his privacy.

1. The motion must explain the relevance and importance of the examination and specify any tests or procedures that will be performed.
2. The motion includes an identification of the physician or psychologist proposed to conduct the examination, who must be appointed by the court.

B. Because of the special nature of mental examinations, no one other than the examiner and the party may be present at an examination, but it may be recorded.

C. The rules requiring exchange of reports and remedies for noncompliance are the same whether the examination is pursuant to court order or by right.

VI. Other IMEs in State Court Actions

A. Leave of court must be obtained for

1. a second examination of the plaintiff by the defendant.
2. an examination of someone other than the named party by either the plaintiff or defendant.
3. an examination of the defendant by the plaintiff.

VII. Federal Court IMEs

A. IMEs may be obtained in federal courts of parties or persons in the custody or control of a party (such as minor children in the control of a parent party).

B. A court order is necessary in the event the parties fail to stipulate between themselves on the conditions of the examination.

1. The motion to the court will specify what is sought, when, and why, as well as the identity of the examining physician.
2. If the court grants the motion, its order will specify the conditions for the examination.

VIII. The Paralegal's Role in IMEs

A. The paralegal for the party demanding the IME can help by interpreting the medical records from treating physicians for use by the firm.

1. Several medical dictionaries and even multivolume sets designed for attorneys working on personal injury matters describe medical language and reports.

B. The paralegal can help to locate a health care professional to perform the examination, by consulting a variety of professional associations and clearinghouses for professional witnesses.

1. The paralegal can provide a summary of the case to the examiner so he knows the legal and factual issues presented.

C. After the examination is completed, the paralegal can work with the examiner to prepare him for his deposition and his testimony at trial.

D. The paralegal for the examined party can work with the party's own physicians to understand the proper scope of the examination and to prepare the client for the examination; the paralegal also may attend the IME.

E. After the examination, the paralegal can review the examiner's report and compare it with his notes of the scope of the examination, to make sure that the examiner's conclusions are based on the examination.

   1. The paralegal can communicate the substance of the examination and report to the client's consultants and experts, so that they will be prepared for their depositions and trial.

CHAPTER OBJECTIVES

1. Under what circumstances are physical or psychiatric IMEs appropriate?

____

____

____

2. What are the elements of a request for IME?

____

____

____

3. What does a motion for psychiatric IME have to show?

____

____

____

4. What would you do to prepare yourself to accompany a client to an IME?

   What would you do to prepare the client for an IME?

____

____

____

REVIEW EXERCISES

Fill in the Blanks:

1. An IME may be obtained from whom?

____

____

____

2. Where would a claim justifying an IME be found?

____

____

____

3. When are court orders required for state court IMEs?

a. ______________________________

b. ______________________________

c. ______________________________

4. What are two disadvantages of an IME?

a. ______________________________

b. ______________________________

5. Name four types of physical examinations that could be required to comply with an appropriate IME demand.

a. ______________________________

b. ______________________________

c. ______________________________

d. ______________________________

6. When deciding what tests might be given at an IME, with whom should the demanding attorney consult?

____

____

7. What happens if no report is provided to the parties in a state court case following the examination?

____

____

8. The plaintiff has an obligation to produce ____________________ if he demands reports from the defendant.

9. A mental IME requires state court approval because ____________________, and requires that the court ____________________ the examining health care professional.

10. A paralegal may be present during a(n) ____________________ IME but not during a(n) ____________________ IME.

KEY WORDS AND PHRASES

Provide a Definition for Each of the Following:

Physical IME: ________________________________

____

Mental IME: ________________________________

____

Mental and emotional distress: ________________________

____

Punitive damages: ______________________________

____

Licensed health care professionals: ______________________________

____

ONLINE PROJECTS

1. Using the official California courts Web site **(http://www.courtinfo.ca.gov/)**, access and read carefully the court's opinion in *Vinson v. Superior Court* (1987) 43 C3d 833. Is there any way the plaintiff can avoid or limit the scope of the examination, given the decision of the court? What could be done in pleading the case to avoid this result? How might this affect the advice given to a potential plaintiff in a similar situation, before a case is filed? Are there any circumstances when counsel might be permitted to attend a mental IME? If so, what are they?

2. Using the official California courts Web site **(http://www.courtinfo.ca.gov/)**, access and read carefully the court's opinion in *Grover v. Superior Court* (1958) 161 CA2d 644. Are stipulations for examinations a good idea? What does this case suggest is the best way to enter into stipulations regarding examinations?

3. Using the official California courts Web site **(http://www.courtinfo.ca.gov/)**, access and read carefully the court's opinions in *Munoz v. Superior Court* (1972) 26 CA3d 643 and *Scharff v. Superior Court* (1955) 44 C2d 508. Does the court have any discretion to exclude counsel from a physical IME? Why not? What is the purpose of permitting counsel to be present at an IME? What does this tell you about how a paralegal should prepare himself to accompany a client to an IME?

4. Access the Federal Rules of Civil Procedure **(http://www.law.cornell.edu/)**, and review rule 35. Under what circumstances could a party require another to submit to an IME without a court order? How does the federal rule treat reports of the examiner?

5. Using the Official California Legislative Information Web site **(http://www.leginfo.ca.gov/)**, locate Code of Civil Procedure sections 2032.010–650. Review the sections, and make a list of the circumstances where a court must take action in connection with an IME.

ADDITIONAL RESEARCH

The following are cases accessible on the official California courts Web site **(http://www.courtinfo.ca.gov/)** on various topics of interest relating to this chapter.

California Shellfish, Inc. v. United Shellfish Co. (1997) 56 CA4th 16 (service before "hold")

Shapira v. Superior Court (1990) 224 CA3d 1249 (number of examinations)

Mercury Casualty Company v. Superior Court (1986) 179 CA3d 1027 (examiner may be biased)

Kennedy v. Superior Court (1998) 64 CA4th 674 (reports)

QUIZ

1. The plaintiff claiming emotional injuries
   a. cannot provide credible evidence of his condition.
   b. is not qualified to provide a medical opinion about his condition.
   c. is required to submit to an IME.
   d. must identify his consultants before he is examined.

2. The plaintiff suffering mental or emotional distress
   a. is always subjected to a mental IME because his condition is not observable by the judge and jury.
   b. is subjected to a mental IME only if the defendant requests it.
   c. is examined only if the court so orders.
   d. must produce his own therapist's records upon demand.

3. In state court matters, the records of the plaintiff's physician
   a. can be obtained by subpoena duces tecum, after notice.
   b. can be obtained by notice for consumer records.
   c. can be produced if plaintiff demands the IME report from defendant.
   d. all of the above.

4. An IME may include
   a. only the examination by a licensed physician.
   b. only the examination by a licensed physician and tests he may order.
   c. only the examination by a licensed physician and tests by others whom he supervises.
   d. only the examination by a licensed physician or other licensed health care professional, and tests by others whom he supervises.

5. In state court, the IME
   a. must take place after the 30-day cutoff.
   b. must take place after the 30-day cutoff but before the 15-day cutoff.
   c. may take place at any time after service of summons on the defendant.
   d. must take place at least 45 days before the cutoff to permit time for the examiner's deposition.

6. In federal court practice,
   a. every IME requires a court order.
   b. the parties must stipulate to all aspects of the examination.
   c. a written demand and response is required before the examination.
   d. if the parties don't stipulate, the court may order an IME.

7. The state court defendant
   a. can demand the plaintiff's IME as a matter of right if physical injury is claimed.
   b. can demand the plaintiff's IME through a motion if emotional injury is claimed.
   c. is the only party who can demand a physical IME if physical injuries are claimed.
   d. a and b.

8. If the state court plaintiff demands the defendant's examiner's report,
   a. he must produce all past reports by his doctors.
   b. he must produce all future reports by his doctors.
   c. he must identify all consultants who have not produced reports.
   d. a, b, and c.

9. The disadvantages of IMEs include
   a. cost, timing, and delay.
   b. cost and the possibility the report may support the opposition.
   c. cost and the threat to the plaintiff's emotional state.
   d. timing, delay, and the threat to the plaintiff's emotional state.

10. Persons who may be compelled to submit to an IME include
    a. the plaintiff only.
    b. the plaintiff and defendant only.
    c. the plaintiff, defendant, and third parties.
    d. only one plaintiff, one defendant, and no third parties.

ALTERNATE ASSIGNMENTS

1. *Auntie Irma's v. Rilling Enterprises:* At the time the Lacy Irma license agreement was signed in *Auntie Irma's v. Rilling Enterprises,* Alice Rilling was undergoing psychotherapy as a result of stress on the job. In fact, she was temporarily committed in a psychiatric facility against her will as a result of an apparent suicide attempt. In a memorandum to your supervising attorney, outline whether an IME is appropriate. If so, why? If not, why not? Describe the procedure to be followed to obtain one.

2. *Whetstone v. Brian:* Outline all of the reasons that Brian should be subject to a mental IME in *Whetstone v. Brian.*

CHAPTER 19

EXPERT WITNESS DISCOVERY

After completing the chapter reading, Discussion Questions, Online Projects, and Assignment, review the material in the following Chapter Outline, then complete the Chapter Objectives, Review Exercises, and Key Words and Phrases. When these are mastered, complete the Online Projects, Additional Research, Quiz, and the Alternate Assignments.

CHAPTER OUTLINE

I. Experts Educate Counsel on the Technical Issues Raised in the Case and the Best Evidence Available to Prove His Case.

A. They may also advise on possible methods of presenting the case to the judge and jury, including

1. essential oral testimony.
2. charts and graphs.
3. physical evidence such as replicas of spinal columns and other demonstrative devices.

B. During the trial, the experts can observe the testimony and advise counsel on the weak points presented by the opposition and the best methods for countering adverse testimony.

C. After the trial, they can advise whether the evidence presented by the opposition supports the findings of the judge and jury, forming the basis of appeal.

II. Expert Discovery in State Court

A. The identity and written reports of a plaintiff's medical expert are discoverable if

1. the defendant obtains an IME.
2. the plaintiff's expert prepares a report on plaintiff's condition.
3. the plaintiff demands a copy of the defense medical report.

B. Once one side demands disclosure of other types of experts, it must provide a list of its own experts.

III. Demand for Expert Exchange

A. Any party may make a demand for an exchange of expert witness lists.

1. Once demanded, all parties must exchange lists simultaneously on a timetable set in the code.

B. A demand may be made after the case is set for trial and before the 70th day before the trial date.

1. The trial date is usually set at least 120 days before the trial date.
2. If the court gives less than 120 days' notice for trial, it will set a date for demand and exchange.

C. The demand caption is entitled "Demand for Exchange of Expert Lists."

1. The code section authorizing the exchange and the intended date must be cited in the demand.
   a. The date for exchange can be no earlier than 20 days after the date of service of the demand.
2. The demanding party retains the original and serves copies of the demand on all parties who have appeared in the action.

D. The demand can request exchange of expert lists only, or ask for all reports and writings of the experts.

1. All parties must participate, by a simultaneous exchange of expert lists, and if demanded, all reports and writings of all experts of all parties.
2. Demanding expert reports obligates the demanding party to disclose his own experts' writings and reports.

E. Any party may demand an exchange of reports and writings after the first party has requested merely a list exchange.

IV. The Response to Demand for Exchange

A. Counsel must prepare, verify, and sign an expert witness declaration and attach it to a list of expert names and addresses.

B. The declaration includes

1. the qualifications of each expert, such as his area of expertise, relevant education, employment and experience, and professional associations.
2. the general substance of the expert's testimony, the expert's opinion, and the information on which it is based as the anticipated testimony.
3. the expert's hourly and daily fee for deposition testimony.
4. a statement that the expert has agreed to testify at trial and is sufficiently familiar with the case to provide meaningful deposition testimony.

C. The respondent can trap opposing counsel by

1. listing far more experts than he actually intends to call to testify at trial, forcing opposing parties to choose whom to depose before trial.

2. requesting that experts refrain from preparing written reports.
   a. Doctors and psychologists are required to prepare written reports, or they may be precluded from testifying.
   b. But other experts—engineers and dentists, for example—are not precluded from testifying without written reports.

D. The exchange may be made in person or, more likely, by mail.

E. The exchange must be made on the date designated.

1. There is no explicit extension of time to respond if the demand is served by mail, so prudent practice suggests that opposing counsel is *not* allowed the additional five days to respond.

V. "Late-Disclosed" Experts: Experts Discovered After the Exchange

A. Experts who will testify on the same issues as described in the initial exchange may testify at trial if, within 20 days of the exchange, the party with the new expert serves

1. a supplemental list containing the same types of information about the new expert.
2. a supplemental declaration.
3. relevant reports and writings by the expert.

B. If the initial exchange discloses a type of expert testimony which counsel did not anticipate, he may retain a new expert on that area and serve a supplemental list within 20 days of the initial exchange.

C. If a previously unavailable expert becomes available after the 20-day period allowed for supplemental disclosure, a motion must be made for leave to amend the initial and supplemental lists.

1. Such motions can be made up to and during the trial.
2. The court's ruling will depend on
   a. the disruption of trial.
   b. opportunity to depose.
   c. the value of the testimony.
   d. the reasons for late disclosure.
3. The expert testimony will not be permitted unless the party seeking the evidence permits immediate deposition.
   a. Depositions of experts may be going on at night during the trial.

D. If the party offering expert testimony at trial has not complied with the exchange requirements, all testimony of the expert may be excluded.

1. The objection can be
   a. failure to disclose.
   b. inadequate or misleading disclosure.
   c. failure to provide writings and reports.
   d. failure to make the expert available for deposition.

VI. Expert Discovery in Federal Court

A. Federal rules do not have a provision for an exchange of expert witness lists.

B. Experts are disclosed at a time set by the court, no later than 90 days before the trial date.

C. The disclosure must include

1. a complete statement of all opinions to be expressed and their bases.
2. the data or information considered in forming the opinions.
3. any exhibits to be used as a summary of or support for the opinions.
4. the qualifications of the witness, including a list of all publications authored by the witness within the preceding 10 years.
5. the compensation to be paid for the study and testimony.
6. a listing of any other cases in which the witness has testified as an expert at trial or by deposition within the preceding four years.

D. Federal rules do permit interrogatories seeking

1. the identity of experts the respondent expects to call to testify at trial.
2. the subject matter of the experts' expected testimony.
3. the substance of the facts and opinions about which the expert is expected to testify.

E. Parties are specifically required to update responses to expert interrogatories.

F. Additional discovery of experts may be accomplished through a court order.

G. The federal rule

1. distinguishes between consultants, who are persons with expertise who are retained to advise counsel but do not testify at trial, and experts, who are retained to testify at trial.
2. The information discoverable through interrogatories is limited to experts.
   a. Discovery concerning consultants is not available unless they are examining physicians or psychologists who have prepared discoverable reports or, by leave of court for exceptional circumstances.

H. Experts or consultants whose identities are known may be deposed at the deposing party's expense.

I. Experts or consultants in federal matters must be deposed before the pretrial discovery date set by the court.

1. The usual deposition procedures are followed for this type of deposition.

VII. State Court Expert Depositions

A. The disclosing party must make his experts available for deposition before trial.

B. Experts who have been disclosed in the exchange procedure may be deposed until the 15th day before trial.

1. *These depositions are not affected by the 30-day cutoff.*
2. Depositions of experts disclosed by other discovery means remain subject to the cutoff and must be completed on or before the 30th day before trial.

C. Motions to enforce expert discovery pursuant to the exchange procedure must be made by the 10th day before trial (rather than by the 15 days allowed for other discovery motions).

D. Scheduling depositions can be difficult.

1. Depositions require 10 or 15 days' notice, lists are not exchanged until 50 days before trial, motions to compel expert deposition questions must be made by 10 days before trial and require 15 or 20 days' notice, so the least amount of time to allow for resolution of disputes is 25 days before trial.

E. The deposition of a disclosed expert must be taken within 75 miles of the courthouse where the action will be tried.

1. The parties may stipulate to another location and may be forced to do so to accommodate busy experts who cannot travel to the geographic area designated in the code.
2. If counsel fail to stipulate, the disclosing party may make a motion for leave to take deposition outside geographical limits to "protect" his witness from extreme hardship.

F. No subpoena is necessary to compel attendance at deposition; the notice of deposition served on counsel is sufficient.

G. The expert's fees for testimony at deposition are paid by the deposing party.

1. If the expert is not retained for testimony but is an employee of a party or the party's treating physician, the expert's fees need not be paid by deposing counsel.
2. The expert's fee for deposition testimony may accompany the notice of deposition served on disclosing counsel.
   a. Fees may be paid at the deposition.
   b. Deposing counsel estimates the total length of the deposition and provides the entire fee.
      (i) If the deposition is longer than expected, and the fees tendered are insufficient, the expert must provide an itemized statement to deposing counsel, who then has five days in which to pay the remainder.
   c. If the expert requires payment for travel time or expenses, it is paid by disclosing counsel.

CHAPTER OBJECTIVES

1. What is contained in a request for exchange of expert lists and reports?

____

____

____

2. What is the difference between a consultant and an expert?

____

____

____

3. Why, when, and how does one supplement an expert disclosure?

____

____

____

REVIEW EXERCISES

Fill in the Blanks:

1. Give three examples of how consultants can be used in litigation.

a. ______________________________

b. ______________________________

c. ______________________________

2. Give three examples of how experts can be used in litigation.

a. ______________________________

b. ______________________________

c. ______________________________

State Cases

3. A medical expert hired by the plaintiff and her reports are discoverable if

a. ______________________________

b. ______________________________

c. ______________________________

4. Why is an expert demand required to discover the identities of experts to be used at trial?

____

____

____

____

5. Expert disclosure in a state case may be demanded by ____________________, and once demanded, expert disclosure must be made by ____________________ according to a timetable set by ____________________.

6. The first day the demand can be made pursuant to the code in a state case is ____________________ after trial setting; the last day is ____________________ before trial, whichever date occurs ____________________.

7. In a state case, the timing of response is unique—it is the only discovery tool that is unaffected by ____ ____________________.

8. A supplemental disclosure is permitted if within 20 days, the supplementing party serves

a. ____

b. ____

c. ____

9. A previously unavailable expert can be permitted to testify at trial if

____

____

10. A disclosed expert may not be permitted to testify at trial if

____

____

11. Expert depositions are unique in discovery because they are permitted until ____________________.

12. Experts are compelled to submit to deposition by service of a(n) ____________________ on ____________________.

13. The party who ____________________ pays the expert for the deposition testimony.

Federal Cases

14. Under the federal rules, a party intending to use expert testimony must disclose

a. ____.

b. ____.

c. ____.

d. ____.

e. ____.

f. ____.

15. Discovery concerning consultants is not permitted unless

a. ____ or

b. ____.

KEY WORDS AND PHRASES

Provide a Definition for Each of the Following:

Fact finder: ______________________________

____

Expert witness declaration: ______________________________

____

Expert list: ______________________________

____

Consultant: ______________________________

____

Expert witness: ______________________________

____

Expert deposition: ______________________________

____

Percipient witness: ______________________________

____

ONLINE PROJECTS

1. Using the official California courts Web site **(http://www.courtinfo.ca.gov/)**, access and read carefully the court's opinions in *Stony Brook I Homeowners' Association v. Superior Court* (2000) 84 CA4th 691 and *Kalaba v. Gray* (2002) 95 CA4th 1416. What do these opinions say is specifically required to comply with a demand to exchange expert disclosures? What are the purposes of expert discovery? Why is it increasingly necessary? What would happen if expert disclosures were not available?

2. Using the official California courts Web site **(http://www.courtinfo.ca.gov/)**, access and read carefully the court's opinion in *County of Los Angeles v. Superior Court* (1990) 222 CA3d 647. Given this decision, how would you preserve your exclusive right to an expert even if you decided not to use him? Why might this be important? Would you hire Dr. Verity as your expert? Why or why not?

3. Using the official California courts Web site **(http://www.courtinfo.ca.gov/)**, access and read carefully the court's opinion in *Bonds v. Roy* (1999) 20 C4th 140. What is the purpose of the declaration requirement in an expert disclosure? What would happen if a party did not comply fully with the declarations requirement?

What was the claim concerning the disclosure in this case? Do you agree with the court's analysis?

4. Access the Federal Rules of Civil Procedure **(http://www.law.cornell.edu/)**, and review rule 26. What is the rule regarding supplemental expert discovery? Why is there a different timetable for disclosure of rebuttal expert testimony? What does that timetable permit?

5. Using the Official California Legislative Information Web site **(http://www.leginfo.ca.gov/)**, locate Code of Civil Procedure sections 2034.010–730. What are the types of abuses that such discovery can impose on a party? Under what circumstances may a court protect a party from a disclosure of experts?

ADDITIONAL RESEARCH

The following are cases accessible on the official California courts Web site **(http://www.courtinfo.ca.gov/)** on various topics of interest relating to this chapter.

Schreiber v. Estate of Kiser (1999) 22 CA4th 31 (declaration requirement)

St. Mary Medical Center v. Superior Court (1996) 50 CA4th 1531 (timing; motions to compel)

Hurtado v. Western Medical Center (1990) 222 CA3d 1198 (status of treating physicians)

Rancho Bernardo Development v. Superior Court (1992) 2 CA4th 358 (variable compensation)

QUIZ

1. An employee of a corporate party need not be paid for his deposition testimony on technical matters because
   a. he is a consultant.
   b. he is an expert.
   c. he is a percipient witness.
   d. a and c.

2. A demand for exchange of expert witness lists
   a. can obtain information not available any other way.
   b. can obtain information available other ways, but can do so earlier in the case.
   c. can be served at any time after the defendant is served.
   d. can be served by the defendant at any time.

3. The state case expert witness list must contain
   a. the identities of the experts.
   b. the verification of counsel.
   c. the code section under which disclosure is sought.
   d. a and b.

4. The state case expert declaration must contain
   a. the qualifications of the experts.
   b. their anticipated testimony.
   c. their reports (if requested) and opinions.
   d. a, b, and c.

5. A supplemental declaration can be served when
   a. an expert who was previously unavailable is available for trial.
   b. the deposition fee is not paid.
   c. an expert in an unanticipated area of expertise is needed in response to the initial exchange.
   d. a and c.

6. The written response to demand for exchange
   a. is always served by hand.
   b. is always served by mail.
   c. is served to be received on the day set in the demand, whether or not the demand was served by hand.
   d. must be served to permit the 50-day window for depositions.

7. In federal practice,
   a. an expert disclosure is required.
   b. an exchange is not required if interrogatories are served.
   c. all parties must participate once the demand is made.
   d. information about experts can be obtained through interrogatories.

8. Once a demand is made which does not require the exchange of reports,
   a. parties may only exchange lists and declarations, with no reports.
   b. any responding party may require the report exchange.
   c. any propounding may require the report exchange.
   d. b and c.

9. If an expert is disclosed in state court interrogatories,
   a. he need not be disclosed in the witness declaration.
   b. his deposition must be concluded before the 30-day cutoff.
   c. his deposition must be started before the 30-day cutoff.
   d. a and c.

10. If the expert's fee is not paid with the notice of deposition,
    a. the notice is defective.
    b. it can be paid later, at the deposition.
    c. his deposition can be delayed until the fee is paid.
    d. costs can be included as a penalty to the noticing party.

ALTERNATE ASSIGNMENTS

1. *Auntie Irma's v. Rilling Enterprises:* Because of your client's contacts in the industry, you are aware that the opposition has retained a scientist with vast experience in developing cookie flavors, marketing cookies, and evaluation of cookie companies.

For your supervising attorney, prepare a memorandum outlining how you would go about learning who the scientist is, whether he has been hired to work on the litigation or to testify at trial, and, if so, the exact nature of his testimony. Include how you would go about taking his deposition. Is it significant that the scientist was hired as a regular employee of your opponent? Why or why not? Is it significant that you learned from a third party that the expert was hired? Why or why not?

2. *Whetstone v. Brian:* Prepare a memorandum to your supervising attorney indicating what experts could be used by each side, and for what purpose.

CHAPTER 20

CALENDARING DISCOVERY

After completing the chapter reading, Discussion Questions, Online Projects, and Assignments, review the material in the following Chapter Outline, then complete the Chapter Objectives and Review Exercises. When these are mastered, complete the Online Projects, Additional Research, Quiz, and the Alternate Assignments.

CHAPTER OUTLINE

I. The Basic Calendaring Rules

A. Days are counted the same way as for pleadings.

B. Mail service usually allows five extra days for response in state court practice, and three extra days in federal practice.

II. Limiting Discovery

A. The plaintiff in a state court action may not engage in discovery for the first 10 days after service of summons on the defendant.

1. With the exception of depositions, discovery cannot be served by the plaintiff on the defendant until 10 days after service of summons.
2. Depositions may not be noticed by the plaintiff before the 20th day.

B. In federal court practice, the plaintiff may initiate written discovery after the initial discovery conference.

C. At the pretrial phase

1. in federal court, all discovery must cease by the day designated by the trial judge.
2. in state court, discovery is cut off 30 days before trial, except for expert witness discovery pursuant to a demand for exchange, which is cut off 15 days before trial.

D. Discovery must be completed on or before the cutoff.

1. Adequate time must be allowed for response before the cutoff.
2. Motions to compel in state court must be heard no later than the 15th day before trial, except for those pursuant to disclosed expert discovery, which must be heard by the 10th day before trial.

E. A stipulation to waive the state court discovery cutoff must be in writing; counsel are probably not permitted to waive the federal court cutoff date.

III. Calendaring Discovery Tools

A. Interrogatories

1. State court: Responses to interrogatories must be served within 30 days, with an additional five days if the interrogatories were served by mail, two if by e-mail.
2. Federal court: Responses to interrogatories must be served within 30 days, with an additional three days if the interrogatories were served by mail.

B. Depositions

1. State court: Depositions require 10 days' notice if service is by hand, 15 if served by mail, 12 if by e-mail.
   a. Additional time is specified in the code when the deponent or his counsel is located more than 300 miles away or out-of-state.
   b. Objections to the deposition notice must be made no later than three days before the deposition.
   c. No deposition (other than that of a disclosed expert) may be started after the 30th day before trial.
   d. The notice must allow adequate notice—10 or 15 days, depending on method of service—before the deposition.
      (i) If the deposition is commenced but not completed before the 30th day, it can continue until completed.
   e. There are two exceptions to the rules previously stated.
      (i) Depositions can be taken before the case is even filed, by order of the court, usually to preserve testimony that might not be available by the time the matter is filed.
      (ii) Depositions may be taken after the trial, by order of the court, usually to preserve evidence in the event of a new trial upon appeal.
   f. Subpoenas compelling attendance must be personally served a "reasonable" time before the deposition.
   g. Subpoenas duces tecum must be served at least 10 days prior to the deposition to allow compilation of documents and evidence.
   h. A notice of deposition for production of consumer records must allow at least 20 days for production.
   i. The subpoena duces tecum must be issued at least 15 days before the deposition and served on the custodian, with a copy to the consumer, at least 10 days before the deposition.
2. Federal court: The written notice of deposition must provide "reasonable" notice to all parties of the deposition.

a. The party may not take a deposition before the initial discovery conference.
b. There are two exceptions.
   (i) Depositions can be taken before the case is even filed by order of the court.
   (ii) Depositions can be taken after the trial by order of the court.
c. Subpoenas compelling attendance must be personally served a "reasonable" time before the deposition.
d. Subpoenas duces tecum must be served at least 30 days prior to the deposition to allow compilation of documents and evidence.
   (i) Subpoenas must be issued by the federal court clerk in the jurisdiction where the witness is found, so they may take extra time to obtain prior to service.
e. Federal courts may follow the state code concerning production of consumer records, which must allow at least 20 days for production.
   (i) The subpoena duces tecum, also issued by the federal court clerk at the location of the witness, must be issued at least 15 days before the deposition and served on the custodian, with a copy to the consumer, at least 10 days before the deposition.

C. Requests for admissions

1. State court: Responses to requests for admissions must be served within 30 days, with an additional five days if the interrogatories were served by mail, two if by e-mail.
2. Federal court: Responses to requests for admissions must be served within 30 days, with an additional three days if the interrogatories were served by mail.

D. Demands for inspection

1. State court: Written responses to a request for inspection must be served within 30 days of a request served by hand, with an additional five days if the request is served by mail, two if by e-mail.
   a. The request for inspection may not state a date for the inspection earlier than 30 days from the date of service by hand, 35 days if by mail, 32 if by e-mail.
2. Federal court: Written responses to a request for inspection must be served within 30 days of service by hand, with an additional three days if the request was served by mail.
   a. The date for inspection may be any time after the 30th day after service by hand, or after the 33rd day for service by mail.

E. IMEs

1. State court: The physical examination cannot be demanded earlier than 30 days from service of the demand by hand, 35 for service by mail, 32 if by e-mail.
2. Federal court: The physical or mental examination is obtained by leave of court, which will specify the date and timing of the examination.

F. Expert witness disclosure

1. State court: A demand for expert witness disclosure cannot be made before the case is set for trial and must be made at least 70 days from the trial date.
   a. The demand specifies a date for the exchange, which must be at least 20 days after service of the demand.
   b. Supplemental disclosures may be made within 20 days of the date of exchange.
   c. Depositions of disclosed experts require the same notice as other depositions but may take place up to the 15th day before trial.
2. Federal court: Expert identities and opinions are discoverable through initial disclosure and written interrogatories, with depositions subject to the usual deposition procedures.

CHAPTER OBJECTIVES

1. What are the considerations of a discovery plan that require calendaring?

____

____

____

2. When may plaintiff's discovery be served in a state court case?

____

____

____

3. When may discovery be served in a federal case?

____

____

____

4. When are responses to written discovery due in a state court case?

____

____

____

____

5. When are responses to written discovery due in a federal court case?

____

____

____

6. How are depositions calendared?

____

____

____

REVIEW EXERCISES

Fill in the Blanks:

1. In state court cases, deadlines for completion of discovery are set by the ______________________; in federal court, they are more commonly set by the ______________________.

2. When serving written discovery, the propounding party must keep in mind the ______________________, the last day by which responses must be served; in a deposition setting, the deposition must be ______________________ by the last day to complete discovery.

3. If the parties decide to serve discovery beyond the last date in a state court case, their agreement ______________________.

4. What state court discovery requires responses within 30 days if the discovery was propounded by hand?

a. ______________________

b. ______________________

c. ______________________

5. What federal court discovery requires responses within 33 days if served by mail?

a. ______________________________

b. ______________________________

c. ______________________________

6. A state court deposition notice must be served by hand at least ______________ days before the deposition; a federal court deposition notice must be served by hand at least a ______________ before the deposition.

7. Notices for production of consumer records provide an additional ______________ days for production, to permit ______________.

8. Subpoenas must be served ______________ before the deposition.

9. Discovery can be taken before a case is filed or after trial if the party obtains a(n) ______________.

10. Subpoenas duces tecum for state court cases are served at least ______________ days before the deposition to permit compilation of the documents; federal court rules provide ______________ days' notice.

ONLINE PROJECTS

1. Using the official California courts Web site **(http://www.courtinfo.ca.gov/)**, access and read carefully the court's opinion in *Professional Career Colleges, Magna Institute, Inc. v. Superior Court* (1989) 207 CA3d 490. What does this case say about the extent of calendaring for discovery? Should the court's opinion pose serious problems for most cases, even if a motion to compel deadline is missed? Why or why not?

2. Using the official California courts Web site **(http://www.courtinfo.ca.gov/)**, access and read carefully the court's opinion in *Sipple v. Foundation for National Progress* (1999) 71 CA4th 226. What is a SLAPP suit? How are the discovery holds different in a potential SLAPP suit? Why?

3. Access the Federal Rules of Civil Procedure **(http://www.law.cornell.edu/)**, and review rule 27. What is the rule regarding depositions pending appeal? Why is such a rule necessary?

4. Using the Official California Legislative Information Web site **(http://www.leginfo.ca.gov/)**, locate Code of Civil Procedure section 2024.010–060. What factors will a court consider before granting a motion to permit a party to perform discovery beyond the discovery cutoff? Are there any discovery tools that should not be calendared to extend the time to the business day following a court holiday? Why or why not?

ADDITIONAL RESEARCH

The following are cases accessible on the official California courts Web site **(http://www.courtinfo.ca.gov/)** on various topics of interest relating to this chapter.

> *Department of Fair Employment and Housing v. Superior Court*, 225 CA3d 728 ("pending" case)
>
> *California Shellfish, Inc. v. United Shellfish Co.* (1997) 56 CA4th 16 (service before "hold")

QUIZ

1. Service of discovery responses
   a. is extended five days if service of the demand was by hand.
   b. is extended three days if service of the demand was by mail.
   c. must be by hand if service was by hand, and by mail, if service was by mail.
   d. is by mail in federal court; by mail, e-mail, or hand in state court.

2. State court rules
   a. prohibit plaintiff's discovery prior to filing the complaint, except by court order.
   b. prohibit defendant's discovery prior to filing the complaint, except by court order.
   c. prohibit discovery prior to filing the complaint.
   d. a and b.

3. The final discovery cutoff
   a. only applies to state court.
   b. is 30 days before trial in state court.
   c. only applies to federal court.
   d. is 15 days before trial in state court.

4. Responses in state court must be served 30 days after service of
   a. interrogatories, by hand.
   b. interrogatories and IMEs, by mail.
   c. interrogatories and document requests, by hand.
   d. a and c.

5. Depositions
   a. in state court require 10 days' notice if service is by hand.
   b. in federal court require 10 days' notice if service is by hand.
   c. in state court require 15 days' notice if service is by hand.
   d. in federal court require 15 days' notice if service is by hand.

6. Responses to demands for inspection
   a. are filed 30 days after service by hand.
   b. are filed 30 days after service by mail or by hand.
   c. are served 33 days after mail service of the demand in federal court.
   d. are served 30 days after mail service of the demand in superior court.

7. The two discovery tools which require written responses as well as performance are
   a. document demands and site inspections.
   b. document demands and IMEs.
   c. document demands and depositions.
   d. IMEs and depositions.

8. A motion to compel further answers
   a. must be filed no later than 45 days after responses were served in federal court, plus three days if service was by mail.
   b. must be filed no later than 45 days after responses were served in state court, plus five days if service was by mail.
   c. must be filed no later than 50 days after responses were served in state court, plus five days if service was by mail.
   d. must be filed no later than 50 days after responses were served in federal court, plus three days if service was by mail.

9. State court depositions
   a. may not be started after the 30-day cutoff unless the deponent is an expert.
   b. must be completed by the 30-day cutoff, unless the deponent is an expert.
   c. may not be started after the 30-day cutoff.
   d. must be complete before the 30-day cutoff.

10. State court notices for deposition must provide at least 10 days' notice except for
    a. expert depositions.
    b. depositions for consumer records.
    c. those requiring a subpoena duces tecum.
    d. a and b.

ALTERNATE ASSIGNMENTS

1. Recalculate the answers to the sample problems in the text as if the cases were filed in federal court. Note the aspects that are not relevant to federal practice.

2. Recalculate the answers to the sample problems in the text, with the following changes:

SAMPLE PROBLEM 1: The case was filed November 25 but served November 27.
SAMPLE PROBLEM 2: The summons and complaint were served December 1.

SAMPLE PROBLEM 4: The trial is set for February 26.
SAMPLE PROBLEM 5:

a. Interrogatories are served by mail December 11.
b. Interrogatories are served by hand December 19.
c. Requests for admissions are served by hand December 30.
d. Requests for admissions are served by mail December 18.
e. A request for production of documents is served by hand December 12.
f. A request for inspection is served by mail December 12.

3. Recalculate the answers to Question 2 as if the cases were filed in federal court. Note the aspects that are not relevant to federal practice.

CHAPTER

21

LAW AND MOTION

After completing the chapter reading, Discussion Questions, Online Projects, and Assignment, review the material in the following Chapter Outline, then complete the Chapter Objectives, Review Exercises, and Key Words and Phrases. When these are mastered, complete the Online Projects, Additional Research, Quiz, and the Alternate Assignments.

CHAPTER OUTLINE

I. Pleading and Discovery Disputes Present Problems for Immediate Resolution by the Law and Motion Court.

A. Law and motion matters are heard on a law and motion calendar.

1. State court law and motion calendars are set differently in each jurisdiction.
   a. Direct calendar system jurisdictions assign each case to a trial judge at the outset, and usually require that judge to handle law and motion matters.
   b. Master calendar jurisdictions provide one or more departments to hear and decide law and motion matters.
      (i) These law and motion departments may consist of one or more judges, depending on the workload of that jurisdiction.
2. Federal court law and motion matters are heard by the trial judge.

B. Local rules govern much of law and motion practice in both state and federal court.

1. Local rules are the best source for information about scheduling, preparing, and filing law and motion matters.
2. In practice, some issues may not be clearly administrative or procedural; the local rules or court clerk will clarify which department should hear them.
3. Examples include when one or more of the parties seek changes in the trial schedule, seeking
   a. a continuance (delay).
   b. preference (expedited trial date).
   c. special setting (specific date for trial).

II. Motions Are Really a Process.

A. Motions are made up of

1. moving papers filed with the court by the moving party.
2. opposition papers filed by the opposition.
3. an optional reply by the moving party.

B. The motion is argued at a hearing before the court, followed by the order of the court.

C. The order either grants or denies the request of the moving party.

1. The order is served on all parties to the action.
    a. A copy of the signed order is usually served on all parties with a notice of entry of order, which informs each party of the outcome of the motion.

D. Motions have calendaring limitations.

E. Paralegals often prepare motions and must understand them to properly participate in the litigation.

III. General Caption and Format Rules

A. Governing rules are in the Rules of Court, the Code of Civil Procedure, and case law.

1. Always consult all applicable rules, including the local rules.
2. Defective papers may not be filed, or may result in sanctions against counsel or the client.

B. The caption is the same as the most recently filed pleading.

1. The parties may be abbreviated by using "et al."
2. Cross-actions may be described in a one-line caption: "and related cross-actions."

C. The motion title appears directly below the case number on the right side of the caption.

1. It must identify each document attached to that document.
    a. For example, a title could be "Notice of Motion and Motion for Order Compelling Production of Documents" or "Notice of Motion for Order Compelling Production of Documents, Memorandum of Points and Authorities in Support thereof, and Declaration of Arthur Advocate in Support thereof."
    b. The choice is usually one of the firm's style and custom, and expediency.

D. Immediately below the title must appear the date, time, and department of the court where the matter will be heard, and the trial date.

E. State and most federal local rules require footers on each page, and the date of the next status conference and the name of the trial judge in the caption.

F. Scheduling the motion

1. Courts differ on whether they require counsel to schedule appearances before selecting hearing dates.
2. Confirm with the court clerk the time of the law and motion calendar.

G. If the date or time specified in the caption is not a time during which the motion can be heard, the court will not correct the error or even notify counsel that an error has been made.

H. Motion papers are bound with staples in the top left-hand corner and page numbers appear in the center at the bottom.

1. Pages are consecutively numbered.

I. Local rules may require that paragraphs be consecutively numbered or that holes be punched at the top of the document to facilitate filing.

IV. The Three Features of Motions

A. The notice of motion must state the time and place of the hearing.

1. "Notice" refers to the document; a motion hearing is "noticed."
2. The date, time, and place of the motion is traditionally given in the first paragraph of the notice, though court rules require it in the caption, underneath the case number and document title.
   a. State court motions must allow for service of the moving papers at least 16 days before the hearing, with an additional five days for mailing, two for e-mail service.
   b. The FRCP require a minimum of five days, but local rules may extend this period.
      (i) The FRCP permits an additional three days if served by mail.
3. The moving party must determine the days on which such matters are heard by the court, the type of service that will be used, and the time required to permit adequate notice.
4. The nature of and the grounds for the order must be stated and described in the first paragraph of the notice.
   a. The court cannot give any relief not requested in the notice.
5. The notice also must state the evidence and papers upon which the motion is based.
   a. The notice refers to "all papers and pleadings on file herein," so that counsel can refer to them if necessary in oral argument.

B. Law and legal argument are presented in the memorandum of points and authorities.

1. "Points" are argument, and "authorities" are citations to the law.
2. A memorandum must be filed with every motion; a motion without a memorandum may be deemed frivolous.
3. A memorandum of points and authorities should contain a concise statement of fact relevant to the motion and the law and evidence upon which the motion is based.
4. Memos more than 10 pages must have a table of contents and a table of authorities; memos may not exceed 15 pages.
5. The memorandum contains statements of law followed by citations to appropriate legal authorities.
   a. California citation style, defined in the *California Style Manual*, should be followed in state court.

b. Federal courts require use of federal citation style, defined in the Harvard *Citator*, also called the Harvard *Bluebook*.
c. Primary authorities, such as court opinions and law journal articles, are favored while secondary sources are disfavored.

C. Statements of fact are supported by evidence.

1. Usually that evidence is documents or a declaration by anyone competent to provide sworn testimony.
2. The evidence is cited in the memorandum.
3. Declarations may be included, with documents bound together or filed separately.
4. Documentary evidence is usually attached to a declaration stating that the exhibits are true and accurate copies of the documents listed.

D. The memorandum also contains argument.

1. The drafter usually states the issues, the rules of law, and argues that the rule applies to the facts.
2. The drafter argues that the facts of his case are either consistent with facts in other cases that held in his favor or inconsistent with cases holding against him.
3. Argumentative statements advocate an application of the cited law to the facts cited.

E. Memoranda are cite checked.

1. Each citation is reviewed for content and style.

F. Memoranda should also be fact cite checked.

1. Each factual reference is reviewed for content and presentation.

V. Service and Filing

A. Motions must be served on all parties to the action who have appeared.

B. Original moving papers are filed with the court clerk when served on the opposing parties.

1. A proof of service form must be filed with the court.

VI. Opposing Motions

A. Attacks may be that the format is defective, or they may be made on substantive grounds.

1. Both should be included in the opposition, to increase persuasive value.

B. The opposition is entitled "Opposition to," stating the motion title, followed by a memorandum of points and authorities.

1. No notice of motion is required.
2. Declarations and exhibits may be prepared and filed with the opposition memorandum.

3. No factual summary is required.
   a. A factual summary is advisable when the moving party's summary is inaccurate or incomplete.

C. All opposition papers must be filed at least 10 calendar days before the hearing of the motion.

VII. Replying to the Opposition

A. The moving party can reply to respond to the opposition's arguments and evidence
   1. at least five days before the hearing in state court.
   2. five to seven days before the hearing in federal court, depending on the district.

B. Replies respond to arguments and evidence presented in the opposition.
   1. They are not restatements of the moving party's position.

C. There are two schools of thought about the efficacy of replies.
   1. Any motion worth making is worth defending with a reply.
   2. Since the reply is filed so close to the hearing date, it has little influence over the judge, and should only be filed where the opposition has seriously misstated the facts or law.

VIII. Tentative Rulings

A. State courts generally publish their tentative rulings a day or two before the hearing.
   1. Counsel can evaluate whether to appear to challenge the ruling of the court.
   2. If counsel do not appear at the scheduled hearing, the tentative ruling becomes the order of the court.
   3. A dissatisfied party must call the court and all other parties to inform them that the tentative ruling will be challenged, and on what grounds.

B. Tentative rulings are published in the legal newspaper, on a telephone tape recording, and online.

IX. Law and Motion Hearings

A. The court usually takes a roll of the contested rulings.

B. The challenging party usually speaks first, arguing why the tentative ruling is incorrect.

C. When both sides have completed their argument, they submit the matter for adjudication.

D. Federal judges are notorious for rules about how matters are presented in their courtrooms.
   1. In federal court, the courtroom clerk often has written "courtroom rules" that set forth that judge's requirements.

E. The paralegal visits the courtroom to observe the judge and note how his interests might be incorporated into the party's presentation.

X. Orders of the Court

A. Service of the court's order triggers time limits to comply.

1. The proposed order may be signed at the hearing, or another order may be drafted after the hearing.
   a. Counsel also may prepare orders based on the tentative ruling and take two copies to the argument.
      (i) One copy will be kept by the court as the original; the other is provided to counsel to serve.
2. If the motion is modified at or after the hearing, it can be modified by hand for the judge's signature.
3. If the order is not signed at the hearing, it can take a considerable amount of time to have such an order signed and filed.

B. An order prepared after the hearing is usually submitted to the opposition to sign "approved as to form" before submitting to the court.

1. Some local rules now require that all orders be "approved as to form" by all counsel before submission.

C. The court clerk checks counsel's proposed order against the minute order book.

1. The original is retained for the court's files, and the copies are returned to the party who submitted them.

D. The signed copies are served on all other counsel, attached to a "Notice of Entry of Order."

1. Any act required by the order within a specified time frame is usually calculated from the date of service, so it should be served as soon as possible.

XI. Sanctions Are Penalties for Causing Harassment or Delay in Bad Faith.

A. Sanctions are usually fines against a party, its lawyer, or both.

B. The court also may dismiss a complaint or strike an answer where the burden has been severe.

1. Usually the "burden" is the time and expense involved to one party when the other fails to comply with court rules.

C. Sanctions are usually in the amount of the fees and costs associated with bringing or defending an unnecessary motion.

D. The award of financial sanctions is almost automatic, except when the court can make an affirmative finding that the noncompliance was inadvertent or in good faith.

1. Sanctions are mandatory for an unreasonable failure to respond to requests for admissions.

E. The moving party must specifically request them in the motion.

1. A noticed motion is required for an award of sanctions, or the opposition requests sanctions as part of the opposition papers.

F. The request for sanctions should be included in the title of the document and in the notice of motion if made by the moving party.

1. It is explained in the memorandum of points and authorities, with appropriate rules and cases cited in the body of the memo.
2. The memorandum should be supported with a declaration by counsel stating the amount of time spent in compelling compliance by the moving party or defending the frivolous motion by the defending party, with
   a. the hourly rate charged the client.
   b. any costs (such as photocopying, messenger costs, and filing fees) required for the motion.

G. The award of sanctions is included in the order on the merits.

XII. Ex Parte Motions

A. An ex parte motion does not require the presence of opposing counsel and may be made on less than the required notice.

B. Ex parte motions occur when an extreme emergency exists, or where giving notice to the opposition will result in the destruction of evidence.

C. Routine ex parte applications are occasionally made to shorten time for a noticed motion, or to file a brief exceeding the normal page limit.

D. Ex parte motions follow the same format as noticed motions.

1. Notice is usually by telephone at least 24 hours before the motion will be presented for adjudication.
   a. State court local rules specify the exact length of notice required, usually at least 24 hours.
   b. Federal court rules require notice but do not specify a minimum time for notice.
2. Notice includes
   a. the date, time, and place of the motion.
   b. the nature and type of order sought.
   c. the evidence upon which it will be based.

E. Ex parte motions concerning filing other motions or pleadings must have them attached.

1. The court will evaluate the underlying motion as part of the ex parte application, although there will be no ruling on it.

F. Ex parte orders are on the ex parte application, not on the underlying motion.

G. If the ex parte motion is granted, the application papers are filed, and the party seeking the order may file the underlying matter.

1. The underlying motion can then be served on all parties with a copy of the ex parte order.

H. If the ex parte application is denied, neither it nor the underlying brief are filed.

I. If a paralegal receives notice of an ex parte application by another party, he must obtain complete information.

1. If counsel is unavailable, the paralegal should telephone the court.

XIII. Specific Types of Motions

A. Amending pleadings

1. Amendment after the answer is filed can only be done by order of the court.
2. Calendaring rules for motions for leave to amend are the same as for ordinary motions.
3. The motion must include a copy of the proposed pleading for the court to review.
4. If the motion is granted, the proposed amended pleading may be filed in the court file, served, and usually
   a. the court's order requires a response within a specified period of time or 10 days if none is ordered.

B. Discovery motions

1. Motions to compel discovery compliance where no response has been provided may be made at any time after the response is due, without necessity to "meet and confer."
2. Motions to compel further responses require a meet and confer attempt.
   a. It is usually documented in the motion by either a copy of a letter confirming the attempt or by counsel's declaration.
3. In state court, the motion must be noticed within 45 days of the service of the responses, with an additional five days if they were mailed.
4. There is no time limit for motions to compel further responses in federal court.
5. Motions to compel further responses to discovery requests must be filed with a "*separate* statement," containing each request, the answer, and a short argument explaining the facts and law which support the motion for further answers.
   a. It effectively replaces the memorandum of points and authorities, but the memorandum is still required.
   b. The opposing party must prepare the same document, arguing why his response is adequate.
   C. Motions for protective order must be accompanied by a document outlining the discovery sought and explaining why protection is justified.

XIV. Motions for Reconsideration and Renewing Motions

A. A motion for reconsideration is the same motion before the same judge based on a different set of facts.

1. In state court, such a motion must be brought within 10 days of counsel's knowledge of the order denying his initial motion and before the same judge.
2. In federal court, local rules set forth the specific motion requirements.

B. A motion to renew is the same as the original motion.

1. Such motions need not be made before the same judge and can be made whenever new facts can be shown justifying the relief sought.

C. A motion for rehearing is made when the court has made a mistake.

XV. The Litigation Paralegal Can Perform All of the Tasks Involved in Law and Motion Except Signing the Moving Papers and Appearing in Court.

A. Drafting (or responding to) a motion involves calendaring skills so that the motion provides adequate notice and is properly filed.

B. Drafting the supporting or opposing memoranda of points and authorities requires mastery of the factual background, as well as an understanding of the issue posed by the dispute and the legal authorities that both support and oppose the desired outcome.

CHAPTER OBJECTIVES

1. What are the parts of a motion to compel discovery, and what is contained in each?

____

____

____

2. What are the elements of an opposition to a motion to compel, and what is contained in each?

____

____

____

3. What is the format of motion papers, and how are they prepared for filing?

____

____

____

REVIEW EXERCISES

Fill in the Blanks:

1. In a direct calendar jurisdiction, the __________________________ judge hears law and motion matters; in a __________________________ jurisdiction, they are heard by the __________________________ judge.

2. In federal court cases, the ____________________________ judge hears law and motion matters.

3. The best source of information about how a court manages law and motion is found in the ____________________________.

4. Motions are always served on ____________________________, even though they may directly affect only one.

5. Care in setting forth the date and time on the motion must be taken because ____________________________.

6. Most state court motions require a minimum of ____________________________ days' notice before the hearing; the Federal Rules of Civil Procedure require a minimum of ____________________________ days.

7. The proof of service is attached to the original motion filed with the court because ____

____

____

8. Why do state law and motion courts provide tentative rulings?

____

____

____

9. Sanctions are imposed in law and motion court when the court finds ____________________________, but they usually are not imposed unless the opposing party ____________________________.

10. Motions that are made on less than required notice are called

____________________ because ____________________; they are made when either

a. ____ or

b. ____.

11. Most ex parte applications require at least ____________________ notice to all parties; since no written papers will be served, counsel receiving notice must be careful that she obtains the following information about the application:

a. ____

b. ____

c. ____

d. ____

12. If the court grants a motion to amend a complaint and does not specify the time to respond, it is ____________________.

13. In state court, the deadline to file a motion to compel further discovery responses is ____________________; in federal court matters, the deadline to file a motion to compel further responses is ____________________.

14. A party serving a state court motion to compel further discovery responses must first ____________________ with the responding party; this requirement is not necessary if the moving party seeks an order ____________________.

15. A motion to compel further responses must include a

________________________ that sets forth

a. ____

b. ____

c. ____.

16. A motion for ________________________ is the same motion made a second time on different facts.

17. A motion to ________________________ is the same as the original motion.

18. A motion for ________________________ is made when the court has made a mistake.

19. A motion for protective order must include

a. ____

b. ____.

20. The two first steps to drafting a memorandum of points and authorities include:

a. ____

b. ____

KEY WORDS AND PHRASES

Provide a Definition for Each of the Following:

Department: ____

____

Continuance/continue: ____

____

Preference: ______________________________

____

Special setting: ______________________________

____

Motion: ______________________________

____

Cite checking: ______________________________

____

Notice of motion: ______________________________

____

Points: ______________________________

____

Authorities: ______________________________

____

Memorandum of points and authorities: ______________________________

____

Reply: ______________________________

____

Tentative ruling: ______________________________

____

E-filing: ______________________________

____

Submission: ______________________________

____

Minute order: ______________________________

____

Minute order book: ______________________________

____

Sanctions: ______________________________

____

Sua sponte: ______________________________

____

Motion for reconsideration: ______________________________

____

Motion to renew: ______________________________

____

Motion for rehearing: ______________________________

____

Ex parte motion: ______________________________

____

ONLINE PROJECTS

1. Using the official California courts Web site **(http://www.courtinfo.ca.gov/)**, access and read carefully the court's opinion in *Stanton v. Superior Court* (1990) 225 CA3d 898. Could this dispute have been avoided? If so, how? If not, why not? What lesson can be learned from this case about making, supporting, and overcoming objections to discovery requests? What guidance does this court provide for interpreting discovery statutes?

2. Using the official California courts Web site **(http://www.courtinfo.ca.gov/)**, access and read carefully the court's opinion in *Steele v. Barlett* (1941) 18 C2d 573. What is the consequence of an opposition due on a weekend or holiday? How would you avoid this situation?

3. Using the official California courts Web site **(http://www.courtinfo.ca.gov/)**, access and read carefully California Rules of Court rules 3.1110–1116. Outline these requirements for law and motion filings. What do these rules suggest is the first resource for preparation and filing of documents with the court?

4. Access the Federal Rules of Civil Procedure **(http://www.law.cornell.edu/),** and review rule 37. What are the consequences of a failure to comply with discovery requirements? Which of these consequences must be imposed in law and motion activity, and which in trial?

ADDITIONAL RESEARCH

The following are cases accessible on the official California courts Web site **(http://www.courtinfo.ca.gov/)** on various topics of interest relating to this chapter.

Kalivas v. Barry Controls Corporation (1996) 49 CA4th 1152 (local rules)

Marriage of Hegge (2002) 99 CA4th 28 (declarations)

Rosenberg v. Superior Court (1994) 25 CA4th 897 (deadline to file)

Medix Ambulance Service Inc. v. Superior Court (2002) 97 CA4th 109 (tentative rulings procedures)

QUIZ

1. Motions made to change the ruling of a previous motion include motions
   a. to renew, for reconsideration, and for continuance.
   b. to renew, for reconsideration, and for rehearing.
   c. to renew, for rehearing, and for continuance.
   d. for rehearing, for continuance, and for preference.

2. The court clerk records the court's orders in the
   a. tentative ruling.
   b. minute order book.
   c. submission.
   d. authorities.

3. A calendar system which assigns the matter to a trial judge for all purposes including law and motion has a
   a. law and motion calendar system.
   b. a direct calendar system.
   c. a master calendar system.
   d. preference system.

4. "Calendar" motions
   a. are usually heard by the presiding judge.
   b. include motions for preference.
   c. include motions for special setting.
   d. a, b, and c.

5. To file a proper motion for sanctions, the moving party must include
   a. reference to the request in the notice of motion.
   b. a bill for counsel's time.
   c. a declaration from the client showing prejudice or harm.
   d. evidence showing attempts to meet and confer.

6. To file a proper motion to compel further responses, the moving party must include
   a. reference to the request in the notice of motion.
   b. a bill for counsel's time.
   c. a declaration from the client showing prejudice or harm.
   d. evidence showing attempts to meet and confer.

7. Memoranda of points and authorities
   a. must be filed with each motion.
   b. need not be filed if the discovery motion includes a separate statement.
   c. contain sworn statements by counsel.
   d. a and b.

8. A notice of motion
   a. tells the date, time, and place of the motion.
   b. tells the nature of the motion and the grounds on which it is based.
   c. indicates what documents are filed to support the motion.
   d. a, b, and c.

9. The decision to file a reply should be based on
   a. the importance of the motion and the arguments being made.
   b. the fact that the judge will not read it anyway.
   c. they are always too expensive to be part of current practice.
   d. a declaration of necessity by counsel.

10. Motions to compel further responses
   a. can be made at any time in state court.
   b. can be made at any time in federal court.
   c. must be made before the 50th day after responses were due in state court.
   d. b and c.

ALTERNATE ASSIGNMENTS

1. *Auntie Irma's v. Rilling Enterprises:* Draft a motion to compel further responses to interrogatories.

IF YOU REPRESENT AUNTIE IRMA'S: Auntie Irma's is suing Rilling Enterprises and Alice Rilling for breach of contract and fraud. In the complaint, Lucille Fitzhugh, on behalf of Auntie Irma's, alleges that five or six years ago she was contacted by a business broker, Judy Roberts, who wanted to sell Auntie Irma's a Rilling Roll license to permit Auntie Irma's to market the Rilling Roll anywhere, and to sell in Fremont County. Fitzhugh negotiated a permanent license with Williams over the telephone, for five annual payments of $50,000. Auntie Irma's was not required to pay any royalty. The agreement was the standard agreement but with the royalty language crossed out and initialed. Before entering into the agreement, Fitzhugh was aware of representations made to the public, including Auntie Irma's, and she confirmed with Rilling that Rilling Enterprises did not and would never compete directly with its licensees by marketing cookies directly to the public. As soon as the last license payment was made, and Rilling Enterprises could anticipate no more income from the license, it wrongfully terminated Auntie Irma's license, opened a shop in Fremont County, and sold the Rilling Roll directly to the public. Auntie Irma's believes that the damage to the company exceeds $500,000, including the $250,000 license fee.

Two years ago, Fitzhugh and Rilling discussed Rilling's desire to market the Lacy Irma. They executed an exclusive license for Rilling Enterprises to sell sublicenses to cookie shops selling the Rilling Roll, so that they could also sell the Lacy Irma. This agreement was drafted by Fitzhugh. It required that Rilling Enterprises obtain a nondisclosure agreement with each sublicensee, provide a copy of the nondisclosure agreement to Auntie Irma's within 30 days of signature, and pay a 7 percent royalty on gross sales each year. Rilling has never obtained the nondisclosure agreements, has never sent any to Auntie Irma's, believes that the royalty would exceed $100,000.

Rilling Enterprises has also filed a counterclaim against Auntie Irma's and Fitzhugh, also with causes of action for breach of contract and fraud. The counterclaim alleges that Auntie Irma's contacted a business broker, Judy Roberts, to negotiate a license to market the Rilling Roll anywhere, and to sell in Fremont County. Rilling agreed to a permanent license for five annual payments of $50,000. Auntie Irma's was not required to pay any royalty. The agreement was the standard agreement but with the royalty language crossed out and initialed. About three years into the agreement, Auntie Irma's sales fell below minimum standards for the license. Two years ago Rilling Enterprises terminated the license for this breach of the agreement.

A year ago Fitzhugh and Rilling discussed Rilling's desire to market the Lacy Irma. Fitzhugh agreed that Auntie Irma's would develop a new flavor of the cookie each year and expand the line. This was an essential part of the agreement for Rilling Enterprises. They executed an exclusive license for Rilling Enterprises to sell sublicenses to cookie shops selling the Rilling Roll, so that they could also sell the Lacy Irma. Auntie Irma's has never provided additional flavors of the Lacy Irma and a few months ago, wrongfully terminated the license.

Rilling Enterprises seeks damages of $250,000 for the breached license agreement for the Rilling Roll, and $500,000 in damages for the breached license for the Lacy Irma.

The license agreement for the Rilling Roll provides for recovery of attorneys' fees by the prevailing party in the event of a dispute about the agreement, which both sides seek. The Lacy Irma license agreement does not.

Fitzhugh has told you that the facts alleged in the Rilling Enterprises counterclaim concerning the Rilling Roll are essentially accurate, but that since the license fee was paid, there should be no breach for less than minimum sales; she points out that the reason for a minimum sales standard is to maintain a royalty stream. Since she doesn't pay royalties, it should not apply to her.

Fitzhugh also acknowledges that she and Rilling did discuss new flavors for the Lacy Irma but that this was not a condition of the agreement. New flavors are expensive and time consuming, and no one can predict how long it may take to develop a winner.

The procedural posture of the case is as follows: The action is in the Federal District Court, Western District. You are the attorney, using your own name, address, and telephone number where appropriate on pleadings. You propounded interrogatories to Rilling Enterprises by hand on August 3, 2007. Numbers 1 through 5 were personal background questions, such as name, address, corporate status, etc. These were answered fully. The remaining interrogatories and responses were as follows:

6. Identify each attorney's fee for which you seek payment pursuant to the Rilling Roll license agreement, including a description of the date, amount of time, rate, and activity represented by the fee.

Response: Objection. Seeks information protected by the attorney-client and attorney-workproduct privileges, and violates format requirements of the FRCP and local rules.

7. State all facts upon which you base your denial that you wrongfully terminated the Rilling Roll license agreement.

Response: Objection. Vague and ambiguous.

8. Identify all persons having knowledge of each fact upon which you base your denial that you wrongfully terminated the Rilling Roll license agreement.

Response: Objection. Seeks attorney-workproduct and violates attorney-client privilege.

9. Identify all documents referring or relating to each fact upon which you base your general denial that you wrongfully terminated the Rilling Roll license agreement.

Response: Objection. Appropriate method of discovery is a request to produce; defendant has no obligation to provide such information.

10. Identify all amounts of damage you have suffered as a result of the lack of additional flavors of the Lacy Irma.

Response: Unknown.

You were served the responses by mail on September 13, 2007. After receiving these responses, you called Rilling Enterprises' attorney on September 14, 2007 and requested additional answers. She said she would pull the file and review the responses and call back. On September 24, 2004 you called her again, and she was not available. Two more calls were made on September 29, 2007. On October 4, 2007 you finally got to speak to her again and she told you that she had reviewed the file and decided not to provide any additional responses. You decide to file a motion to compel.

IF YOU REPRESENT RILLING ENTERPRISES: Rilling Enterprises is suing Auntie Irma's and Lucille Fitzhugh for breach of contract and fraud. In its counterclaim, Alice Rilling alleges on behalf of Rilling Enterprises that Auntie Irma's contacted a business broker, Judy Roberts, to negotiate a license to market the Rilling Roll anywhere, and to sell in Fremont County.

Rilling agreed to a permanent license for five annual payments of $50,000. Auntie Irma's was not required to pay any royalty. The agreement was the standard agreement but with the royalty language crossed out and initialed. About three years into the agreement, Auntie Irma's sales fell below minimum standards for the license. Rilling Enterprises terminated the license for this breach of the agreement.

A year ago, Fitzhugh and Rilling discussed Rilling's desire to market the Lacy Irma. Fitzhugh agreed that Auntie Irma's would develop a new flavor of the cookie each year and expand the line. This was an essential part of the agreement for Rilling Enterprises. They executed an exclusive license for Rilling Enterprises to sell sublicenses to cookie shops selling the Rilling Roll, so that they could also sell the Lacy Irma. Auntie Irma's has never provided additional flavors of the Lacy Irma and a few months ago, wrongfully terminated the license.

Auntie Irma's complaint against Rilling Enterprises consists of counts of breach of contract and fraud. Its complaint alleges that a few years ago she was contacted by a business broker, Judy Roberts, who wanted to sell Auntie Irma's a Rilling Roll license to permit Auntie Irma's to market the Rilling Roll anywhere, and to sell in Fremont County. Fitzhugh negotiated a permanent license with Roberts over the telephone, for five annual payments of $50,000. Auntie Irma's was not required to pay any royalty. The agreement was the standard agreement but with the royalty language crossed out and initialed. Before entering into the agreement, Fitzhugh was aware of representations made to the public, including Auntie Irma's, and she confirmed with Rilling that Rilling Enterprises did not and would never compete directly with its licensees by marketing cookies directly to the public. As soon as the last license payment was made, and Rilling Enterprises could anticipate no more income from the license, it wrongfully terminated Auntie Irma's license, opened a shop in Fremont County, and sold the Rilling Roll directly to the public. Auntie Irma's believes that the damage to the company exceeds $500,000, including the $250,000 license fee.

The complaint also alleges that a year ago, Fitzhugh and Rilling discussed Rilling's desire to market the Lacy Irma. They executed an exclusive license for Rilling Enterprises to sell sublicenses to cookie shops selling the Rilling Roll, so that they could also sell the Lacy Irma. This agreement was drafted by Fitzhugh. It required that Rilling Enterprises obtain a nondisclosure agreement with each sublicensee, provide a copy of the nondisclosure agreement to Auntie Irma's within 30 days of signature, and pay a 7 percent royalty on gross sales each year. Rilling has never obtained the nondisclosure agreements, has never sent any to Auntie Irma's, and has never paid a royalty. Auntie Irma's believes that the royalty would exceed $100,000.

Rilling Enterprises seeks damages of $250,000 for the breached license agreement for the Rilling Roll, and $500,000 in damages for the breached license for the Lacy Irma.

The license agreement for the Rilling Roll provides for recovery of attorneys' fees by the prevailing party in the event of a dispute about the agreement, which both sides seek. The Lacy Irma license agreement does not.

Rilling has told you that the facts alleged in the Auntie Irma complaint concerning the Rilling Roll are essentially accurate, but that all licensees have to maintain sales standards in order to keep a market presence of the Rilling Roll in the marketplace. Even though the license fee from Auntie Irma's was paid, minimum sales standards must be maintained. Rilling acknowledges that the drop in sales occurred before the final license fee payment, and that Rilling waited to terminate until after the final payment. She estimates the injury to Rilling Enterprises to be about $50,000.

Rilling insists that she and Fitzhugh did discuss new flavors for the Lacy Irma, and it was a condition of the agreement. Fitzhugh told her that several flavors had already been developed and would be added to the cookie line one at a time to maximize public exposure. She acknowledges that Rilling Enterprises did not get nondisclosure agreements from the sublicensees and did not tell Auntie Irma's who they are. Rilling Enterprises did not pay any royalties because, by the time the first one was due, Auntie Irma's had already fallen below minimum sales standards, so Rilling regarded the nonpayment of royalties as a setoff against the damages to Rilling Enterprises.

You propounded interrogatories to Rilling Enterprises by hand on August 9, 2004. Numbers 1 through 5 were personal background questions, such as name, address, corporate status, etc. These were answered fully. The remaining interrogatories and responses were as follows:

6. State all facts upon which you base your first count in this action.

Response: Objection. Vague and ambiguous.

7. Identify all persons having knowledge of each fact upon which you base your first count in this action.

Response: Objection. Burdensome and oppressive.

8. State whether you contend that you performed pursuant to the license agreement that is the subject of this action.

Response: Objection. Vague and ambiguous, since responding party cannot determine to which contract the interrogatory refers.

9. Identify gross sales figures for each year of sales of the Rilling Roll by responding party.

Response: Not applicable.

10. Identify all witnesses to the alleged representations concerning non-competition by propounding party, including their names, addresses, and telephone numbers.

Response: Objection. Interrogatory violates the FRCP and local rules by asking compound question with subparts.

You were served the responses by mail on August 25, 2007. After receiving these responses, you called Murphy's attorney on September 3, 2007 and requested additional answers. She said she would pull the file and review the responses and call back. On September 10, 2007 you called her again, and she was not available. Two more calls were made on September 20, 2004. On September 24, 2007 you finally got to speak to her again, and she told you that she had reviewed the file and decided not to provide any additional responses. You decide to file a motion to compel.

BOTH PARTIES: The action is in the Federal District Court, Western District. You are the attorney using your own name, address, and telephone number where appropriate on pleadings. Notice a motion to compel further responses to interrogatories. Prepare the notice of motion and motion, the memorandum of points and authorities, and any necessary declarations and attachments. Consider the limitations on the date for service of the notice, and show the date by which it must be served beside the date of counsel's signature.

2. *Whetstone v. Brian:*

IF YOU REPRESENT WHETSTONE: You served a notice of deposition on Brian's attorney by hand September 6, 2007, noticing Brian's deposition for September 21, 2007 at 10:00 A.M. While her attorney arrived in your office and said that she expected Brian, Brian failed to appear.

Brian's attorney called the next day to say that Brian had misunderstood the time of the deposition. The attorney offered to make her available at your convenience; you confirm in writing an agreed date and time of September 28, 2007 at 10:00 A.M. Brian appeared 30 minutes late; she explained to you and her attorney that she had been unable to sleep the night before from her continuing distress caused by Whetstone, and that she is unable to participate in the deposition. Her attorney speaks to her briefly privately. Brian stops on her way out the door and announces that she simply cannot be deposed, that the strain would be too much.

Prepare a motion to compel.

IF YOU REPRESENT BRIAN: You advised your client that her deposition would be taken on September 21, 2007. You worked with her the day before, and she seemed nervous but prepared for the deposition. She did not appear at the deposition. You were embarrassed and offered to make her available at the convenience of opposing counsel September 28, 2007.

You again prepared your client, who seemed increasingly agitated and incoherent. You calmly advised her to appear at her deposition September 28, 2007. She did appear but refused to be deposed. Privately she shows you a letter from her psychotherapist saying that she was extremely distressed, experiencing an acute episode, and should not be deposed for at least a month. Brian then leaves the offices, announcing that she cannot be deposed.

Whetstone's counsel is furious and says that unless Brian is deposed within the next week, he will seek a dismissal of her case.

Prepare a motion for protective order.

CHAPTER 22

SUMMARY JUDGMENT

After completing the chapter reading, Discussion Questions, Online Projects, and Assignment, review the material in the following Chapter Outline, then complete the Chapter Objectives, Review Exercises, and Key Words and Phrases. When these are mastered, complete the Online Projects, Additional Research, Quiz, and the Alternate Assignments.

CHAPTER OUTLINE

I. Summary Judgment Motions Seek Adjudication of the Entire Action on the Merits without Trial.

A. If granted, the action ends.

B. If denied, the litigation continues to trial.

C. The fact finder is a jury in a jury trial, the judge in a bench trial.

1. The judgment is the application of the law to the facts determined by the fact finder.
2. A fact finder is necessary when facts are in dispute, so the matter may be decided by a judge without trial.
3. The only issues remaining—what law applies, and how—are issues for the judge.

II. Grounds for Summary Judgment

A. Summary judgment may be granted where there is no triable issue of any material fact.

1. A material fact is a fact that *matters* to the outcome.

B. The moving party in state court must present

1. evidence establishing the material facts.
2. a separate statement listing each fact and its evidentiary support.
   a. The evidentiary support is primarily documents and declarations that go to the heart of the issues.

C. The federal rules do not require a statement of undisputed material facts, but some local rules do require them.

D. To successfully oppose, the defendant must present evidence sufficient to raise at least one issue of triable fact on at least one element of plaintiff's cause of action.

1. The defendant must show that the plaintiff cannot establish at least one material fact.

E. The judge cannot evaluate the evidence or decide any issue where the evidence is in controversy.

1. The opposition is entitled to a jury to decide any factual issue.

III. Motions for Summary Adjudication Can Dispose of Individual Cause of Action or Defenses.

A. Parties are allowed—even encouraged—to obtain adjudication of individual causes of action by motion.

B. These issues are conclusively decided for the entire litigation even if there is a trial on the remaining issues.

C. Motions for summary adjudication are routinely made with motions for summary judgment, so that individual claims can be adjudicated even if complete adjudication is not possible.

IV. The Two Advantages of Summary Adjudication

A. Even if summary judgment is denied, the moving party might obtain adjudication of some causes of action or defenses to reduce the length and expense at trial.

B. The opposition is forced to present all his evidence in defense of his position.

V. The Four Disadvantages of Summary Adjudication

A. The moving party must begin by revealing his case.

B. The moving party's witnesses will be less able to change their stories at trial.

C. The motions can be expensive, since they require the presentation of all the evidence in written form.

1. But, they are less expensive than presentation at trial.

D. Motions for summary judgment are very rarely granted.

VI. Form and Format of Summary Judgment Motions

A. Motions for summary judgment and summary adjudication can be made simultaneously or independently.

B. Motions for summary judgment or summary adjudication consist of a notice of motion, memorandum of points and authorities, and supporting evidence.

1. State court motions must be accompanied by a separate statement of material facts not in dispute, with references to the evidence.
2. Local federal rules may require a separate statement.

VII. Timing Limitations

A. State court rules

1. A motion for summary judgment cannot be filed without a court order until at least 60 days after the general appearance of the party against whom judgment is sought.
   a. Courts disfavor early motions for summary judgment, since late-discovered evidence may be grounds for overturning the decision.
2. The 30-day cutoff before trial also applies to motions for summary judgment.
   a. Such motions must be heard on or before the 30th day before trial.

B. Federal court rules

1. Federal court rules 20 days from filing of the action.
2. Local rules generally set a pretrial cutoff for motions for summary judgment.
   a. The trial judge will likely set a date by which such motions must be brought before trial.

VIII. Notice Requirements

A. In state court 75 days' notice must be provided if service is by hand, 80 if by mail.

1. The supporting memorandum of points and authorities and copies of all the supporting documentation must be served with the notice.
2. Moving papers must be filed with the court clerk 15 days before the hearing, but the better practice is to file the motion as it is served.

B. Federal rules require 10 days' notice rather than the usual five, but the local rules may extend the time to 21 and 28 days for personal service, depending on the jurisdiction.

C. The notice must state the date, time, and department of the hearing on the motion.

D. The notice also must state

1. the specific order sought.
2. the grounds upon which it is based.
3. the evidence upon which the moving party will rely.

E. A motion for summary *judgment* must specify against which party the judgment is sought.

F. A motion for summary *adjudication* must recite the precise fact or facts for which adjudication is sought.

G. If both motions are combined, the notice must say so

1. in its title.
2. in its description.
3. in the body of the notice, which also must state
   a. the party against whom judgment is sought.
   b. the facts for which adjudication is sought.

H. Unless the notice and other moving papers clearly show that summary adjudication of facts is sought in addition to summary judgment, a court denying the motion for summary judgment will be powerless to adjudicate individual facts.

IX. Memorandum of Points and Authorities

A. Memoranda of points and authorities are required.

B. T he memorandum follows the same format as other memoranda and includes

1. a brief statement of the facts of the case.
2. an analysis of the law.
3. argument.

C. The memo also should include

1. a statement of the procedural posture of the case, describing
   a. who the parties are.
   b. what motions have been brought and their outcomes.
   c. the status of discovery to inform the court about the propriety of summary judgment or adjudication.

D. Statements of fact in the memorandum are cited to the evidence submitted in support of the motion.

X. Supporting Evidence

A. Declarations, admissions, discovery responses, depositions, and matters of which judicial notice may be taken are appropriate evidence to support a motion for summary judgment.

B. The evidence submitted in support of motions for summary judgment is subject to the same limitations as evidence presented at trial.

C. Declarations

1. Each witness must have personal knowledge of the events about which he will testify, to be competent to testify.
2. The declarant must set forth facts explaining his qualifications.
3. The declarant begins the declaration by stating his name and
   a. "I know each of the facts set forth herein from my own personal knowledge, and if called to testify as a witness, I could completely and competently testify thereto."
4. The declaration consists of specific statements describing how the declarant comes to know of the matters about which he testifies.

D. The most common evidentiary issue with respect to declarations is hearsay, when the declarant presents testimony about a statement that he did not make.

1. If his testimony is used to prove the truth of the statement, it is inadmissible, because he did not make the statement and has no knowledge that the statement is true.

2. Exceptions include
   a. admissions.
   b. spontaneous statements.

E. Response to requests for admissions or interrogatories may support a motion for summary judgment.

1. An excerpt should be prepared as an exhibit to the motion, with a short declaration identifying the exhibit as a true copy of the actual written discovery.

F. Documentary evidence must be prepared and presented to the court in admissible form.

1. The documentary evidence must be authenticated by a declaration that identifies it and states that the evidence is what it appears to be.

G. Judicial notice may be made of facts accepted as true because they are of indisputable accuracy and not subject to reasonable contradiction.

1. Some facts are mandatorily noticeable, some are discretionary.

XI. Separate Statement of Undisputed Fact

A. A separate statement of undisputed fact must be filed with the motion in state court and most federal jurisdictions.

B. The moving party must set forth

1. each individual fact necessary to prove his case.

2. each fact referenced to the evidence filed with the motion.

XII. Opposing Motions for Summary Adjudication

A. The opposing party must prove to the court that there is a triable issue of fact.

1. The opposing party need not prove he is correct, he need only provide evidence to show a dispute, with some fact offered by the moving party.

B. If the opposing party accepts the statement of undisputed fact offered by the moving party, summary judgment may be desirable.

C. The opposition prepares

1. a memorandum of points and authorities opposing the motion for summary judgment or adjudication.

2. supporting evidence establishing issues of fact.

3. a statement of disputed facts.
   a. It states whether the opposition agrees or disagrees with each fact set forth by the moving party.
   b. It references the evidence upon which any disagreement is based.
   c. It contains objections to the evidence offered by the moving party.

D. The same rules of evidence apply to the opposition as to the moving party.

E. The opposing papers must be served and filed.

1. In state court, the deadline is the 14th day before the hearing.
2. In federal court, papers may be served and filed at anytime prior to the day of hearing.
3. In state court, there is no extension, even if the moving papers were mailed.
4. Untimely opposition papers may be ignored by the court, leading to a judgment against the client!
5. Oral objections may be made at the hearing, but a court reporter must be present.

XIII. Replying to the Opposition

A. The moving party in a state court matter may serve and file a reply to the opposition at least five days before the hearing.

1. The reply may include a memorandum of points and authorities, evidentiary objections, and additional evidence.

B. The moving party in a federal matter must file his reply in the time permitted by local rule for all replies.

XIV. Orders

A. If the motion for summary judgment is granted, a simple order may be filed.

1. Since there are no issues of fact, the court need not explain its reasoning in its order.

B. If the motion for summary adjudication is granted, the order will state the precise facts determined.

C. If the motion is denied, the state court must specify each issue where there is a dispute of fact, and all evidence that shows a controversy exists.

D. If a federal court denies a motion for summary judgment, it must specify the issues upon which it bases its determination "if practical."

E. This specification by the court enables the moving party to

1. appeal the order.
2. prepare additional evidence on that issue before making the motion again.
3. prepare to try the case.

CHAPTER OBJECTIVES

1. What is a motion for summary judgment?

____

____

____

2. What is a motion for summary adjudication?

____

____

____

3. What are the documents that comprise a motion for summary judgment and the purpose(s) of each?

____

____

____

REVIEW EXERCISES

Fill in the Blanks:

1. Give two advantages of summary judgment motions.

a. ____

b. ____

2. Give two disadvantages of summary judgment motions.

a. ____

b. ____

3. What happens to the case if

a. a motion for summary judgment is granted?

____

b. a motion for summary adjudication is granted?

____

4. What happens to the case if

a. a motion for summary judgment is denied?

____

b. a motion for summary adjudication is denied?

____

5. The judge is the fact finder in a ____________________ trial because she determines all issues of ____________________.

6. The principal procedural difference between a state court motion for summary judgment and one in federal court is that

____

____

____.

7. In state court, the moving party must provide at least ____________________ days' notice of a motion for summary judgment or adjudication; in federal court, the moving party must provide at least ____________________ days' notice.

8. Evidence offered in support of a motion for summary adjudication is subject to the same rules as ____________________.

9. A party opposing a motion for summary judgment must present evidence showing a dispute of at least ____________________.

10. A state court party opposing summary adjudication must prepare a

____________________, which contains ____________________

____.

11. A state court order denying a motion for summary judgment must contain

____

____

____.

12. A state court order granting a motion for summary adjudication must contain

____

____

____.

13. If the parties are in agreement about the facts in a case, the dispute will be an issue of ____________________; summary judgment is appropriate because ____________________.

14. If the motion combines summary judgment and adjudication, it must say so in the

a. ____

b. ____

c. ____.

15. The failure to adequately identify a motion for summary adjudication in a combined motion will result in

____

____.

KEY WORDS AND PHRASES

Provide a Definition for Each of the Following:

Summary judgment motion: ______________________________

____

Summary adjudication: ______________________________

____

Bench trial: ______________________________

____

Material fact: ______________________________

____

Competency: ______________________________

____

Hearsay: ______________________________

____

Authentication: ______________________________

____

Judicial notice: ______________________________

____

Spontaneity: ______________________________

____

Separate statement of undisputed fact: ______________________________

____

ONLINE PROJECTS

1. Using the official California courts Web site **(http://www.courtinfo.ca.gov/)**, access and read carefully the court's opinion in *Chevron USA, Inc. v. Superior Court* (1992) 4 CA4th 544. Given the facts of this case, is there any way the moving party could have obtained summary judgment? What evidence was necessary to obtain summary judgment?

2. Using the official California courts Web site **(http://www.courtinfo.ca.gov/)**, access and read carefully the court's opinion in *Aguilar v. Atlantic Richfield Co.* (2001) 25 C4th 826, especially section III. What is the purpose of summary judgment in federal court? What is the purpose of summary judgment in state court? What must the moving party do to prove that he is entitled to summary judgment? What must an opposing party do to show that summary judgment is inappropriate?

3. Using the Official California Legislative Information Web site **(http://www.leginfo.ca.gov/)**, access and read carefully California Code of Civil Procedure section 437c. What is the court's role in a motion for summary judgment? What is contained in an order granting summary judgment? Denying summary judgment?

4. Using the official California courts Web site **(http://www.courtinfo.ca.gov/)**, access and read carefully California Rules of Court rules 3.1350–1354. These rules govern the preparation of evidence as exhibits for summary judgment motions. Make an outline of these requirements.

5. Access the Federal Rules of Civil Procedure **(http://www.law.cornell.edu/)**, and read rule 56. What are the consequences of failing to offer evidence in opposition to a motion for summary judgment? Can a federal court adjudicate liability summarily, without determining damages?

ADDITIONAL RESEARCH

The following are cases accessible on the official California courts Web site **(http://www.courtinfo.ca.gov/)** on various topics of interest relating to this chapter.

Zavala v. Arce (1997) 58 CA4th 915 (material facts)

FPI Development, Inc. v. Nakashima (1991) 231 CA3d 367 (relationship of pleadings to summary judgment)

Montrose Chemical Corporation of California v. Superior Court (1993) 6 C4th 287 (coverage dispute amenable to summary judgment)

Lopez v. Superior Court (1996) 45 CA4th 705 (premises liability amenable to summary judgment)

United Community Church v. Garcin (1991) 231 CA3d 327 (separate statement)

Bahl v. Bank of America (2001) 89 CA4th 389 (continuance to respond)

QUIZ

1. The disadvantages of summary judgment motions include
   a. cost, delay, and revealing the evidence.
   b. cost and delay.
   c. delay.
   d. cost and revealing the evidence.

2. State court calendaring rules concerning summary judgment motions
   a. prohibit service by the plaintiff for 65 days after service of the complaint.
   b. are the same as those in federal court.
   c. prohibit service by mail.
   d. require 75 days' notice for hand service.

3. Federal court calendaring rules concerning summary judgment motions
   a. prohibit service by the plaintiff for 65 days after service of the complaint.
   b. are the same as state court.
   c. do not permit an extra three days to respond to service by mail.
   d. require 10 days' notice.

4. Motions for summary adjudication
   a. may be filed with motions for summary judgment.
   b. must specify the issues for which adjudication is sought.
   c. require a separate statement of undisputed fact.
   d. a, b, and c.

5. The judge must
   a. not weigh disputed evidence submitted with a summary judgment motion, but may do so for summary adjudication.
   b. weigh disputed evidence submitted with a summary judgment motion, but may not do so for summary adjudication.
   c. not weigh disputed evidence submitted with a summary judgment motion, nor do so for summary adjudication.
   d. provide a statement of decision in the event the motion is granted.

6. In motions for summary judgment,
   a. hearsay is not a problem because the testimony is in declaration form.
   b. hearsay is not a problem because the evidence is in documentary form.
   c. hearsay can be a problem in both declarations and documents.
   d. a and b.

7. The purpose of the content of an order denying a motion for summary adjudication is to
   a. permit the moving party to appeal.
   b. permit the moving party to better prepare his case for trial.
   c. permit the opposing party to appeal.
   d. a and b.

8. If there is a dispute of material fact, summary judgment cannot be granted because
   a. the moving party is entitled to a jury.
   b. the opposing party is entitled to a jury trial.
   c. a judgment would be incomplete.
   d. a, b, and c.

9. If summary adjudication is granted,
   a. the case is over.
   b. the issue is decided for all purposes for the litigation.
   c. the opposing party may immediately appeal.
   d. a and c.

10. The separate statement of disputed fact
    a. supports the opposing party.
    b. supports the moving party.
    c. refers only to the evidence contradicting the evidence of the moving party.
    d. a and c.

ALTERNATE ASSIGNMENTS

1. *Auntie Irma's v. Rilling Enterprises:* Analyze the facts of Auntie Irma's and Rilling Enterprises' cases, and decide whether either can move for summary judgment. If either or both has grounds to move for summary judgment, prepare a statement of undisputed fact for that party (without caption); if not, prepare a short explanation of the contradictions of fact precluding summary judgment. In other words, prepare *TWO* documents, one for each party. For both documents cite to the following facts, which are summaries of interrogatory and deposition responses. Distinguish between relevant, material facts, and irrelevant, immaterial facts.

AUNTIE IRMA'S INTERROGATORY RESPONSES:

1. Fitzhugh's allegations of fraud concerning the Rilling Roll license agreement are based on her knowledge through newsletters and the Rilling Enterprises operations manual that Rilling Enterprises did not and would not compete with a licensee by marketing or selling cookies to the public. Fitzhugh knew at the time the agreement was entered into that one license had received a letter indicating that Rilling Enterprises would compete in the future.

2. Fitzhugh negotiated a permanent license with Judy Roberts over the telephone, for five annual payments of $50,000. The agreement was the standard agreement, but with the royalty language crossed out and initialed.

3. The damage from the competition by Rilling Enterprises is based on the lost sales, loss of reputation, and stolen wholesale and commercial customers who were given special deals to change suppliers.

4. The damage prayed for violation of the Lacy Irma license agreement is based on the estimated lost royalties for the duration of the license, the lost opportunities that the royalties represent, and the damage to the Lacy Irma trade secrets, since Rilling Enterprises failed to obtain nondisclosure agreements from sublicensees.

5. The Rilling Roll license was obtained after Judy Roberts solicited Auntie Irma's.

6. At the time the Lacy Irma license agreement was entered into, Auntie Irma's had one new cookie flavor which had completed development, and two in final stages of development. The flavors were not released because Auntie Irma's decided not to expand the Lacy Irma line.

7. The failure to meet minimum sales standards does not constitute a breach of the agreement since the parties knew at the time the agreement was executed that since the license fee was fixed, and no royalties were required by the contract, there is no reason to require minimum sales standards to maintain a royalty stream.

8. Fitzhugh and Rilling discussed new flavors for the Lacy Irma at the time the license was entered into, with Robin Fitzhugh and Ray Rouse present.

9. The stockholders are presently Lucille Fitzhugh (8.5 percent), Robin Fitzhugh (1.5 percent), and Monster Cookie Company (90 percent).

10. Fitzhugh does not remember anything about the representations from Rilling to her concerning the noncompetition policy, other than that it was made before the license agreement was entered into.

RILLING ENTERPRISES' ANSWERS TO INTERROGATORIES:

1. The Rilling Roll license agreement with Auntie Irma's was terminated because three years into the agreement, Auntie Irma's sales fell below minimum standards for the license.

2. Fitzhugh represented to Rilling that, as part of the Lacy Irma license agreement, Auntie Irma's would develop a new flavor each year to add to the Lacy Irma line.

3. At the time the parties entered into the Rilling Roll license agreement, Rilling Enterprises had never competed directly with its licensees by marketing cookies directly to the public. It had acknowledged this policy in newsletters.

4. At the time the parties entered into the Rilling Roll license agreement, Rilling Enterprises had a policy whereby Rilling Enterprises would open stores in license areas where existing licenses had been terminated, until a new licensee was found. The policy is not in writing except in one letter. Rilling Enterprises had informed at least one other licensee of its policy of opening up shops in areas where a license has been terminated, but the letter has been lost, and no one remembers who the licensee was.

5. Rilling Enterprises never obtained a nondisclosure agreement with each sublicensee, never provided a copy of the nondisclosure agreement to Auntie Irma's within 30 days of signature or otherwise, nor paid a 7 percent royalty on gross sales each year.

6. Seven percent of gross sales of the Lacy Irma by Rilling Enterprises sublicensees for the duration of the agreement is $87,900.02.

7. The drop in Auntie Irma's Rilling Roll sales occurred before the final license fee payment, and Rilling waited to terminate until after the final payment. No notice was given to Auntie Irma's about this breach until the notice of termination, two years after the breach.

8. The Rilling Roll license agreement provides for recovery of attorneys' fees by the prevailing party in the event of a dispute about the agreement.

9. The Rilling Enterprises shop in Fremont County opened on December 15 of last year. The lease for the space was signed on November 1 last year.

10. Auntie Irma's Rilling Roll license was terminated on March 12 of this year.

SUMMARY OF ROUSE'S DEPOSITION:

(use cites to lines as if from deposition transcript)

Rouse says he knew Rilling for a long time and was happy to work with her, since the Rilling Roll was such a special and high-quality cookie. Rouse had worked for Rilling Enterprises for about 6 years by the time he was fired. Rouse had given Rilling the best years of his professional life and is very angry that he was fired. Not only that, but he was fired because Rilling thought he was an industrial spy for Monster Cookie Co., which he was not, and she should have known better. The reason for his firing made it nearly impossible for him to get another job. He has no respect for Rilling and nothing but contempt for Rilling Enterprises, but this does not affect his ability to tell the truth and does not affect his testimony. He is now employed by Monster Cookie Co., which is paying him almost twice what Rilling paid him. He has no contact with Auntie Irma's, however. Rouse remembers a conversation between Rilling and Fitzhugh, which took place at the time they were discussing the Lacy Irma license agreement. Rilling asked if Fitzhugh had plans for additional cookie flavors, to expand the line over time. Fitzhugh said "We have one new flavor ready to go, and two more in the oven. One new flavor a year would be good, but I'm not convinced that's the way we should go. Of course, if we had a healthy royalty stream coming in, that would help." Rilling did not respond. Rouse, who has 20 years' experience in the cookie licensing business, says that he reminded Rilling to get nondisclosure agreements from the Lacy Irma sublicensees, and to pay the royalties, and she said, "I'm not going to do anything about Irma. Irma is flirting with Monster, and if I pay, she'll be even more attractive for a takeover. I don't need the competition. I'd be just as happy if she folded up and blew away."

2. *Whetstone v. Brian:* If you represent Whetstone, prepare a motion for summary judgment on a breach of contract cause of action, for Brian's nonpayment of Whetstone's bill for legal services, based on the fact that there is no dispute of material fact.

If you represent Brian, prepare a motion for summary judgment on Whetstone's cause of action for breach of contract, based on the assertion that Whetstone cannot establish the facts necessary to prove his cause of action.

CHAPTER 23

TRIAL-SETTING PROCEDURES

After completing the chapter reading, Discussion Questions, Online Projects, and Assignment, review the material in the following Chapter Outline, then complete the Chapter Objectives, Review Exercises, and Key Words and Phrases. When these are mastered, complete the Online Projects, Additional Research, Quiz, and the Alternate Assignments.

CHAPTER OUTLINE

I. Case Disposition Is an Important Consideration for Both State Courts and Federal Courts.

A. State courts attempt the disposition of 90 percent of all matters within one year of filing.

B. Federal trial judges attempt to meet similar disposition rates through local rules and active case management.

C. Rapid disposition for both courts is balanced by the need for planning.

1. Courtrooms and jury panels must be available when the case is ready for trial.

II. Trial-Setting Procedures in State Court

A. The clerk enters complaint date into a computer.

1. The computer triggers case management conference date, about 120 days after filing.

B. State law requires completion of a case management statement form and filing no less than 15 days before the conference.

C. The case management judge determines whether the case is making adequate progress; when the case is ready, she sets it for trial.

III. State Court Motions for Preference

A. Preference entitles the party to priority at trial setting by advancing his case to the top of the list.

B. Preference is based upon the characteristics of the case or the circumstances of the party.

1. Cases seeking injunctions or declaratory relief are entitled to preference and may obtain a trial within days of filing, depending upon the urgency of the issue.
2. A party may be entitled to preference because of age and if delay may prejudice his interests.
3. The court may also grant preference at its discretion in the interests of justice.

C. Preference is obtained by following the usual motion procedures, but it is made to the presiding judge.

1. The case management conference statement indicating the intention to seek preference should be filed with the motion.
2. A declaration of counsel is required.

IV. Mandatory Settlement Conferences (MSCs) Are Required in Every State Court Jurisdiction with More than Three Judges, in All Cases Other than Short-Cause Matters.

A. The MSC must be scheduled for the three weeks preceding the trial date.

B. The settlement conference is supervised by the case management judge.

C. Each party claiming damages must serve a mandatory settlement conference statement on all other parties.

1. The statement is a demand for damages upon all appropriate parties, itemizing the amounts and types of damages sought.
2. It must be served and filed with the court at least five days before the conference.

D. Trial counsel must attend the conference.

1. Counsel must have settlement authority.

E. The client's attendance is required, or the client can be placed on telephone standby.

F. Failure to comply with any of the court or local rules concerning MSCs may result in an award of sanctions, including:

1. payment of fees and costs to all parties in attendance
2. reimbursement to the county for the use of the court's time.

G. Paralegals are usually excluded from the actual conference by the judge.

H. The conferences consist of discussions between the judge and counsel.

1. Counsel usually discuss their settlement authority amount to the judge, who keeps it confidential while pressuring the opposition to adjust its position.
2. The judge may also ask to talk to the clients individually, with or without counsel, to pressure the clients to compromise.

I. If a settlement is achieved, the court reporter is usually requested to attend and record the agreement, to avoid later disagreement about the terms.

1. If any party fails to perform pursuant to a settlement agreement stated on the record, the agreement may be enforced by motion.
2. If the agreement is not on the record, it must be enforced by a motion for summary judgment.

V. Voluntary Settlement Conferences

A. The parties may engage in voluntary settlement conferences at any point in the litigation.

VI. CCP Section 998 Allows Any Party to Extend a Formal Settlement Demand or Offer on the Opposition Prior to Trial.

A. A party may offer to allow judgment to be entered at a dollar amount without the necessity of trial.

B. The offer can be made at any point in the litigation up to the 10th day before trial.

C. If the recipient accepts, the clerk enters judgment on the terms specified.

D. If acceptance of the offer is not communicated within 30 days of service or by the first day of trial, whichever is earlier, the offer is deemed rejected and expires.

E. It cannot be used as evidence at trial.

F. If the plaintiff rejects the offer and obtains a judgment for less than the offer,

1. he cannot recover his own costs incurred after the offer was made.
2. he must also pay defendant's costs incurred after the offer was made.

G. If the defendant rejects plaintiff's offer, and plaintiff obtains an award higher than that offered,

1. plaintiff is entitled to 10 percent interest on the judgment amount calculated from the date of the offer.
2. plaintiff may also recover the fees charged by his expert witnesses, at the discretion of the court.

VII. Partial Settlements

A. A settling party may also seek an order confirming good faith settling by circulating an application for good faith determination and a proposed order.

B. Any other party may file and serve a notice of motion consenting the good faith determination.

C. The court will consider

1. the likely amount of plaintiff's recovery.
2. the proportion of liability between all defendants.
3. the financial status of the settling defendant.
4. any evidence of fraud or collusion between the plaintiff and settling defendant designed to shift a disproportionate share of the damages.

D. When the court has rendered its order, it must be signed, filed, and served as any other law and motion order.

VIII. Trial-Setting Procedures in Federal Court

A. Since cases are managed by the trial judges from the date of filing, the progress of the case is monitored through conference rather than through computer-driven procedures.

B. Initial status conferences

1. Deadlines for completion of the pleading, discovery, and pretrial stages are set at the initial status conference.
    a. The deadlines are made part of a scheduling order, and enforced by imposing sanctions on the attorneys or parties who fail to meet them.
        (i) The scheduling order must be entered within 120 days of filing of the complaint.
    b. The scheduling order can only be modified by an order of the court.

C. Pretrial conferences

1. Pretrial conferences are to inform the trial judge about
    a. the pace and status of discovery.
    b. any changes in issues.
    c. settlement.
    d. any other issues affecting the preparation for trial.
2. A final pretrial conference must be set as close to the trial date as possible, to advise the trial judge on the status of settlement and the plans for trial.

D. Settlements

1. Settlement discussions are encouraged at all status conferences.
2. The trial judge usually assigns another judge or magistrate to preside over the negotiations.
3. Defendants may serve on plaintiffs, no later than the 10th day before trial, a demand to enter judgment at a given dollar amount.
    a. The demand expires after 10 days.
    b. The plaintiff must pay the defendant's postdemand costs, if
        (i) he rejects the demand, and thereafter loses the trial.
        (ii) he wins but receives an award less than that offered.
    c. There is no reciprocal right for plaintiffs.

CHAPTER OBJECTIVES

1. How are cases set for trial in state court?

____

____

____

2. How are cases set for trial in federal court?

____

____

____

3. What is the key language of a section 998 demand/offer?

____

____

____

4. How is a case management conference statement drafted?

____

____

____

REVIEW EXERCISES

Fill in the Blanks:

1. The objective of case management is

____

____

____

2. Cases seeking injunctive relief are entitled to ____________________ that may permit trial within ____________________ of filing the action.

3. A motion for preference is made to the ____________________.

4. Three weeks before a state court trial date, the case is probably involved in a

____________________; 15 days before that date, the parties are required

to file and serve a ____________________.

5. Sanctions, including

a. ____ and

b. ____,

may be awarded against a party who fails to participate in settlement conferences in good faith.

6. If a settlement is reached during a settlement conference, it is usually put on the record because

____

____

____.

7. A party who rejects a section 998 offer takes the risk that

____

____

____.

8. Partial settlements are allowed, but they are subject to challenge, so the settling parties may seek a determination of ____________________ from the court.

9. In federal court, the case management judge is usually the

____________________, so the case is assigned to another judge or magistrate for settlement activities.

10. In federal court, a demand to enter judgment is permitted, but only by the ______________________ against the ______________________.

KEY WORDS AND PHRASES

Provide a Definition for Each of the Following:

Order to show cause: ______________________

____

Case management system: ______________________

____

Mandatory settlement conferences: ______________________

____

Settlement authority: ______________________

____

Telephone standby: ______________________

____

ONLINE PROJECTS

1. Using the official California courts Web site **(http://www.courtinfo.ca.gov/)**, access and read carefully the court's opinion in *Winet v. Price* (1992) 4 CA4th 1159. What would the release have stated if the parties intended to exclude one or more claims? Is there any additional language that this release could have included to make it clear that all claims were released?

2. Using the official California courts Web site **(http://www.courtinfo.ca.gov/)**, access and read carefully the court's opinion in *First State Insurance Company v. Superior Court* (2000) 79 CA4th 324. What is a complex case? What is the purpose of designating cases as "complex cases"?

3. Using the Official California Legislative Information Web site **(http://www.leginfo.ca.gov/)**, locate Code of Civil Procedure section 36. What are the specific grounds for preference? What is required to demonstrate a right to preference? What is the court required to do if the motion is granted?

4. Using the Official California Legislative Information Web site **(http://www.leginfo.ca.gov/)**, locate Code of Civil Procedure section 877.6. What parties may seek good faith determination of a partial settlement? When and how do they do it?

5. Using the official California courts Web site **(http://www.courtinfo.ca.gov/)**, access and read carefully California Rules of Court rules 3.1380. What does the rule tell you about the objective of the case management process? Counsel's role in preparing for case management conferences?

6. Access the Federal Rules of Civil Procedure **(http://www.law.cornell.edu/)**, and read rule 16. What are the issues that the court deals with in managing cases before trial? How are these different from the issues a state court judge deals with in managing a case before trial? Why are their roles different?

ADDITIONAL RESEARCH

The following are cases accessible on the official California courts Web site **(http://www.courtinfo.ca.gov/)** on various topics of interest relating to this chapter.

Roe v. Superior Court (1990) 224 CA3d 642 (preference)

Rutherford v. Owens-Illinois, Inc. (1997) 16 C4th 953 (court power to manage cases)

Stell v. Jay Hales Development Company (1992) 11 CA4th 1214 (998 offer)

Robertson v. Chen (1996) 44 CA4th 1290 (settlement conference statements)

Bice v. Stevens (1958) 160 CA2d 222 (settlement authority)

Tech-Bilt, Inc. v. Woodward-Clyde & Associates (1985) 38 C3d 488 (good faith settlements)

QUIZ

1. A case is technically ready for trial
   a. as soon as all allegations have been answered.
   b. as soon as the parties have completed discovery.
   c. as soon as the trial judge says so.
   d. when the presiding judge issues the trial-setting order.

2. A state case is set for trial
   a. when the case management judge sets it.
   b. when the parties request it.
   c. when the court administrator orders it.
   d. when the presiding judge orders it.

3. Cases are removed from the trial list when
   a. they are tried.
   b. they settle.
   c. an amended complaint is filed.
   d. a, b, and c.

4. Case management conference statements
   a. are judicial counsel forms.
   b. can preserve the right to jury trial.
   c. are required of all parties.
   d. a, b, and c.

5. Motions for preference are proper
   a. when the plaintiff is more than 70 years old and her health makes delay prejudicial.
   b. only when any party is more than 70 years old.
   c. only when all parties are more than 70 years old.
   d. only when the court specifically determines that it furthers the interests of justice.

6. A defendant who rejects an offer to enter judgment at a specific amount
   a. is not in state court.
   b. is taking a risk that he may have to pay the opposition's expenses.
   c. will be liable for the plaintiff's fees and costs if he loses.
   d. will be liable for the plaintiff's fees and costs if he loses a lesser amount than demanded.

7. A federal court party can expect the trial judge to
   a. set discovery deadlines.
   b. refer the case to another judge for settlement discussions.
   c. ask about settlement at each status conference.
   d. a, b, and c.

8. Federal court scheduling orders
   a. can be modified by court order.
   b. can only be modified by court order.
   c. can be modified by stipulation of the parties.
   d. are made by the clerk to keep the judge informed of the status of the case.

9. Settlements
   a. must be approved by the court.
   b. must be approved by the federal court judge.
   c. must be approved by the state court judge.
   d. must be approved by the state court only if it involves less than all the parties.

10. Cases must be dismissed
   a. if the case management is not filed on time.
   b. if the conference statement is incomplete.
   c. if the case is not tried within five years.
   d. if the case is not prosecuted within two years.

ALTERNATE ASSIGNMENTS

1. *Auntie Irma's v. Rilling Enterprises:*

A. Prepare a settlement conference statement for your client for a conference set for three weeks from today in the Western District of the United States District Court.

The settlement conference statement should set forth the facts, the procedural posture (i.e., motions for summary judgment, if any, should be mentioned), and status of discovery. Assume that depositions have been taken of Fitzhugh, Rilling, and Rouse; interrogatories have been propounded to both parties and responses obtained. Assume also that documents have been produced, including the letter to the licensee noting Rilling Enterprises' policy to compete with licensees. The document exchange has also revealed an internal memo from Rouse to Rilling dated before the Lacy Irma license agreement stating that in his opinion, the standard Rilling Enterprises nondisclosure agreement would not protect the Lacy Irma recipe from disclosure by sublicensees, and Auntie Irma's form ought to be used in addition to Rilling's standard form; also uncovered is an undated, handscrawled note in unidentifiable handwriting on Fitzhugh's office memo pad "cancelling new flavors—no need to sweeten the Rilling pot!" No serious settlement discussions have occurred.

As you will recall from earlier facts, Auntie Irma's wants royalties and damages for the breach of the Lacy Irma license and the Rilling Roll license, and damages for fraud. Rilling Enterprises wants the same. They both seek attorneys' fees for the breach of the Rilling Roll license.

Decide in your own mind what your client would accept, or offer, to settle the entire case, which will involve an objective analysis of the likelihood of recovery for both cases. Consider the possibility of "setoff," that is, the offset of recovery in one case against the other, if both prevail in any amount. Your statement will be evaluated more on its style and content than the precise figures proposed.

Exhibits to the statement are not required.

B. Draft a settlement demand letter to your opponent.

2. *Whetstone v. Brian:*

A. Prepare the first settlement demand letter for your opponent.

CHAPTER 24

ARBITRATION AND ADR

After completing the chapter reading, Discussion Questions, Online Projects, and Assignment, review the material in the following Chapter Outline, then complete the Chapter Objectives, Review Exercises, and Key Words and Phrases. When these are mastered, complete the Online Projects, Additional Research, Quiz, and the Alternate Assignments.

CHAPTER OUTLINE

I. ADR Is Usually One of Three General Types:

1. arbitration (determines outcome of case based on facts and law, binding or nonbinding by nonjudicial third parties)

2. mediation (voluntary, nonbinding negotiations like a settlement conference)

3. neutral evaluation (by experienced third party recommending reasonable settlement approaches, or helping the parties to identify areas for additional discovery).

A. There are three types of arbitration:

1. mandatory judicial
2. voluntary judicial
3. voluntary nonjudicial, including alternative dispute resolution.

B. Judicial arbitration is supervised by the judicial system.

1. State court cases in controversy with amounts less than $50,000 are automatically diverted to arbitration.

C. Voluntary judicial arbitration is available for any case under any conditions or circumstances agreeable to the parties.

D. ADR notices are required to be served with complaints by many local jurisdictions.

II. Voluntary Nonjudicial Arbitration

A. The parties may agree to arbitration at any point in the litigation.

B. Many contracts require that disputes be submitted to binding arbitration.

  1. The parties forfeit their right to litigate in the judicial system.

C. The arbitrator can be anyone agreeable to the parties.

D. The American Arbitration Association (AAA) and Judicial Arbitration and Mediation Service (JAMS) provide procedures and arbitrators, and are specified in many contracts.

  1. They have their own rules of evidence and procedures similar to those used in civil litigation.

  2. If a case is subject to such arbitration, the rules must be obtained and followed carefully.

E. The Code of Civil Procedure also describes arbitration procedures.

F. Awards in nonjudicial arbitrations can be vacated, confirmed, or corrected by the courts.

  1. The grounds to vacate include corruption and misconduct causing substantial prejudice.

G. The judgment is binding and nonappealable.

  1. The judgment can be appealed to a higher court if the parties agree.

III. Judicial Arbitration

A. Judicial arbitration is arbitration supervised by the judicial system.

B. It is required in cases in which there is less than $50,000 in controversy.

C. It is not available in cases where no financial recovery is sought, such as unlawful detainer (eviction) actions and marital dissolutions.

D. Parties in cases exceeding $50,000 may voluntarily submit to judicial arbitration, but having done so, they are required to follow all of the procedures for mandatory arbitration.

E. Assignment to arbitration

  1. The parties may stipulate to any person arbitrating their case.
     a. If the parties fail to agree, the court administrator will provide each party with a list of three or more prospective arbitrators.
     b. Each party may strike one name from the list within 10 days.
        (i) The parties research the prospective arbitrators for their types of practice and reputations.

F. Assignment to arbitration

  1. After the parties have responded, there will be at least one arbitrator remaining on the list.
     a. If there is only one person left, he will be appointed.
     b. If more than one name remains, the court administrator will select one at random for assignment.

2. After assignment, the arbitrator can be disqualified.
   a. Grounds for disqualification include
      (i) former representation of a party.
      (ii) affiliation with one of the attorneys.
      (iii) having an interest in the action.
   b. The parties can also exercise their single peremptory challenge of a judge against the arbitrator.

3. The administrator notifies each party of the assignment of the arbitrator.

4. Within 15 days of appointment, the arbitrator must notify the parties.
   a. Parties must be notified of the court's notice.
   b. Parties must be notified of the date, time, and place of the arbitration hearing.
   c. The arbitrator must allow at least 30 days' notice of the hearing, 35 if the notice is mailed.

G. The arbitration

1. The arbitrator must set the arbitration hearing for a date occurring between 35 and 60 days from his appointment.
   a. Failure to timely hold the hearing automatically disqualifies the arbitrator.

2. The case may be continued up to 90 days from the original hearing date.
   a. Any further continuance requires a court order.

3. All discovery except expert discovery must be completed 15 days before the hearing.

4. The arbitrator has the same powers and immunities as a trial judge.
   a. The arbitrator may
      (i) administer oaths.
      (ii) rule upon evidentiary objections.
      (iii) render a judgment and make an award.
      (iv) sanction parties or witnesses.

5. The arbitration is informal.
   a. Usually the arbitration is held in the law offices of the arbitrator.
   b. No record is kept of the proceedings, so no court reporter is present.
   c. No clerk is present.
   d. Special evidentiary rules apply.
   e. The rules specifically state the hearing is to be as private as possible.

6. The rules of evidence apply to arbitration hearings, with some startling exceptions.
   a. Copies of documents must be admitted into evidence if a copy is served to all other parties at least 20 days before the hearing, 25 days if service is by mail.
   b. Testimony need not be given by witnesses if their declarations or affidavits are served on all parties 20 days before the hearing if served by hand, 25 days if service is by mail.
   c. Deposition transcripts must be admitted into evidence if a notice of intention to use the transcripts is served on all parties 20 days before the hearing if service is by hand, 25 days if service is by mail.

d. Other discovery may be used subject to the same rules as trial.
e. The purpose of the special notices is to allow opposing parties to prepare opposing testimony.
   (i) The opposition may subpoena a witness.
      (a) The subpoena form must be modified to reflect testimony at arbitration rather than at trial or deposition.

7. The arbitrator must decide the law and facts, make an appropriate award, and serve the award on all parties within 10 days after the hearing.
   a. The arbitrator may request an additional 20 days if the case is unusually lengthy or complex.

H. Trial de novo

1. After the judgment is entered, the court clerk notifies all parties.
2. All parties except the plaintiff who elected arbitration and received the maximum award may seek a trial de novo within 30 days.
   a. The trial de novo is permitted because all parties have an absolute right to trial by jury, which would otherwise be limited.
   b. The request for trial de novo need not be in any particular form.
   c. If the request is not made within 30 days of the filing of the arbitrator's award, the judgment becomes final automatically.
      (i) Later requests for trial de novo may be granted with a showing of mistake, inadvertence, surprise, or excusable neglect explaining the delay.
3. There are strategic disadvantages and risks associated with requesting a trial de novo.
   a. The only discovery permitted from the cutoff 15 days before arbitration to trial is expert discovery pursuant to Code of Civil Procedure 2034.010–730.
   b. At the trial, no reference may be made to the arbitration or the award.
   c. There is no record of testimony or statements made to the arbitrator.
      (i) A witness may change his testimony at the trial and not be impeached by his arbitration testimony.
   d. If the requesting party does not receive a more favorable judgment or award,
      (i) he may not recover the costs of suit.
      (ii) he must pay the expert witness and other costs of the other parties.
      (iii) he must also reimburse the county for the cost of the arbitrator.

CHAPTER OBJECTIVES

1. What is the mandatory judicial arbitration process?

____

____

____

2. What are the various forms of alternative dispute resolution?

____

____

____

3. What is a request for trial de novo?

____

____

____

REVIEW EXERCISES

Fill in the Blanks:

1. What are the three types of arbitration?

a. ______________________________

b. ______________________________

c. ______________________________

2. An example of a private ADR provider is ______________________________

______________________________.

3. The only condition of voluntary nonjudicial arbitration is that

______________________________.

4. Judicial arbitration is supervised by the ______________________________.

5. In judicial arbitration, the ______________________________ proposes a list of arbitrators greater than the number of parties; each party can strike one name, and if more than one arbitrator is left on the list, the selection is made by the

______________________________.

6. An arbitrator can be disqualified if

a. ______________________________

b. ______________________________

c. ______________________________

7. All discovery except ______________ must be completed ______________ days before a state court judicial arbitration.

8. At a judicial arbitration, deposition transcripts may be used instead of live testimony, if

____

____

____

9. If a party requests a trial de novo, she takes a risk that

____

____

____

10. A trial de novo is required because every party has a right to ______________.

KEY WORDS AND PHRASES

Provide a Definition for Each of the Following:

Arbitration: ______________________________

____

Voluntary arbitration: ______________________________

____

Neutral evaluation: ______________________________

____

Binding arbitration: ______________________________

____

Trial de novo: ______________________________

____

Mediation: ______________________________

____

ONLINE PROJECTS

1. Using the official California courts Web site **(http://www.courtinfo.ca.gov/)**, access and read carefully the court's opinion in *Robinson v. Superior Court* (1984) 158 CA3d 98. When should the motion to withdraw from arbitration have been made? Would there have been arbitration anyway? What does this case illustrate about discovery schedules and arbitration? Is there a limit to the arbitrator's award when the court orders arbitration?

2. Using the official California courts Web site **(http://www.courtinfo.ca.gov/)**, access and read carefully the court's opinion in *Garstang v. Superior Court* (1995) 39 CA4th 526. Is anything about the mediation process discoverable? Is any part of the mediation process admissible at trial? Why or why not?

3. Using the official California courts Web site **(http://www.courtinfo.ca.gov/)**, access and read carefully the court's opinion in *Mercury Insurance Group v. Superior Court* (1998) 19 CA4th 332. What is the difference between judicial and contractual arbitration? What determines the arbitration procedure to be used? Under what circumstances do the parties have a right to discovery?

4. Using the Official California Legislative Information Web site **(http://www.leginfo.ca.gov/)**, locate Code of Civil Procedure section 1141.10. What are the purposes of judicial arbitration? What are the legislature's objectives in requiring judicial arbitration?

5. Using the Official California Legislative Information Web site **(http://www.leginfo.ca.gov/)**, locate Code of Civil Procedure sections 1775–1775.15. What program do these sections establish? How does it work?

6. Review the local rules for your state court jurisdiction. Are there any special forms provided relating to ADR?

ADDITIONAL RESEARCH

The following are cases accessible on the official California courts Web site **(http://www.courtinfo.ca.gov/)** on various topics of interest relating to this chapter.

Pratt v. Gursey, Schneider & Company (2000) 80 CA4th 1105 (stipulation to arbitrate)

Howard v. Drapkin (1990) 222 CA3d 843 (ADR provider immunity)

Hebert v. Harn (1982) 133 CA3d 465 (trial de novo)

Blanton v. Womancare, Inc. (1985) 38 C3d 396 (counsel authority to stipulate to arbitration)

QUIZ

1. An arbitrator
   a. can be anyone acceptable to the parties.
   b. must be an attorney.
   c. should be a judge.
   d. b and c.

2. An arbitrator
   a. must set the hearing within 10 days of his appointment.
   b. must set the hearing within 15 days of his appointment.
   c. must set the hearing within 30 days, or he will be disqualified.
   d. must set the hearing within 60 days, or he will be disqualified.

3. A plaintiff in a case which is within six months of the expiration of the five-year statute and is sent to arbitration
   a. should be concerned that the delay will cause him to miss the deadline.
   b. should be concerned that his case is off the trial list.
   c. should not be concerned because the five-year statute does not apply to cases diverted for arbitration.
   d. should be aware that the time toward the five-year statute is suspended for arbitration.

4. Mandatory judicial arbitration
   a. is required in every court in California.
   b. applies to state court cases with a limited amount in controversy.
   c. can be elected by parties in state court cases with less than $50,000 in controversy.
   d. a, b, and c.

5. The evidentiary rules unique to judicial arbitrations include
   a. permitting declarations instead of live testimony.
   b. use of the court reporter's notes for final argument.
   c. entering copies of documents into evidence, even if they were discovered the day before the arbitration.
   d. not requiring testimony under oath, since there is no court reporter to give oaths.

6. Appeals from binding arbitration awards
   a. can be based on corruption of the arbitrator.
   b. are only possible from mandatory judicial arbitration awards.
   c. are only possible from nonjudicial arbitration awards.
   d. are only possible in unlimited civil cases.

7. Requesting a trial de novo can backfire because
   a. the requesting party can be impeached by his arbitration testimony.
   b. a plaintiff receiving the full amount of damages sought can't get more.
   c. a defendant later found liable for the same or more damages is required to pay some costs to the prevailing plaintiff.
   d. b and c.

8. In mandatory judicial arbitration, the parties
   a. need not worry about completing trial discovery, because they can resume discovery after the arbitration award.
   b. are required to complete all discovery except expert discovery by the 15th day before the arbitration.
   c. are required to complete all discovery in the case by the 30th day before the arbitration.
   d. are not permitted to stipulate to the appointment of a specific arbitrator.

9. A plaintiff awarded in excess of $50,000 by an arbitrator
   a. stipulated to mandatory judicial arbitration.
   b. was ordered to mandatory judicial arbitration.
   c. was involved in alternative dispute resolution.
   d. b or c.

10. A court determining which cases are subject to mandatory arbitration
    a. will look only to the prayers in the pleadings.
    b. will review the case management statements.
    c. will consider the settlement figures and affirmative defenses.
    d. will decide how many trials it can keep active on the trial list.

ALTERNATE ASSIGNMENTS

1. *Auntie Irma's v. Rilling Enterprises:* Using the evidence described in the Assignment for Chapter 22 (Summary Judgment), prepare a notice of intention to submit evidence for your client in *Auntie Irma's v. Rilling Enterprises* for a voluntary arbitration.

2. *Whetstone v. Brian:* Prepare an arbitration brief on the legal issues involved in the contract dispute.

CHAPTER 25

TRIAL PREPARATION

After completing the chapter reading, Discussion Questions, Online Projects, and Assignments, review the material in the following Chapter Outline, then complete the Chapter Objectives, Review Exercises, and Key Words and Phrases. When these are mastered, complete the Online Projects, Additional Research, Quiz, and the Alternate Assignments.

CHAPTER OUTLINE

I. The Key to Successful Litigation Practice Is Thorough Preparation.

A. Relaxed, exhaustive preparation simply does not occur because of the time pressures involved in maintaining a profitable practice.

1. Few cases financially justify thorough preparation.
2. The most profitable case is one that has minimal preparation, resulting in minimal fees and costs and maximum recovery.
3. The least profitable case is one that is continually prepared, to the point where fees and costs dwarf the recovery.

B. Prematurely incurring costs through preparation

1. educates and informs counsel about the strengths and weaknesses of his case.
2. increases the settlement amount required.

C. The natural tension between over- and underpreparation translates into daily judgments about the necessity and justification for time and resources.

II. Anticipating the Trial Date

A. The state case management judge usually sets the trial at the second or third case management conference.

1. The trial date is usually within one year of the complaint filing date.

B. The federal trial judge usually sets the trial at the second or third conference.

C. The court administrator or calendar clerk can advise counsel about the average number of continuances from the initial trial date.

1. Even with a date set for trial, the trial may be continued because of court congestion, and may not occur until two additional trial settings, eight additional months, or more.

D. Once the trial date is set, all aspects of the case should be reviewed immediately and in detail.

E. Every conceivable date should be calendared to define what can still be done in the case.

1. Dates for propounding and responding to all types of discovery, including expert witness disclosures, should be calendared.
2. Moreover, the pretrial calendar may serve as a checklist for all remaining activity.

III. Trial Strategy Memo

A. The trial team must understand the trial strategy.

1. Each essential allegation in the pleadings must now be proven.

B. The trial strategy memorandum is a list of allegations, each followed by a reference to the type of proof to be presented at trial.

1. It might look very much like a statement of undisputed fact prepared in connection with a motion for summary judgment.

IV. Reviewing Existing Workproduct

A. Workproduct is any and all types of summary and analysis of the facts and law accumulated throughout the litigation, such as:

1. deposition outlines and summaries
2. document indices and summaries
3. legal memoranda and analyses.

B. The workproduct and its organization is usually not appropriate for trial, for the simple reason that it was not prepared for that purpose.

1. Document reorganization eliminates unimportant evidence and makes room for documents which will be used at trial.
2. Evaluation of existing workproduct will benefit the trial team by saving substantial amounts of time by reducing the workproduct to manageable size.
3. An additional master document collection is created using the same format as the original master collection.
4. Smaller subfiles for issues and witnesses should be evaluated,
   a. as to whether the issue or witness is still important.
   b. to reduce the documents in the subfile to those which remain relevant documents.

C. Each type of workproduct—indices, lists, issue files, and chronologies—should be updated to reflect the changes made to the documents selected for the trial set.

1. Deposition summaries must be reevaluated to determine whether they contain potential impeachment testimony.

D. Legal memoranda may be applicable to trial issues.

V. Creating New Workproduct for Trial Use

A. The trial strategy memo is probably the first workproduct created specifically for trial preparation and trial.

B. The raw materials of the case are the witnesses' testimony, documents, and other tangible evidence which have been identified in the trial strategy memo.

C. The principal trial workproduct will be the organization and analysis of the expected oral testimony and documents, which assist trial counsel in presenting the case to the judge and jury.

VI. Witness-Related Workproduct

A. The first trial workproduct is organization of oral testimony.

B. The trial strategy memo determines which witnesses will be required to testify at trial, and to what.

1. Their files must be reviewed to prepare for examination, impeachment, and rehabilitation.

C. The existing workproduct becomes the witness examination outline.

1. The outline is augmented with
   a. the deposition transcript.
   b. copies of all references made about the witness by other parties or prospective third-party witnesses.
   c. copies of all documents about which the witness will be asked to testify.

2. The outline contains all of the essential testimony to be obtained from the witness, with
   a. cross-references to any deposition testimony.
   b. statements made under oath.
   c. written discovery responses.

3. Any tangible evidence to be admitted based upon the witnesses' testimony is included at the point at which it should be entered, with necessary authentication and identification questions.
   a. Copies of the tangible evidence should be placed with the outline.

D. All client-parties and third-party friendly witnesses must be prepared to provide testimony at trial.

1. A complete list of witness names, telephone numbers, and addresses should be available in the event they must be contacted quickly.

2. Each witness should have the name and telephone number of the trial team to communicate any emergencies during the trial.

VII. Tangible Evidence

A. A complete set of intended exhibits and a copy of the trial document chronology are then prepared for use during trial.

1. Copies of the exhibits are required, and trial counsel must have virtually instantaneous access to all potential exhibits.
2. Each copy set should be placed into its own individual file, in an order corresponding to the trial document chronology.
    a. Each exhibit file should be labeled with a number so that it can be readily pulled and filed.
    b. The copy of the document in the trial document chronology should be assigned the same number, so that loose exhibit copies can be easily identified and refiled.

VIII. Demonstrative Evidence

A. Demonstrative evidence is workproduct prepared specifically for presentation to the judge and jury, to demonstrate some aspect of the disputed facts.

B. Demonstrative evidence is expensive but may be very effective at trial.

C. If demonstrative evidence is to be used, foundation evidence must be prepared.

D. Lists of anticipated demonstrative evidence should be made which indicate when they are to be used and with what testimony.

1. The witness outlines should be augmented with examination questions establishing the authenticity of any demonstrative evidence.
2. Equipment necessary to present the evidence, such as overhead and PowerPoint projectors, must be anticipated.

IX. Compelling Attendance of Witnesses and Production of Evidence at Trial

A. The attendance of third-party witnesses at trial is compelled by subpoena.

1. Subpoenas for trial witnesses must specify
    a. that their testimony is required at court.
    b. the time and courtroom or department number of the trial.
2. The subpoena must be served "a reasonable time" prior to the appearance, which may be as little as a few days.
    a. Additional witnesses can be served during the trial for later appearances.
    b. Public entity employee witnesses may require much more time.
3. Federal court subpoenas are issued by the court clerk, requiring additional time for preparation and issuance.
4. The date for attendance is usually specified as the first day of trial.
5. Even friendly witnesses should be subpoenaed, since service of the subpoena requires a delay in the trial or later testimony when the witness is available.
6. If the third-party witness is required to bring documents or things to court, a subpoena duces tecum must be served.
    a. The subpoena must specify the exact items to be produced, rather than general categories.

B. Attendance of parties is compelled by a notice to appear.

1. The notice must be served at least 10 days before the date the appearance is required.
2. If the party witness is to bring documents or things to court, the notice must so specify and must be served to permit adequate notice before the appearance.

X. Jury Fees

A. Client and counsel must carefully consider whether or not to request a jury, and once the decision is made, to preserve it.

B. The right to jury is preserved three ways.

1. It is preserved by so specifying in the case management conference statement in state court, in the first pleading in federal court, or within 10 days of the final pleading.
2. The second way the right is preserved is by specifying it at the trial-setting conference.
3. There is one critical additional step in state court: the right to jury trial is preserved by payment of jury fees, which are not required in federal court.

C. Jury fees are the fees paid to state court jurors during their service.

1. Jury fees are paid by the party requesting the jury.
   a. During the trial, the party requesting the jury will also pay for the jurors' meals and mileage.
2. The amount of jury expense for one day of service for 20 jurors must be deposited with the clerk of the court 25 days prior to the date set for trial.
3. If the fees are not paid, any other party may submit them within five days of the day the deposit was required.
4. The fee is refundable if the case settles before trial.

XI. Preparation of the Trial Book

A. The trial book should include

1. a complete set of all relevant pleadings provided in chronological order.
2. any court orders concerning trial.
3. a complete set of all discovery and responses.
4. any motion affecting the trial, and every motion intended to be made at trial.
5. a chart to aid in jury selection.
6. a list of each witness expected to testify, in order of the expected testimony.
7. trial strategy memorandum.
8. the brief setting forth the facts and law, which summarizes the entire case for the trial judge.
9. the outline of the statement to be given to the judge and jury at the outset of the trial.

10. an outline of the questions to be asked of each witness to be called in support of the attorney's case, and copies of appropriate exhibits.
11. an outline of the questions to be asked of each witness to be called by the opposing side, and copies of appropriate exhibits.
12. an outline of the argument to be made to the judge or jury at the end of the trial.
13. a set of instructions to be given to the jury.
14. a copy of relevant legal memoranda, cases, and statutes to which counsel may refer during the trial.

XII. Even Though Technology Advances Make The "Paperless Office" Possible, Trial Preparation Requires Organization of Documents and Files.

CHAPTER OBJECTIVES

1. What is the difference between document organization during discovery and during trial?

____

____

____

2. Why prepare a trial strategy memorandum?

____

____

____

3. What is in a trial book?

____

____

____

4. What is involved in scheduling appearances at trial by witnesses?

____

____

____

REVIEW EXERCISES

Fill in the Blanks:

1. Prematurely incurring costs before trial increases the ______________________ and also risks ______________________.

2. Evidence that is created to illustrate some aspect of the case is ______________________ and requires preparation of ______________________.

3. Even friendly third-party witnesses should be ______________________ to make sure that they appear at trial.

4. Parties are compelled to attend trial by service of a ______________________.

5. The right to a state court jury trial is preserved in the following three ways:

a. ______________________

b. ______________________

c. ______________________.

6. The right to a federal jury trial is preserved by

a. ______________________.

b. ______________________.

7. The raw materials of the trial include

a. ______________________.

b. ______________________.

c. ______________________.

8. To require that documents be brought to trial, a party serves a ______________ on a party and a ______________ on a nonparty.

9. If documents are required of a third party at a federal court trial, the ______________ must be issued by the ______________.

10. Witness files must be reviewed to prepare for examination, ______________, and ______________.

KEY WORDS AND PHRASES

Provide a Definition for Each of the Following:

Trial strategy memorandum: ______________

____

Trial book: ______________

____

Workproduct: ______________

____

Examination: ______________

____

Identification: ______________

____

Foundation evidence: ______________

____

Rehabilitation: ______________

____

Notice to appear: ______________________________

____

Demonstrative evidence: ______________________________

____

Admitted into evidence: ______________________________

____

ONLINE PROJECTS

1. Using the official California courts Web site **(http://www.courtinfo.ca.gov/)**, access and read carefully the court's opinion in *Sacramento and San Joaquin Drainage District v. Reed* (1963) 215 CA2d 60. When should a motion to exclude be made? Why might counsel prefer one opportunity to exclude to another? Are such motions appropriate for all types of evidentiary issues? Why or why not?

2. Using the official California courts Web site **(http://www.courtinfo.ca.gov/)**, access and read carefully the court's opinion in *Taggart v. Super Seer Corporation* (1995) 33 CA4th 1697. If documents are subpoenaed for trial, is it the duty of the subpoenaing party to notify other parties? Why or why not?

3. Access the Federal Rules of Civil Procedure **(http://www.law.cornell.edu/)**, and review rule 38. How does the process of preserving a right to jury work for all parties in the case?

4. Using the Official California Legislative Information Web site **(http://www.leginfo.ca.gov/)**, locate Code of Civil Procedure sections 607. What does this code section suggest about the organization of the trial strategy memorandum and the trial book? What does it suggest about scheduling witnesses?

5. Using the Official California Legislative Information Web site **(http://www.leginfo.ca.gov/)**, locate Code of Civil Procedure sections 2025.010–620. When are objections made to deposition questions? What can be done now about objectionable deposition questions that may be read at the trial? How are deposition transcripts prepared for trial? Who conveys them to the court? What does this code section suggest should be done at the time the deposition is taken, and what should be included on the list of trial preparation tasks?

ADDITIONAL RESEARCH

The following are cases accessible on the official California courts Web site **(http://www.courtinfo.ca.gov/)** on various topics of interest relating to this chapter.

Miller v. Los Angeles County Flood Control District (1973) 8 C3d 689 (expert testimony at trial)

Twin Lock Inc. v. Superior Court (1959) 52 C3d 754 (notices to appear)

New York Times Company v. Superior Court (1990) 51 C3d 453 (violation of subpoena)

QUIZ

1. Workproduct created during the discovery process may not be suitable for trial because
   a. there are not enough copies.
   b. it is not admissible.
   c. it was developed to obtain information, not present it.
   d. it is too detailed.

2. Examination outlines should contain
   a. impeachment sources.
   b. foundation questions.
   c. demonstrative evidence.
   d. a and b.

3. Demonstrative evidence requires
   a. foundation evidence.
   b. authentication evidence.
   c. impeachment evidence.
   d. a and b.

4. Attendance at trial is compelled by
   a. subpoena.
   b. notice to appear.
   c. subpoena duces tecum.
   d. a, b, and c.

5. A witness who contradicts his deposition testimony at trial
   a. can be impeached.
   b. can be rehabilitated.
   c. can be authenticated.
   d. a and b.

6. Friendly witnesses should be subpoenaed because
   a. they have no obligation to appear without a subpoena.
   b. the trial cannot conclude without their testimony.
   c. a notice to appear is ineffective for them.
   d. a and b.

7. The methods of preserving the right to a state court jury trial include
   a. a statement at the status conference.
   b. a statement in the case management conference statement.
   c. a statement at the mandatory settlement conference.
   d. a statement at the pretrial conference.

8. The method of preserving the right to a federal court jury trial is
   a. a statement at the status conference.
   b. a statement in the at-issue memorandum.
   c. a statement at the mandatory settlement conference.
   d. a statement in the last pleading.

9. A party who has not paid jury fees but nevertheless is in a jury trial
   a. is in federal court.

b. is in state court.
c. waived his right to jury trial which was preserved by another party in the case.
d. a and c.

10. The trial book contains
a. pleadings.
b. motions to compel.
c. authentication.
d. a and c.

ALTERNATE ASSIGNMENTS

1. *Auntie Irma's v. Rilling Enterprises:*

A. Review all of the pleadings and workproduct you have prepared for your client. Draft a memo for your supervising attorney outlining which is useful at trial and why.
B. Prepare a trial strategy memo for your client.
C. Revise your deposition summary in *Auntie Irma's v. Rilling Enterprises* to conform to the proofs required at trial.
D. Draft a pretrial calendar for federal court matters.

2. *Whetstone v. Brian:*

A. Review all of the pleadings and workproduct you have prepared for your client. Draft a memo for your supervising attorney outlining which is useful at trial and why.
B. Prepare a trial strategy memo for your client.
C. Determine what demonstrative evidence might be useful in trial, and draft a memorandum to your supervising attorney describing it in detail.
D. Draft a pretrial calendar for state court matters.

CHAPTER 26

TRIAL PROCEDURES

After completing the chapter reading, Discussion Questions, Online Projects, and Assignments, review the material in the following Chapter Outline, then complete the Chapter Objectives, Review Exercises, and Key Words and Phrases. When these are mastered, complete the Online Projects, Additional Research, Quiz, and the Alternate Assignments.

CHAPTER OUTLINE

I. Assignment to Trial Department

A. The trial judge is assigned at the time of filing to cases in state courts having a direct management system, and to cases in federal courts.

1. In these cases, the trial judge sets the trial date.

B. In case management jurisdictions of the state court, the trial date is set at the trial-setting conference.

C. The trial usually does not occur on the date set, however.

1. Each case therefore usually has more than one setting.
2. Cases may go through one to eight settings, or even more, as courts become more and more congested.

D. In state court case management systems, trials are set for appearance at the presiding judge's courtroom for the master calendar.

1. In direct calendar systems, the trial court contacts the parties to inform them whether the trial will take place as set.

E. Cases which will be tried during the week of the trial date may "trail" until a courtroom becomes available.

1. Counsel may be placed on telephone standby for trial assignment.
   a. The trial team must remain in constant contact while counsel is on telephone standby.
2. Some jurisdictions use a beeper system.

II. Challenging the Trial Judge

A. In state court, each side has one peremptory challenge to disqualify the judge without a specific showing of bias.

B. State and federal courts permit motions to disqualify the judge for specific bias, called cause.

C. Peremptory challenges of state court judges require an affidavit that the party (or counsel) does not believe the judge can render a fair judgment in the case.

1. Each side has one challenge to assert before the judge has ruled on any evidence.
2. In a master calendar jurisdiction, this challenge must be made when the case is first sent out to trial by the presiding judge.
3. In direct calendar jurisdictions, the trial judge is assigned at the time the pleadings are filed, so the challenge must be made then.

III. Peremptory Challenges in State Courts

A. In master calendar jurisdictions, counsel must decide at the moment they are told their trial department by the presiding judge whether they wish to make a peremptory challenge.

1. The challenge, under oath, is that the party does not believe that the judge can render a fair judgment in the case.
   a. It can be made orally by counsel if necessary.
2. If counsel leave the presiding judge's courtroom, they have waived their right to challenge.
   a. The trial book should include a list of judges by department.
   b. Once the trial court is committed, counsel and the parties proceed to the trial department.

B. In a direct calendar jurisdiction, the trial judge is assigned when the pleadings are filed.

1. The peremptory challenge must be made within 15 days of the challenging party's first appearance.
2. The challenge must be made before the assigned trial judge.
3. The matter will be assigned to another trial judge and will not be delayed.

IV. Challenging the Trial Judge for Cause

A. State court motions for disqualification for cause are referred to the judicial council.

1. The motion may be opposed by the opposing parties and the judge against whom the motion is directed.
2. The judge assigned to resolve the matter may entertain oral argument at his discretion.
   a. If he grants the motion, another judge must be assigned to try the case.
   b. If he denies the motion, the case will be tried by the judge against whom the motion was directed.

B. Federal court motions for disqualification for cause require an affidavit stating the facts and reasons demonstrating the judge's bias.

1. Another judge is immediately assigned to hear the matter.

C. The federal rules require a judge to disqualify himself in a proceeding where his impartiality may be questioned, or where there is a personal knowledge of the case or the parties.

1. No motion is required, and a judge who recognizes that grounds exist must disqualify himself.
2. The parties may raise the issue by motion.

V. Recusal

A. A judge may also choose to disqualify himself if

1. he has some interest in the case which is unknown to counsel.
2. he has some interest in one of the firms involved.
3. he served as a public official in some capacity related to the issues involved.

VI. Pretrial Conferences

A. The pretrial conference educates the judge about the case, alerts him to any administrative problems, and advises counsel of any rules or procedures required by the judge during the trial.

B. The pretrial conference is also the time when the judge begins making rulings on issues that will be presented in the case.

C. In master calendar jurisdictions, the pretrial conference takes place after the case is referred to the trial department by the presiding judge.

1. The pretrial conference is conducted before the formal proceedings begin, usually in chambers.
2. The judge will review the trial brief.
   a. All documents, including the trial brief, are now filed with the clerk of the department.
3. The judge will also ask about any administrative problems, such as witnesses who have conflicts or counsel with commitments during the trial.
4. The judge should also be made aware of any evidentiary disputes, so he can begin his own legal research before ruling on its admissibility.

D. In direct calendar jurisdictions, the trial judge was assigned at the time of filing and so is familiar with the case.

E. Local rules specify

1. when the pretrial conference will be held, either a few weeks prior to the trial itself or the first day of trial.
2. what motions must be made.

3. what documents must be filed with the judge.
   a. For example, many local rules require that counsel provide witness lists, indexed copies of exhibits, and jury instructions at the time of the conference.

F. Pretrial conferences in federal court must be held as close to the trial as possible.

1. The trial judge will inquire into the status of settlement discussions.
   a. If settlement appears possible, he will assign a magistrate or another judge to preside over the negotiations.
2. The conference also prepares the court and the parties for trial.

G. Federal local rules specify the documentation which must be filed at the final pretrial conference, which may include

1. a trial brief.
2. all exhibits (in chronological order, indexed and marked by the parties).
3. pretrial motions.
4. jury instructions.
5. witness lists with an outline of expected testimony and time estimates.

VII. Issues for Pretrial Resolution

A. Motions in limine are motions to exclude certain evidence, although they can also be used to urge the admission of evidence at trial.

1. The original and several copies of each motion in limine should be included in the trial book.
2. The original is filed by the court clerk, with copies distributed to the judge and opposing counsel.
3. Since the motions are now being made at trial, notice is not required.
   a. Opposing counsel may request an opportunity to oppose the motion in writing before a ruling is made or may make his opposing argument orally.
   b. The judge may also request opposing briefs or argument.
4. Rulings are made directly on the record.
   a. Counsel should take care that all argument and rulings are reported.
   b. The only record of the trial is the reporter's transcript, so all rulings must be contained in that record or in the minute book.

B. Jury instructions are the statements of law that guide the jury in determining the facts.

1. Each side prepares a set that favors his case, and presents them to the judge at the pretrial conference.
2. Based on arguments from counsel, the judge decides which will be given to the jury.
3. These instructions are the only guidance the jury will receive and are the single most important legal effort in the entire case.
4. The primary source for standard jury instructions is *California Civil Jury Instructions,* although the instructions can be drafted.

C. The judge and counsel must also anticipate the form of the judgment.

1. The jury may be asked to provide a general verdict, which specifies only which side prevails and, if damages are to be awarded, the amount.
2. The alternative is a special verdict, a series of questions about its findings.
   a. A special verdict is proposed along with the jury instructions for argument and decision by the trial judge.

D. The judge will review the prospective jury voir dire.

1. The judge may rule on the questions during the pretrial conference or wait until the voir dire begins.

VIII. Jury Selection

A. At the conclusion of the pretrial conference, the jury panel is sent to the courtroom.

B. Juries are generally made up of 12 people selected at random and a number of alternates.

C. The entire panel is sworn in by the clerk, so that their answers to voir dire questions are under oath.

D. As the jurors are questioned, each party may exercise peremptory challenges and challenges for cause.

1. If a juror shows an actual conflict of interest in the case, the judge quickly excuses him and the clerk selects another name at random.
2. If the juror has some small prejudice, the judge may rehabilitate him.

E. During this process, counsel must recall each juror to make his challenges.

F. After the jury is selected, alternates are selected the same way.

G. The jury is then sworn in and given basic instructions by the judge.

H. The trial begins with plaintiff's opening statement.

IX. The Trial

A. The defendant may make a statement immediately after plaintiff or reserve it until the conclusion of plaintiff's case.

B. After the opening statement or statements, the plaintiff presents his case.

1. He calls and examines witnesses regarding the case.
2. He submits tangible evidence.
   a. He requests that tangible evidence be marked for identification.
   b. When the witness has identified the exhibit, counsel asks that it be admitted into evidence.
   c. Opposing counsel may object, and the judge rules on the objection on the spot.

C. Each side calls friendly witnesses for direct examination.

1. Opposing examination is called cross-examination.
2. After cross-examination, the calling party may redirect, which may be followed by recross, until no questions remain.
3. Questions may not exceed the scope of the previous round of questions.

D. If deposition testimony is required, the original must be presented to the clerk in an envelope sealed by the court reporter who prepared it.

1. Any written discovery submitted must be with the originals of both the propounded discovery and the responses.

E. At the conclusion of plaintiff's case, defendant may make a motion for a nonsuit or directed verdict.

1. If plaintiff has failed to have evidence admitted to prove any of the essential allegations, it may be granted.
2. Plaintiff may also move for directed verdict following defendant's case.

F. The defendant calls his own witnesses and presents his own evidence in support of his case, which may either be

1. an attack on plaintiff's case by contradicting evidence presented by plaintiff or
2. a presentation of evidence supporting his own affirmative defenses.

G. At the conclusion of defendant's case, plaintiff makes a closing argument, followed by the defense's closing argument and plaintiff's rebuttal.

H. The judge reads the jury instructions to the jury, and the jury retires to deliberate.

1. The jury often has questions for the judge that require discussion with counsel.

I. Counsel must be present when the jury renders its verdict at the conclusion of its deliberations.

CHAPTER OBJECTIVES

1. What is the chronology of a trial?

____

____

____

2. What is a Code of Civil Procedure 170.6 challenge?

____

____

____

3. How are documents organized for trial?

____

____

____

REVIEW EXERCISES

Fill in the Blanks:

1. In direct case management systems, which include all ____________________ and some ____________________ courts, the ____________________ sets the trial date.

2. The first date that the trial is scheduled to begin is the first trial ____________________; the trial may be ____________________ several times before it actually commences.

3. Cases that are on standby awaiting trial are said to be ____________________.

4. Each party in a state court case is permitted one ____________________ to disqualify a judge without specifying the precise reason that the party believes the judge cannot be fair; in a master calendar system, this disqualification must take place within ____________________ days of the appointment of the trial judge; in a case management jurisdiction, the disqualification must be made ____________________.

5. In state court cases, judicial challenges for cause are referred to the ____________________ for determination.

6. Any judge may ______________________________ himself from serving as the trial judge.

7. The first time the trial judge makes rulings on the conduct of the trial is at the ______________________________.

8. Once the trial begins, any documents to be filed are given to the ______________________________.

9. A federal trial judge will not have as much need to review the trial brief as a state court judge in a case management jurisdiction because

____

____

____.

10. Federal rules require that the following documents be filed at the pretrial conference:

a. ____

b. ____

c. ____

d. ____.

11. Motions to include or exclude evidence are ______________________________.

12. The single most important legal effort in the entire case is the ______________________________, the importance of which is that

____

____.

13. A party examining his own witnesses is performing a ______________________________ examination and must ask ______________________________ questions; a party examining the witnesses of the other side is performing a ______________________________ -examination and may ask ______________________________ questions.

14. CACI means ______________________________ and is a source of ______________________________.

15. Prospective jurors are questioned by the judge and counsel in a process known as ______________________________.

16. Each side is given a number of ______________________________ to excuse jurors whom they do not wish to have on the jury.

17. An exhibit is marked for ______________________________ by ______________________________, but it must be ______________________________ before it can be considered by the jury as part of the case.

18. At the conclusion of plaintiff's case, the defendant may make a motion for ______________________________.

19. Closing arguments are made first by the ______________________________, then by the ______________________________, and finally by the ______________________________.

20. The jury renders a ______________________________, which results in the outcome of the case.

KEY WORDS AND PHRASES

Provide a Definition for Each of the Following:

Trail: ______________________________

____

Peremptory challenge: ______________________________

____

For cause: ______________________________

____

Recusal: ______________________________

____

Trial brief: ______________________________

____

Jury trial: ______________________________

____

Motions in limine: ______________________________

____

Reporter's transcript: ______________________________

____

Jury instructions: ______________________________

____

California Civil Instructions (CACI): ______________________________

____

General verdict: ______________________________

____

Special verdict: ______________________________

____

Voir dire: ____________________

____

Opening statement: ____________________

____

Plaintiff's case: ____________________

____

Statement of the case: ____________________

____

Direct examination: ____________________

____

Cross-examination: ____________________

____

Directed verdict: ____________________

____

Closing argument: ____________________

____

Rebuttal: ____________________

____

Case-in-chief: ____________________

____

ONLINE PROJECTS

1. Using the official California courts Web site **(http://www.courtinfo.ca.gov/)**, access and read carefully the court's opinion in *Deeter v. Angus* (1986) 170 CA3d 241. What does this case demonstrate about the relationship of discovery to trial? Why and how should a recalcitrant client be encouraged to produce all appropriate discovery before trial?

2. Using the official California courts Web site **(http://www.courtinfo.ca.gov/)**, access and read carefully the court's opinion in *People v. Morris* (1991) 53 C3d 152.

What is a motion in limine? What is its purpose? How might the progress of the trial benefit from motions in limine?

3. Access the Federal Rules of Civil Procedure **(http://www.law.cornell.edu/)**, and review rules 47 through 50. What is the minimum number of jurors to decide a federal case? How are they instructed about the applicable law? What are the two types of judgments that can be rendered by the jury?

4. Using the Official California Legislative Information Web site **(http://www.leginfo.ca.gov/)**, locate Code of Civil Procedure sections 170 through 170.6. Under what circumstances must a judge disqualify herself? Under what circumstances may a judge be disqualified by one of the parties? If a judge is not disqualified, what is the judge's duty with respect to a case assigned to her for trial?

ADDITIONAL RESEARCH

The following are cases accessible on the official California courts Web site **(http://www.courtinfo.ca.gov/)** on various topics of interest relating to this chapter.

In re Jeanette H. (1990) 225 CA3d 25 (court power regarding witness lists)
Fight for the Rams v. Superior Court (1996) 41 CA4th 953 (judicial peremptory challenge)
People v. Williams (1981) 29 C3d 392 (jury voir dire)
People v. Green (1956) 47 C2d 209 (opening statement)
McAllister v. George (1977) 73 CA3d 258 (authentication)
Westover v. Los Angeles (1942) 20 C2d 635 (preinstruction)

QUIZ

1. In federal court, judges may be disqualified by the parties
   a. by peremptory challenge and without a specific showing of cause.
   b. by motion for disqualification.
   c. only by recusal.
   d. a and b.

2. In state court, judges may be disqualified by the parties
   a. by peremptory challenge and without a specific showing of cause.
   b. by motion for disqualification.
   c. only by recusal.
   d. a and b.

3. Motions in limine
   a. can only be used to exclude evidence.
   b. are intended to exclude evidence and ensure admission of evidence.
   c. are intended to exclude evidence, ensure admission of evidence, and authenticate demonstrative evidence.
   d. must be filed 10 days before trial in state court master calendar jurisdictions.

4. In federal court, parties must file the following at the pretrial conference:
   a. all exhibits (in chronological order, indexed and marked by the parties).
   b. jury instructions.
   c. witness lists and time estimates.
   d. a, b, and c.

5. Jury instructions
   a. are all taken from a book.
   b. are decided by the attorneys and the judge together.
   c. are decided by the judge after argument by counsel.
   d. a and c.

6. Judicial voir dire questions
   a. are all taken from a book.
   b. are decided by the attorneys and the judge together.
   c. are decided by the judge after argument by counsel.
   d. a and c.

7. A jury may be asked
   a. to fashion its own "special verdict."
   b. for a general verdict which responds to questions.
   c. to decide whether to provide a special verdict or a general verdict.
   d. for a special or general verdict.

8. State court juries
   a. are always made up of 12 jurors and six alternates.
   b. are usually 12 jurors.
   c. may have alternates, depending on the length of the trial.
   d. b and c.

9. If a witness is to be impeached by use of deposition testimony,
   a. counsel only must read from the original deposition transcript.
   b. the clerk must read from the original transcript.
   c. the clerk must be given a copy of the transcript by counsel.
   d. the clerk must be given the original transcript under seal.

10. A defendant's case might be
   a. a motion for directed verdict.
   b. an attack on plaintiff's case.
   c. evidence supporting affirmative defenses.
   d. b and c.

ALTERNATE ASSIGNMENTS

1. Prepare an opening statement outline and an outline of the actual examination of each witness you would call at trial on behalf of your client in *Auntie Irma's v. Rilling Enterprises* and/or *Whetstone v. Brian*, based on the facts you have been given. Remember: you must (1) prove your case and (2) disprove the opposition case.

Your opening statement may be written out or be in outline form. It should be about four pages in length. This is your chance to explain the facts as you see them and talk directly to the judge and jury about your client and the opposition.

Your examination outline should be written as actual questions, as they would be asked at trial. Each should be cross-referenced to the answer as given in discovery, in the event that the witness testifies differently from deposition or other testimony. Each examination should also show what, if any, exhibits you would request entered into evidence, when, and how.

2. Prepare an exhibit foundation sheet for each piece of tangible evidence anticipated at the trial of your case, a jury voir dire, and a motion in limine for the evidence of Rilling's or Brian's emotional state and psychotherapy. If you represent Auntie Irma's or Brian, argue for admission; if you represent Rilling Enterprises or Whetstone, argue against admission.

CHAPTER 27

JUDGMENTS AND POST-TRIAL MOTIONS

After completing the chapter reading, Discussion Questions, Online Projects, and Assignments, review the material in the following Chapter Outline, then complete the Chapter Objectives, Review Exercises, and Key Words and Phrases. When these are mastered, complete the Online Projects, Additional Research, Quiz, and the Alternate Assignments.

CHAPTER OUTLINE

I. The Judgment in State Court

A. When the jury reaches a verdict, counsel go to the courtroom.

1. The verdict is read aloud for the record.
2. Counsel may then ask the judge to poll the jury.
   a. The trial support team should have the jury chart available and make note of how each juror voted.
3. After polling the jury, the judge thanks the jurors and dismisses them.

B. The clerk prepares the verdict or the prevailing party for signature by the judge.

1. The verdict is filed with the clerk of the court and recorded within 24 hours in the judgment book.

C. The judgment is served on the parties by the clerk, or by one party on the others with a notice of entry of judgment.

1. The notice of entry of judgment is served on all parties to the action with proof of service.

D. The judgment may be executed as soon as it is served on all parties.

E. The filing, service, and mailing dates of the notice of entry of judgment are critical in planning and calendaring post-trial motions.

1. Post-trial motions are jurisdictional, so the relevant dates are critical.

II. Post-Trial Motions in State Court

A. The prevailing party is entitled to obtain its costs and sometimes its fees.

1. Costs include expenses incurred for
   a. filing fees, jury fees, and meal expenses.
   b. depositions.
   c. preparation of demonstrative evidence.
   d. service of process.

2. Costs which are not recoverable include
   a. expert fees.
   b. postage and telephone bills.
   c. copying expenses, except for exhibits.

3. Attorneys' fees are generally the fees incurred in the prosecution or defense of the action, whether charged at an hourly rate or on a contingency basis.

B. The prevailing party addresses a cost bill to the trial judge after the jury's verdict, or after the judge's decision if there is no jury.

1. The cost bill must be filed no later than 10 days after notice of entry of judgment.

2. A cost bill is an itemized list of the costs for which reimbursement is sought, prepared on a judicial council form.
   a. The cost bill is accompanied by a declaration from counsel stating that
      (i) the party was entitled to costs.
      (ii) the cost bill is true and accurate.
      (iii) the cost bill reflects actual costs necessarily incurred.

3. The opposing party then files a motion to tax costs, which is generally heard at the convenience of the judge.
   a. The order of the trial judge is appended to the judgment.

4. The court clerk can advise the parties about the local costs procedure.

C. Any party dissatisfied with the verdict may make a motion for judgment notwithstanding the verdict, to change the verdict without a new trial.

1. This motion claims that the jury's verdict is not supported by sufficient evidence.

2. It is important where the jury has rendered a special verdict and the answers to the questions are inconsistent or show that the jury committed error.
   a. Such motions are occasionally appropriate to challenge a general verdict.

3. The motion for judgment NOV cannot be made unless the motion for directed verdict was made before the case was given to the jury.

4. The motion to judgment NOV must be filed either before the entry of judgment or the earliest of the following dates:
   a. within 15 days of mailing the notice of entry of the judgment served by the clerk
   b. within 15 days of service of the notice of entry of judgment by any party
   c. within 180 days of entry of judgment.

5. A party may try to expedite the process by serving the notice immediately by mail.
6. The notice of intention must be supported by the actual moving papers, including memorandum of points and authorities, filed within 10 days of filing the notice of intent.
7. These dates are *not* extended by Code of Civil Procedure section 1013 for mailing.
8. Motions for judgment NOV are appropriate when the judgment is not supported by the evidence.
   a. The trial judge can substitute his own verdict and judgment in place of the verdict of the jury since the weight of the evidence is clear.
9. If the motion is granted, the trial judge will vacate the jury verdict, and replace it with his own verdict, which will be consistent with the weight of the evidence.

D. The losing party may move for a new trial to reexamine the issues after the first trial and decision.

1. If granted, the first judgment is nullified.
2. Motions for new trial are made on the grounds that the moving party's rights were substantially affected by
   a. irregularity in the proceedings.
   b. misconduct of the jury.
   c. accident or surprise.
   d. newly discovered evidence which could not have been discovered prior to the trial.
   e. excessive or inadequate damages.
   f. insufficient evidence to support the verdict.
   g. legal error in the trial.
3. The grounds for the motion justify a new trial because the error or mistake occurred in the presentation or consideration of the facts and can only be corrected by a reconsideration by the fact finder.

E. The trial judge may vacate the judgment and replace it if there is a legal error in applying the law.

1. Since there is no claim that the facts were erroneously presented or decided, there is no reason to require redetermination by the fact finder.

III. Considering State Court Post-Trial Motions

A. As soon as the judgment is announced, counsel must consider post-trial motions.

B. A motion for new trial is suggested by conflict among the jurors during the jury poll.

1. Upon request, the judge may release the jurors' addresses and telephone numbers to counsel to be interviewed about the deliberations.

C. The jurors should be asked for a declaration, or counsel prepares one based on the interview.

IV. Form and Format of State Court Post-Trial Motions

A. The moving party files and serves a notice of intention to move for a new trial.

1. The notice must specify the grounds for the motion.
2. It must be filed either before the entry of judgment or the earliest of the following dates:
   a. within 15 days of mailing the notice of entry served by the clerk
   b. within 15 days of service of the notice of entry by any party
   c. within 180 days of entry of judgment.
3. The notice may always be filed before the judgment is entered.
4. The deadlines for filing are jurisdictional.
5. The clerk is responsible for notifying the parties of the entry of judgment.
   a. If the notice is not served, the parties have 180 days to file.
6. These dates are *not* extended by Code of Civil Procedure section 1013 for mailing.

B. The notice must be supported by the actual moving papers, including memorandum of points and authorities, filed within 10 days of filing the notice of intent.

1. An affidavit outlining the facts must be included if the motion is based upon the grounds of irregularity, misconduct, accident or surprise, or newly discovered evidence.
2. If the ground is insufficient evidence supporting the judgment or the damage award, or legal error, no affidavit is required.

C. The memorandum in opposition to the motion must be served and filed within 10 days of the motion for new trial.

1. If the motion for new trial is made on a ground that must be supported by affidavit, the opposition must include counter affidavits.
2. The dates for the filing of the motion and the opposition may be extended by stipulation or by court order.

D. The motion must be heard by the trial judge.

1. The clerk of the trial department sets the hearing date and provides at least five days' notice of the hearing.

E. The court's power to rule on the motion expires the earlier of

1. 60 days after the notice of entry is mailed by the clerk,
2. 60 days after service of the notice of entry by any party, or
3. within 60 days of the filing of the notice of intention to move if it is filed before the notice of entry.

F. The motion to vacate the judgment is also initiated by a notice of intention, which must be filed and served within the same time requirements as those of a motion for new trial.

1. The moving papers and the decision must also conform to the time requirements of the motion for new trial.
2. The motion to vacate must also be heard by the trial judge and decided before the court's jurisdiction expires.

V. Post-Trial Motions in Federal Court

A. Federal court rules include costs in the judgment as a matter of right, unless the court otherwise directs.

1. Costs are added to the judgment by the clerk on one day's notice.
2. The opposing parties have five days in which to file a motion to challenge the costs.

B. The motion for directed verdict must be made at the close of evidence to preserve the right for a motion for judgment NOV.

1. Within 10 days after the entry of judgment, the party who moved for a directed verdict may move for judgment NOV.

C. Ten days after denial of the motion, the moving party may file a motion for new trial.

D. A motion for new trial may be served within 10 days of entry of judgment.

1. If affidavits were included in the motion, the opposing party has 10 days to file opposing affidavits.
2. The parties may stipulate to an extension of 20 days, or the court may so order upon a showing of good cause.
3. If the trial was a bench trial, the trial judge may resume the trial for additional evidence, and may direct entry of a new judgment, rather than begin a new trial.

E. Parties may also move to amend or alter a judgment within 10 days of entry.

CHAPTER OBJECTIVES

1. What are the post-trial motions, and when is each appropriate? What is the deadline to file each?

____

____

____

2. How is a judgment drafted, and what is a notice of entry of judgment?

____

____

____

REVIEW EXERCISES

Fill in the Blanks:

1. The judgment is entered in the ______________________ by the ______________________.

2. The notice of entry of judgment is served on ______________________ by ______________________.

3. The prevailing party is entitled to recovery of its costs, which include expenditures for

a. ______________________

b. ______________________

c. ______________________

d. ______________________, but not

e. ______________________ and

f. ______________________.

4. To recover costs, the prevailing party in a ______________________ case serves and files a ______________________, which includes a list of the recoverable costs, called a ______________________, no later than 10 days after notice of entry of judgment.

5. In a ______________________ court case, the clerk automatically adds recoverable costs to the judgment on ______________________ day's/days' notice; opposing parties have ______________________ days to file a challenge to the cost award.

6. Any party dissatisfied with the jury's verdict may file a motion to change the judgment without retrying the case, called a ______________________, within

__________ days of service of the notice of entry of judgment by the clerk, __________ days of service of the notice of entry of judgment by any party, or __________ days of entry of judgment.

7. Grounds for a motion for new trial include

a. __________.

b. __________.

c. __________.

d. __________.

8. The first clue that a post-trial motion might be appropriate occurs when __________.

9. Post-trial motions are __________, which means that the court loses jurisdiction to decide them if they are not filed timely.

10. Post-trial motions differ from other types of motions because the time deadlines __________; the court's power to rule on the motion expires __________ days after notice of entry is mailed by the clerk, __________ days after services of the notice of entry by any party, or __________ days after filing the notice of intention to move if it is filed with the notice of entry.

11. NOV means

__________.

12. Post-trial motions must be heard by

____.

13. If a motion for new trial is granted, the initial judgment is

____.

14. A party dissatisfied with the outcome of the trial may move to request another one, called a motion ____________________.

15. In federal court, a motion for ____________________ must be made at the close of evidence to preserve the right to make a motion for JNOV after the verdict.

KEY WORDS AND PHRASES

Provide a Definition for Each of the Following:

Judgment book: ______________________________

____

Judgment debtor: ______________________________

____

Tax costs: ______________________________

____

Motion for judgment notwithstanding the verdict: ______________________________

____

Motion for new trial: ______________________________

____

Poll the jury: ______________________________

____

Motion to vacate the judgment: ______________________________

____

Notice of entry: ______________________________

____

ONLINE PROJECTS

1. Using the official California courts Web site **(http://www.courtinfo.ca.gov/)**, access and read carefully the court's opinion in *Nazemi v. Tseng* (1992) 5 CA4th 1633. How could the parties have avoided the timing problem? What does the case suggest regarding post-trial motions? What does the case suggest is appropriate support for a motion for attorney's fees?

2. Using the official California courts Web site **(http://www.courtinfo.ca.gov/)**, access and read carefully the court's opinion in *Bank of San Pedro v. Superior Court* (1992) 3 C4th 797. What does this court say is the purpose of Code of Civil Procedure section 998? What was the effect in this case?

3. Using the official California courts Web site **(http://www.courtinfo.ca.gov/)**, access and read carefully the court's opinion in *Serrano v. Priest* (1977) 20 C3d 25. What is the basis for the attorney's fees claim in this case? What is the legal rationale for awarding such fees? What is the societal rationale for awarding such fees?

4. Access the Federal Rules of Civil Procedure **(http://www.law.cornell.edu/)**, and review rules 54 and 59. Under what circumstances are federal judgments modified?

5. Access the Federal Rules of Civil Procedure **(http://www.law.cornell.edu/)**, and review rule 58. How are federal judgments recorded?

6. Using the Official California Legislative Information Web site **(http://www.leginfo.ca.gov/)**, locate Code of Civil Procedure sections 664, 668, 668.5, and 670. In what form does the court keep judgments? What documents are made part of the judgment? Under what circumstances is the judgment modified?

ADDITIONAL RESEARCH

The following are cases accessible on the official California courts Web site **(http://www.courtinfo.ca.gov/)** on various topics of interest relating to this chapter.

Maxwell v. Power (1994) 22 CA4th 1596 (jury deliberations)

Texas Commerce Bank v. Garamendi (1994) 28 CA4th 1234 (prevailing party)

Garcia v. Hyster (1994) 28 CA4th 724 (costs)

Sharples v. Chloe (1994) 29 CA4th 1221 (effect of arbitration on costs)

Hauter v. Zogarts (1975) 14 C3d 104 (judgment notwithstanding the verdict)

Beverly Hospital v. Superior Court (1993) 19 CA4th 1289 (motion for new trial)

QUIZ

1. The jury poll is important because
   a. it is an indication of which jurors might provide support for a motion for new trial.
   b. it triggers the dates for post-trial motions.
   c. it is the jurors' opportunity to discuss potential jury misconduct.
   d. the absence of the jury poll is an appealable error.

2. The filing dates for state court post-trial motions are important because
   a. the timing is jurisdictional.
   b. the trial court has limited time to grant the motions.
   c. the trial court has no ability to extend them.
   d. a, b, and c.

3. To get its costs of suit awarded, the prevailing party
   a. makes a motion for costs.
   b. submits a cost bill to the court.
   c. serves and files a cost bill.
   d. sends whatever bills the client has paid to the losing party for reimbursement.

4. The grounds for motions for new trial include
   a. irregularity in the proceedings.
   b. misconduct of the jury.
   c. accident or surprise.
   d. a, b, and c.

5. No matter what may happen, the last possible day a post-trial motion must be filed is
   a. immediately after the judgment is entered.
   b. within 15 days of mailing the notice of entry served by the clerk.
   c. within 180 days of entry of judgment.
   d. within 30 days of the notice of entry of judgment.

6. A party serving a notice of intention to move for a new trial
   a. should be aware that he has an extra five days if the notice of entry was mailed.
   b. should be aware that he has an extra five days if the clerk mailed the judgment to the parties.
   c. should be aware that there is no extra five days for mailing.
   d. a and b.

7. An opposition to a motion for a new trial
   a. must be filed and served within 10 days of the filing of the motion.
   b. must contain affidavits and declarations opposing those filed by the moving party.
   c. is filed with the law and motion court.
   d. a and c.

8. A state court motion for judgment NOV
   a. is preceded by a motion for directed verdict.
   b. is the same as a motion for new trial.

c. is heard by the trial judge.
d. a and c.

9. A federal court motion for judgment NOV
   a. is preceded by a motion for directed verdict.
   b. is the same as a motion for new trial.
   c. is heard by the trial judge.
   d. a and c.

10. In federal court, a judge who grants a motion for new trial after a bench trial
   a. may order a new trial date.
   b. may resume the trial for additional evidence.
   c. may direct entry of a new judgment.
   d. a, b, and c.

ALTERNATE ASSIGNMENTS

1. *Auntie Irma's v. Rilling Enterprises:*

A. During the *Auntie Irma's v. Rilling Enterprises* trial, you overhear three jurors laughing and joking about the poor quality of your client's cookies. What does this fact suggest? What steps could be taken during and after the trial to protect your client's interests?

B. A week after the *Auntie Irma's v. Rilling Enterprises* trial, and judgment for Auntie Irma, Rilling receives a call from Ray Rouse, crowing about the judgment. Among other things, he reminds Rilling that he was present during the very first discussion with Fitzhugh where Fitzhugh and Rilling had discussed whether Rilling Enterprises ever competed directly with licensees for sales to the public. Rouse remembered that Rilling had said they had not but were in the process of changing their policy. The new policy, which would be applicable to Auntie Irma's, required the licensee to maintain sales at a minimum level, or Rilling would come in and take over the area. Rouse says he didn't provide this information since no one ever asked him if he knew anything about that aspect of the case, and he's happy he didn't have to help his old nemesis. What problems does this present to Rilling Enterprises and its counsel? What steps could be taken to protect Rilling's interests?

2. *Whetstone v. Brian:*

A. The attorney for whom you work has concluded a trial, and you are responsible for calendaring post-trial activities. (You won, but you want to be prepared for an appeal from the other side.) Use the calendar on page 123. The jury returned its verdict on November 3. The judgment was entered on November 4. A notice of entry of judgment was mailed by the court clerk on November 5 and received on November 6. You served a notice of entry by hand November 7. Provide the following dates for a matter in state court:

(a) the last date for hearing a motion to vacate
(b) the last day a notice of intent to move for a new trial may be filed
(c) the last date for hearing a motion for new trial
(d) the last date the opposition can file/serve its cost bill
(e) the last date for a hearing to tax costs.

B. Recalculate the previous dates for a federal court matter.

CHAPTER 28

APPEALS

After completing the chapter reading, Discussion Questions, Online Projects, and Assignment, review the material in the following Chapter Outline, then complete the Chapter Objectives, Review Exercises, and Key Words and Phrases. When these are mastered, complete the Online Projects, Additional Research, Quiz, and the Alternate Assignments.

CHAPTER OUTLINE

I. Any Aggrieved Party May Appeal the Judgment.

A. An appeal of an unlimited civil case may be taken to the court of appeal.

1. The court of appeal may assess sanctions for frivolous appeals.

B. An appeal of a limited civil case may be taken to the appellate department of the superior court.

C. In federal court, an appeal may be taken from a district court to a court of appeals.

D. The purpose of appeals is to determine whether the trial court properly applied the law.

1. The appeal requests
   a. reversal of the judgment.
   b. modification of the judgment.
   c. affirmation of the judgment.
   d. the remand of the case to the trial court for further action.

II. Standards of Review

A. The appeal court's standard of review is the extent to which the appellate court will substitute its own judgment for that of the trial court.

B. There are three principal standards of review.

1. Substantial evidence
   a. If substantial evidence supports the judgment, the appellate court will not disturb it.
2. Abuse of discretion
   a. A ruling which is an abuse of discretion exceeds reason and sound rules of law.

3. Independent judgment
   a. When the issue is one of pure law, the appellate court can decide it independently of the trial court's decision.

III. Appeals from State Court Unlimited Civil Cases

A. California is divided into six geographical districts, each of which has its own court of appeal.

1. Each court of appeal is divided into divisions consisting of three or more judges who make up a panel.
   a. Each case is heard by a panel of three judges.

B. A judgment may be executed as soon as it is entered.

1. An appeal does not suspend the judgment,
   a. except where judgment is for attorneys' fees only.
2. A stay of execution of the judgment is obtained by posting a bond.
   a. The appealing party may post either
      (i) a bond from a surety company of 1½ times the judgment amount or
      (ii) the bond in cash in twice the amount of the judgment.
   b. The bond is filed with the court clerk.
3. Judgments remain valid for 10 years and may be renewed easily for an additional 10 years.

C. The notice of appeal is filed with, and the filing fee is paid to, the clerk of the court from which the appeal is taken.

1. The superior court clerk notifies all parties and the clerk of the court of appeal that the notice has been filed.
2. The notice must be filed
   a. within 60 days of the mailing of the notice of entry of judgment by the clerk,
   b. within 60 days of service of the notice of entry by any party, or
   c. if no notice of entry is mailed or served, the notice of appeal must be filed within 180 days of the actual entry of judgment.
3. These deadlines are jurisdictional and are *not* extended by service by mail.
4. An opposing party may then cross-appeal.
   a. The notice of cross-appeal must be filed within 20 days of the mailing of the notice of appeal by the clerk.

IV. Appeals of Limited Civil Cases

A. Appeals of limited cases are processed in general as appeals of unlimited civil cases but with shorter time limits of 30 days rather than 60.

B. The opening brief is required within 20 days of filing the record, the responding brief 20 days after, and the reply 10 days after that.

C. Briefs are prepared in the same way as they are for unlimited civil cases, but they are bound at the top, not the side.

D. Rules for requesting record preparation are similar to those for unlimited civil case appeals.

V. Preparing the Record

A. The clerk's transcript is the court file, consisting of the pleadings and any motions, oppositions, and orders which were filed with the court.

1. The clerk's transcript includes tangible evidence admitted during trial, as well as all potential evidence which the court refused to admit.
2. The clerk's transcript also recorded all of the trial judge's orders in the minute book.
3. The clerk's transcript is always required on appeal.

B. The reporter's transcript is all of the oral proceedings, including oral argument, court rulings, and oral testimony provided by witnesses, as well as the voir dire and jury instructions.

1. The reporter's transcript is usually kept in the form of stenographic notes for the duration of the trial.
2. The reporter's transcript is required if any point made in oral argument will be considered by the court of appeal,
   a. unless the parties agree on a settled statement.

C. The appellant must file a notice to prepare reporter's transcript within 10 days of the filing of the notice of appeal.

D. The reporter files an original and one copy of the completed transcript with the court clerk within 30 days from receipt of payment from counsel.

1. Timely completion of the transcript is unusual.
2. Counsel must request and pay for additional copies from which the briefs are prepared.

E. There are three types of clerk's transcripts.

1. The rule 8.120 election includes everything in the court file.
   a. The clerk prepares a copy of the record and files it with the court of appeal.
2. The rule 8.124 election includes only those items which the parties require.
   a. The electing party prepares the record with the approval of all parties, files it with the court of appeal, and serves it on all parties.
   b. Unless the 8.124 election is made, a rule 5 transcript will be prepared.
3. The rule 8.128 stipulation permits the clerk to index and paginate the original court file and transfer it to the appellate court.
4. The notice to prepare clerk's transcript must be filed within 10 days of the notice of appeal.
   a. It may be included in the same document as the notice to prepare reporter's transcript.
   b. The notice designates each exhibit, pleading, order, instruction, or other written record of the trial which the appellant wishes to include in his appeal.

5. If he wishes to include additional items, the respondent may file and serve a notice to augment clerk's transcript within 10 days of service of appellant's notice to prepare clerk's transcript.
   a. The clerk notifies the appellant of the cost of copying the transcript within 30 days of the notice.
   b. The estimate must be paid within 10 days or the notice is ineffective.
6. The transcript must be completed within 30 days of payment of the estimate.
7. The notice of appeal, judgment, and request to prepare clerk's transcript are included in the clerk's transcript whether requested or not.
   a. Exhibits, jury instructions, and excluded evidence are included only if specified in the notice.
8. The original and one copy are transmitted to the court of appeal.
   a. Additional copies may be provided to counsel upon request.
9. The 8.124 election is made by filing and serving a notice of election within 10 days of filing the notice of appeal.
   a. The appellant prepares an appendix in lieu of clerk's transcript.
   b. Counsel must confer with opposing counsel to attempt to stipulate to a joint appendix to be used by all parties.
   c. Failing a stipulation, opposing parties then may prepare their own appendices to augment the appendix filed by appellant.
10. The appendix is served and filed with the appellant's opening brief.
    a. The court of appeal may impose sanctions if the appendix is inadequate or contains nonconforming copies.

VI. Briefing the Appeal

A. The appeal can be briefed

1. The appeal can be briefed by following the briefing format used for law and motion, that is, a brief prepared by the appellant, opposition brief by the respondent, and a reply by the appellant; it can include a stipulated statement of facts which is accepted by all parties and filed with the appellant's brief.
2. A party can file a stipulation that the parties are attempting to agree on a settled statement.
   a. If the parties fail to agree, the trial court will rule on the proposed settled statement.

B. Appellate briefs are subject to specific form and format rules.

1. Appellate briefs must be typeset or typed.
2. Opening and responding briefs are limited to 8,400 words; replies are limited to 4,200 words.
3. They must include tables of authorities, tables of contents, and certification as to the number of words.
4. They must also be bound with covers in various colors, depending on what type of brief is enclosed.
   a. Opening briefs are green, respondent's briefs are yellow, and replies are tan.

5. The caption is placed on the cover of the bound brief, with a caption modified for the appeal.
   a. The appellate court, instead of the superior court, in which the case will be filed is at the top.
   b. The box indicating the parties designates whether the parties are appellants or respondents as well as plaintiffs or defendants.
   c. The case number is left blank for a new case number to be assigned for the court of appeal, although the case number for the superior court is included in parentheses.
   d. Below the caption box the court from which the judgment is taken is designated, along with the trial judge.
   e. Counsel's name, address, telephone number, and client are placed in the lower right corner.

C. The body of the brief is similar to a motion, with a statement of the case, statement facts, and legal argument.

1. A statement of the case is included after the fact statement.
2. The statement of facts is a detailed review of the trial transcript and clerk's transcript.
   a. Every reference to the facts must be cited to the record.
   b. The review of the transcript and the exhibits which permit the citation to the record can be the most critical in preparing an appellate brief.

D. Following a rule 5 election, within 30 days of the date the record was filed, the appellant files

1. the original and four copies of the appellant's opening brief.
2. the original and one copy of the trial transcript.
3. a single copy of the appendix.

E. Within 70 days after the 5.1 election was filed, the appellant files

1. the original and four copies of the appellant's opening brief.
2. the original and one copy of the trial transcript.
3. a single copy of the appendix.

F. For a 8.128 settled statement, the trial court will set a briefing schedule.

G. The brief must contain a proof of service indicating service of one copy of the brief and appendix on all parties and the trial judge, as well as seven copies of the brief served on the supreme court.

H. The respondent's brief is due 30 days after service of the appellant's opening brief.

I. The appellant's reply is due 20 days after service of the respondent's brief.

J. The parties may stipulate to a 60-day extension of each filing date and file the stipulation with the court.

K. Counsel are notified by the court clerk of the date of the hearing approximately 120 days before oral argument.

1. They may decline oral argument and submit the appeal on the briefs.
2. The time from briefing to oral argument may be a few months to a year and a half, depending on court congestion.

L. Oral argument is limited to 30 minutes per side.

M. The court has 90 days in which to render its opinion, which may be published or unpublished.

VII. Appeals of Limited Civil Cases

A. Clerk's transcript

1. Appellant must request clerk transcript portions within 10 days of filing the notice of appeal.
2. Respondent may give notice to augment the record.
3. The clerk estimates the cost of preparing the record, and appellant must pay the estimate within 10 days.

B. Same procedure for reporter's transcript.

1. If there is no reporter's transcript, appellant may seek a settled statement.

C. Opening brief is due 20 days from notice by clerk that transcript is completed.

1. Respondent's brief is due 20 days thereafter.
2. Reply due 10 days after respondent's brief.
3. No brief may exceed 15 pages, bound at the side.

VIII. Petition for Review by the California Supreme Court

A. The California Supreme Court has the power of discretionary review.

1. If it declines to hear a case, the decision of the court of appeal is final, unless a federal issue is presented which can be appealed to a federal court.

B. The grounds for review by the Supreme Court are

1. that the decision of the court of appeal results in lack of uniformity of decision between courts of appeal in different jurisdictions which can only be resolved by the higher court.
2. that the case presents an important issue of law.
3. that the court of appeal had no jurisdiction over the case.

C. The petitioning party must first convince the court to review the case, and then convince the court to change the decision of the court of appeal.

D. The court of appeal decision becomes final 30 days after filing.

1. The petition for review must be filed within 10 days of the date the decision of the court of appeal becomes final.
2. The answer is filed 20 days later.
3. The reply to the answer is filed 10 days after filing the answer.
4. The page limits are the same as those in the court of appeal.
5. Each must have tables of authorities and contents, and be bound in appropriately colored covers.
   a. No exhibits may be filed without permission of the court.

6. Each must include a proof of service showing service on
   a. all parties.
   b. the court of appeal.
   c. the trial court.
7. The Supreme Court requires 14 copies and one original of each brief.

E. The Supreme Court may
   1. deny the petition, rendering the court of appeal decision final.
   2. grant the petition, and briefing will begin again on the merits.
      a. After briefing, the court will schedule oral argument before a complete panel of seven judges.

F. The court's decision is required within 90 days of submission.

G. The Supreme Court may
   1. affirm, reverse, or modify the decision of the court of appeal.
   2. retransfer the case to the court of appeal for further, and presumably different, disposition.
   3. decertify a published opinion.

H. A party may seek a rehearing by the Supreme Court after the decision is rendered.

I. The decision is final unless
   1. it raises an important federal issue.
   2. it is in conflict with decisions of federal courts.

IX. Appeals from the Federal District Courts

A. A district court judgment may be appealed to the federal court of appeals.
   1. A judgment of a district court located in California is appealed to the United States Court of Appeals for the Ninth Circuit, located in San Francisco, California.

B. This court of appeals has adopted circuit rules that govern the form and format of appellate briefs, and the appellate procedure.

C. The Federal Rules of Appellate Procedure also govern the appellate process.

X. Record on Appeal from Federal Court Judgments

A. A party seeking to appeal
   1. must file his notice of appeal within 30 days of the judgment or order.
   2. must file a bond for the cost of the appeal.
   3. may seek an order to stay the execution of the judgment pending appeal.

B. The appellant must file a request to prepare the reporter's transcript within 10 days of the notice of appeal.
   1. Unless the entire transcript is requested, the appellant must file a statement of the issues on appeal with the clerk within 10 days of the notice of appeal.

2. The appellant must give notice to all of the other parties of the issues on appeal and the parts of the transcript that have been ordered.

3. The opposing parties have 10 days to designate additional portions of the transcript.

C. The parties may stipulate to an agreed statement on the record on appeal.

1. Unless the parties stipulate to an agreed statement, the clerk must prepare the entire court file for transmission to the circuit court.

2. The reporter must prepare and file the transcript with the district court clerk within 30 days of the request.

3. The clerk is required to prepare the clerk's transcript within 40 days of filing the notice of appeal.
   a. It is the appellant's responsibility to see that the transcripts are timely prepared.
   b. The record remains with the district court until requested by the court of appeals.

D. The filing fee for the appeal must be paid within 40 days of filing the notice of appeal.

E. Briefs on appeal

1. Briefs on appeal contain
   a. tables of contents and authorities.
   b. statements of issues.
   c. statements of the case.
   d. legal argument.
   e. a conclusion.

2. Citations must be made to the record as prepared by the clerk.

3. The opening and opposition briefs may not exceed 50 pages, and the appellant's reply may not exceed 25 pages.

4. The opening and opposing briefs shall contain a statement justifying jurisdiction of the appeal, including
   a. the subject matter jurisdiction.
   b. the finality of the underlying judgment from which the appeal is taken.

5. A party seeking an award of attorneys' fees must say so in his brief.

F. The appellant must prepare and file an appendix to the briefs showing

1. relevant docket entries in the record.

2. relevant portions of pleadings or opinions from the lower court.

3. the judgment from which the appeal is taken.

G. A local rule requires preparation and filing of five copies of an excerpts of the record, including:

1. the notice of appeal

2. the court docket sheet

3. the judgment appealed from

4. any court opinion

5. any jury instruction complained of.

H. The appellant's opening brief must be filed by the 40th day after filing the record on appeal.

I. The appellee must file his brief within the following 30 days.

J. Appellant may file a reply within the 14 days after filing of the opposing brief.

K. Local rules require the parties file an original and 15 copies of each brief.

L. The circuit court clerk sets oral argument unless it appears that oral argument is unnecessary.

   1. Both sides have an opportunity to argue the case, and the court may issue a published or unpublished opinion.

XI. A Party Dissatisfied with the Decision by the Circuit Court May Petition to the United States Supreme Court for Review.

A. Matters that reach the U.S. Supreme Court are usually one of the following three types:

   1. cases which have been decided by a state court of last resort, such as the California Supreme Court, in a way that conflicts with decisions of federal courts or the U.S. Supreme Court.
   2. cases which have been decided by a federal court of appeal, such as that in the Ninth Circuit, in a way which conflicts with decisions of other federal courts or the U.S. Supreme Court.
   3. cases decided by either a state court or federal court which raise important questions of federal law which should be settled by the U.S. Supreme Court.

B. Review of these matters is called certiorari.

C. The Rules of the Supreme Court require filing of notice and briefs similar to the Federal Rules of Appellate Procedure and circuit rules.

D. A decision by the U.S. Supreme Court is final.

CHAPTER OBJECTIVES

1. Where are the statutory requirements for appellate deadlines?

____

____

____

2. What is a notice of appeal?

____

____

____

3. What is a request to prepare the record?

____

____

____

4. What are the elements of an appellate brief?

____

____

____

REVIEW EXERCISES

Fill in the Blanks:

1. An appeal from a limited civil jurisdiction case is taken to the ______________________; an appeal from an unlimited civil case is taken to the ______________________.

2. An appeal from a federal trial court is taken from the ______________________ to the ______________________.

3. The purpose of an appeal is to determine if the ______________________ properly applied the ______________________.

4. An appeal requests one of the following:

a. ______________________

b. ______________________

c. ______________________

d. ______________________.

5. The standard of review is the extent to which the

____________________ will substitute ____________________

for that of the trial court.

6. The three principal standards of review are

a. ____.

b. ____.

c. ____.

7. A judgment may be ____________________ as soon as it

is entered, so it is important for the appealing party to obtain a(n)

____________________ as soon as possible.

8. The first step in the appellate process is the filing of the

____________________, which must be done timely because

the deadline is ____________________ and is not extended by

____________________.

9. An appeal from an unlimited civil case must be filed no later than

____________________ days from the clerk's mailing of the notice of

entry; in a limited civil case, the deadline is ____________________

days from the clerk's mailing of the notice of entry.

10. The clerk's record includes

a. ____,

b. ____,

c. ____, but not

d. ____.

11. The reporter's transcript includes

a. ______________________________ but not

b. ______________________________.

12. Unless the parties agree on a ______________, the appellant must file a ______________ the reporter's transcript within ______________ days of the ______________.

13. If an appellant requests everything in the clerk's file be copied for the appellate court, she has made a ______________ election.

14. If the appellant has made a rule 8.128 election, the clerk ______________ the file.

15. If the appellant has made a rule 8.124 election, the record is prepared by ______________.

16. If the parties are unable to agree on a settled statement, the ______________ will decide what the statement will contain.

17. Appellate briefs are subject to format rules, including rules governing the following:

a. ______________________________

b. ______________________________

c. ______________________________

d. ______________________________.

18. Every statement of fact in an appellate brief must be cited to ______________.

19. The unlimited civil case appellant's brief must be served on

a. ______________________________.

b. ______________________________.

c. ______________________________.

d. ______________________________.

20. The Supreme Court of California may ______________ or ______________ a petition for review.

21. The Supreme Court of California may make any of the following rulings with respect to a decision of the court of appeal:

a. ______________________________

b. ______________________________

c. ______________________________

d. ______________________________.

22. A court opinion that is not part of the official record of the court is said to be ______________.

23. The opening brief in a limited civil case appeal must be filed within ______________ days of ______________; the respondent's brief must be filed ______________ days thereafter, and the reply within ______________.

24. The decision of the California Supreme Court is final unless

a. ______________________________.

b. ______________________________.

25. A party dissatisfied with a decision by the Ninth Circuit may appeal it to the ______________.

KEY WORDS AND PHRASES

Provide a Definition for Each of the Following:

Appeal: ______

Reverse the judgment: ______

Modify the judgment: ______

Affirm the judgment: ______

Remand: ______

Standard of review: ______

Substantial evidence: ______

Abuse of discretion: ______

Independent judgment: ______

Notice of appeal: ______

Record: ______

Clerk's transcript: ______

Cross-appeal: ______________________________

____

Joint appendix: ______________________________

____

Nonconforming copies: ______________________________

____

Statement of facts: ______________________________

____

Certify the opinion for publication: ______________________________

____

Discretionary review: ______________________________

____

Retransfer: ______________________________

____

Decertify: ______________________________

____

Agreed statement: ______________________________

____

Excerpts of the record: ______________________________

____

Appellee: ______________________________

____

Certiorari: ______________________________

____

Circuit rules: ______________________________

____

Undertaking: ______________________________

____

Minute book: ______________________________

____

ONLINE PROJECTS

1. Using the official California courts Web site **(http://www.courtinfo.ca.gov/)**, access and read carefully the court's opinion in *Trujillo v. Trujillo* (1945) 71 CA2d 257. What does the opinion suggest about calendaring appeals? How could this result have been avoided? Was the matter adjudicated ever challenged on the merits? Why or why not?

2. Using the official California courts Web site **(http://www.courtinfo.ca.gov/)**, access and read carefully the court's opinion in *Van Beurden Insurance Services, Incorporated v. Customized Worldwide Weather Insurance Agency Inc.* (1997) 15 C4th 51. What does this court say about timely filings of notices of appeal? Why? What does this suggest is the first act upon notice of entry of judgment?

3. Access the Federal Rules of Appellate Procedure by locating the judiciary section of the official United States House of Representatives Web site **(http://www.house.gov/)**, and review rules 7 and 8. What are the procedures an appellant could invoke to avoid paying a judgment pending appeal?

4. Access the Federal Rules of Appellate Procedure by locating the judiciary section of the official United States House of Representatives Web site **(http://www.house.gov/)**, and review rule 29. What is an amicus curiae? How does an amicus curiae file a brief in an appeal?

5. Access the Rules of the Supreme Court of the United States **(http://www.law.cornell.edu/)**, and consider rules 5 and 6. What do these rules suggest an attorney should consider before she agrees to represent a client in a matter pending in the United States Supreme Court?

6. Review the judicial council forms at **http://www.courtinfo.ca.gov/**. What forms are available for appellate practice?

ADDITIONAL RESEARCH

The following are cases accessible on the official California courts Web site **(http://www.courtinfo.ca.gov/)** on various topics of interest relating to this chapter.

Casado v. Sedgwick, Detert, Moran & Arnold (1994) 22 CA4th 1284 (filing deadlines)

Estate of Davis (1990) 219 CA3d 663 (appellant's duty)

Tupman v. Haberkern (1929) 208 C 256 (purpose of appeal)

Stratton v. First National Life Insurance Company (1989) 210 CA3d 1071 (summary judgment)

Clothesrigger Inc. v. GTE Corporation (1987) 191 CA3d 605 (standard of review)

People v. Burgener (1986) 41 C3d 505 (standard of review)

Soule v. General Motors Corporation (1994) 8 C4th 548 (evaluating error on appeal)

Richie v. Bridgestone/Firestone, Inc. (1994) 22 CA4th 335 (retroactivity)

QUIZ

1. Standards of review include
   a. substantial evidence: a measure of whether substantial evidence supports the judgment.
   b. abuse of discretion: a measure of whether the court committed malfeasance.
   c. independent judgment: a measure of whether the appellate court's evaluation of the facts supports that of the trial court.
   d. a, b, and c.

2. A defendant against whom a money judgment has been entered
   a. should not worry if he plans to appeal, since filing the notice of appeal will stay the judgment.
   b. must obtain an undertaking before he can appeal.
   c. must obtain a bond if he wants to keep the prevailing party from executing the judgment during the appeal.
   d. has 10 years, until the judgment expires, to pay the judgment.

3. The state court notice of appeal
   a. is filed with the appellate court clerk.
   b. is filed with the superior court clerk.
   c. must be accompanied by the clerk's transcript.
   d. b and c.

4. The state court notice of appeal
   a. must be served on all parties by the appellant.
   b. is served on the parties by the superior court clerk.
   c. is served on all parties by the appellate court clerk.
   d. must be filed within 90 days of entry of judgment.

5. A cross-appeal
   a. is filed by a party other than the defendant.
   b. is filed by any party opposing the appellant.
   c. is filed by any aggrieved party.
   d. is filed by any aggrieved party other than the appellant.

6. The clerk's transcript includes
   a. the court file, consisting of the pleadings and any motions, oppositions, and orders.
   b. tangible and testamentary evidence.
   c. only evidence admitted during trial.
   d. a and b.

7. The portion of the record which is always required on appeal is the
   a. reporter's transcript.
   b. clerk's transcript.
   c. trial exhibits.
   d. a, b, and c.

8. The 8.124 election
   a. is made by filing and serving a notice of election within 10 days of filing the notice of appeal.
   b. is made after attempting to stipulate to facts with the opposing parties.
   c. results in preparation of excerpts from the record.
   d. is filed 30 days before filing the opening brief.

9. The special format requirements of state court appellate briefs include
   a. velo binding with green covers.
   b. typeset briefs.
   c. tables of authorities in the index.
   d. captions including the trial court case number and name of trial judge.

10. The grounds for review by the California Supreme Court include
   a. lack of uniformity in the courts of appeal.
   b. abuse of discretion by the appellate court.
   c. an important issue of law.
   d. a and c.

ALTERNATE ASSIGNMENTS

1. The attorney for whom you work has concluded an unlimited civil trial, and you are responsible for calendaring post-trial activities. (Your supervising attorney has gone on vacation to recover from his loss.) Use the calendar on page 123. The jury returned its verdict on September 26. The judgment was entered on September 28. (Even court clerks are not infallible.) A notice of entry of judgment was mailed by the court clerk on October 29 and received on November 3. The opposition wasted no time in serving its notice of entry by mail on November 4, which you received this morning, November 5. Provide the following requested dates, citing the code sections or rules that govern:

(a) the first date to file a notice of intent to appeal
(b) the last date to file a notice of intent to appeal
(c) what the filing fee is for the appeal, to whom it is paid, and when.

If the notice of intent to appeal is filed November 6, what

(a) is the last date to make a "rule 8.124 election"?
(b) is the last date to file appellant's opening brief?

2. How would the dates in Assignment 1 change for an appeal from a district court judgment?

3. How would the dates in Assignment 1 change for an appeal from a judgment in a limited civil case?

CHAPTER 29

PROVISIONAL REMEDIES AND EXTRAORDINARY WRITS

After completing the chapter reading, Discussion Questions, Online Projects, and Assignment, review the material in the following Chapter Outline, then complete the Chapter Objectives, Review Exercises, and Key Words and Phrases. When these are mastered, complete the Online Projects, Additional Research, Quiz, and the Alternate Assignments.

CHAPTER OUTLINE

I. Provisional Remedies and Extraordinary Writs Permit Speedy Management of Disputes That Cannot Wait for Trial.

A. Provisional remedies protect the litigants' rights pending a resolution.

B. Extraordinary writs require the lesser tribunal to comply with the law.

C. Neither provisional remedies nor extraordinary writs provide for money damages.

II. Injunctions Are Orders Requiring the Party Against Whom the Order Is Directed to Act or Refrain from Acting.

A. An injunction is appropriate when

1. the remedies available through ordinary litigation are inadequate because the time required renders the issues moot.
2. ordinary litigation does not provide the type of remedy needed.

B. Some types of injunctions are specifically defined in state statute, such as in cases of

1. domestic violence.
2. harassment.

3. unfair business practices.
4. trade secrets violations.

C. Injunctions are equitable remedies allowing a court to fashion a remedy to suit the circumstances.

D. In evaluating a request for injunction, state and federal courts consider

1. whether the legal remedy is adequate, that is, will normal litigation resolve the problem and protect the rights of the parties.
2. whether the party seeking the injunction has exhausted all administrative remedies, such as hearings or appeals to administrative agencies.
3. whether the party seeking the injunction will suffer irreparable harm if the injunction is not granted.
4. whether it is likely that the party seeking the injunction will prove his case after the injunction is granted to preserve the status quo.
5. whether the party seeking the extraordinary relief has clean hands.
6. whether the injunction sought will require continuing supervision by the court, which will tax court personnel and resources.
7. whether the injunction sought is ultimately enforceable.

E. The three types, or levels, of injunctions

1. Temporary restraining orders are designed to preserve the status quo for 15 to 22 days pending a resolution of the underlying dispute.
   a. A superior court may require the party seeking the injunction to post a bond.
   b. A federal court temporary restraining order (TRO) requires a bond.
      (i) The bond protects the rights of the other party who may be injured if the injunction is improperly granted.
2. A preliminary injunction preserves the status quo pending a trial on the underlying dispute.
   a. This type of injunction is a determination of the trial court that the status quo should continue until trial.
   b. Bonds are required at both state and federal courts.
3. A permanent injunction requires permanent compliance as part of a final judgment of the court.
   a. A bond is not required.

F. The court will consider the same seven elements with each level of injunction, requiring stronger showings each time.

G. Actions for injunctive relief have automatic preference on the civil active list and may come to trial in a matter of days or weeks.

III. Receiverships

A. A receiver can manage a business or property during a dispute.

B. The receiver is given specific powers

1. to manage the assets and liabilities of the business.
2. to prevent it from deteriorating during the course of the dispute.

C. Receiverships are expensive but effective.

D. Receiverships are granted upon noticed motion.

1. The order includes a detailed list of powers given to the receiver to protect him from liability.

IV. Claim and Delivery

A. Claim and delivery is a proceeding created by California statute to allow a complainant to obtain the possession of tangible personal property pending the resolution of the underlying dispute.

B. Claim and delivery is appropriate when the plaintiff has an immediate right to possession of tangible personal property and the property has been wrongfully withheld by the defendant.

C. An action for claim and delivery is commonly called a petition for writ of attachment and is obtained in three ways:

1. by noticed hearing
2. by temporary restraining order
3. by ex parte motion.
    a. Ex parte motions are explicitly authorized in cases of
        (i) credit card theft or fraud.
        (ii) in commercial cases where the property is subject to imminent destruction.

D. The complaint must be filed with

1. a proposed order.
2. a bond to protect the defendant in the event that he can prove his possession was rightful.
3. a writ prepared by counsel or the court clerk.

E. The writ may be executed by the sheriff.

V. Attachment

A. Attachment is used to seize defendant's assets to preserve them for resolution of the underlying dispute.

B. Attachment is appropriate only in commercial settings, for unsecured debts of fixed amounts incurred in contract.

C. Attachment is obtained through the same methods as claim and delivery.

VI. Extraordinary Writs

A. Writs challenge the jurisdiction of a lower court or tribunal by petition to a higher court.

1. The higher court can order the lesser tribunal to comply with the law.

B. A writ of mandamus is an order of a higher tribunal to a lesser tribunal, to compel obedience to the law or to rules.

1. It is obtained by filing a verified complaint called a petition.
   a. The complaint must be accompanied by a memorandum of points and authorities and a proposed writ.
   b. It must be served before it is filed.
2. The complainant is the petitioner; the opposing party is the respondent.
   a. Real parties in interest are the third parties affected by the outcome.
3. The petitioner may seek an alternative writ to stop the respondent from performing an act, or compel continued performance pending a hearing on the petition.
4. The court will order the respondent to appear to show cause why the peremptory (permanent) writ should not be granted.
5. If the respondent fails to appear or fails to show cause, the peremptory writ will be granted.

VII. Writ of Administrative Mandamus

A. Writs may be sought to compel an administrative body to comply with the laws or rules governing its activities.

B. In administrative mandamus,

1. all records, documents, and hearing transcripts must be submitted to the court before it will consider the petition.
2. the petitioner must complete all administrative procedures before seeking relief from the judicial system.

VIII. Writ of Prohibition

A. A writ of prohibition prevents a lesser tribunal from exceeding its authority.

B. Writs of prohibition are obtained by following the same general procedure as writs of mandate.

IX. Writ of Certiorari

A. A writ of certiorari is brought to seek review by a higher tribunal of an act, which has already taken place, of a lesser tribunal in excess of its authority.

CHAPTER OBJECTIVES

1. List examples of provisional remedies.

____

____

____

2. List examples of extraordinary writs.

____

____

____

3. Describe the various levels of injunctive relief.

____

____

____

4. Where are the state laws governing injunctions? Writs?

____

____

____

5. Where are the federal laws governing injunctions? Writs?

____

____

____

REVIEW EXERCISES

Fill in the Blanks:

1. Provisional remedies protect ____________________ pending a resolution; extraordinary writs require ____________________ to ____________________.

2. An injunction is appropriate when

a. ____.

b. ____.

3. List five factors considered by both a state and federal court in considering a request for injunction.

a. ______________________________

b. ______________________________

c. ______________________________

d. ______________________________

e. ______________________________

4. When granting an injunction, a state court may require a ______________________________.

5. A preliminary injunction preserves the ______________________________ until ______________________________.

6. At each level in the injunction process, the court will require increasingly ______________________________ showings that the injunction is proper.

7. A ______________________________ manages property or money during a dispute, and is protected from liability as long as he ______________________________.

8. A party who requests possession of tangible personal property seeks a writ of ______________________________, by the process of either a(n)

a. ______________________________,

b. ______________________________, or

c. ______________________________.

9. A writ ordering a governmental agency to comply with its governing rules is a writ of ______________________________.

10. A petition for writ requesting a higher tribunal to review the decision of a lower tribunal seeks a writ of ____________________.

KEY WORDS AND PHRASES

Provide a Definition for Each of the Following:

Provisional remedies:

Extraordinary writ:

Injunction:

Temporary restraining order (TRO):

Preliminary injunction:

Prohibition:

Claim and delivery:

Receivership:

Attachment:

Mandamus or mandate:

Petitioner:

Respondent: ______________________________

____

Administrative mandamus: ______________________________

____

Exhaustion of administrative remedies: ______________________________

____

Permanent injunction: ______________________________

____

Alternative writ: ______________________________

____

Petition: ______________________________

____

ONLINE PROJECTS

1. Using the official California courts Web site **(http://www.courtinfo.ca.gov/)**, access and read carefully the court's opinion in *People v. Mitchell Brothers' Santa Ana Theater* (1981) 118 CA3d 863. What are Gow I and Gow II? How does the court define "irreparable injury"? What does this court hold are the purposes of a temporary restraining order and a preliminary injunction? What is the holding of the court? Why? Is there any other form of litigation that would achieve the result sought in this action?

2. Using the official California courts Web site **(http://www.courtinfo.ca.gov/)**, access and read carefully the court's opinion in *RLI Insurance Company Group v. Superior Court* (1996) 51 CA4th 415. What remedy is being sought? What about the decision of the lower tribunal is unusual? Does that factor into the court's decision? What is the court's authority to decide the matter? What is the outcome? Why?

3. Access the Federal Rules of Civil Procedure **(http://www.law.cornell.edu/)**, and review rule 65. How would a litigant obtain a preliminary injunction? A permanent injunction?

4. Using the Official California Legislative Information Web site **(http://www.leginfo.ca.gov/)**, locate Code of Civil Procedure sections 1068, 1085, and 1102. Compare the remedies provided by these code sections.

5. Using the Official California Legislative Information Web site **(http://www.leginfo.ca.gov/)**, locate Code of Civil Procedure sections 525–527. What are the grounds and procedure for obtaining a preliminary injunction?

ADDITIONAL RESEARCH

The following are cases accessible on the official California courts Web site **(http://www.courtinfo.ca.gov/)** on various topics of interest relating to this chapter.

Oceanside Union School District v. Superior Court (1962) 58 C2d 180 (mandamus)

Dvorin v. Appellate Department (1975) 15 C3d 648 (certiorari)

Greyhound Corporation v. Superior Court (1961) 56 C2d 355 (resolving conflicting decisions)

Oceanside Community Association v. Oceanside Land Company (1983) 147 CA3d 166 (injunction)

Marsch v. Williams (1994) 23 CA4th 238 (receivership)

Lorber Industries of California v. Turbulence, Inc. (1985) 175 CA3d 532 (attachment)

Englert v. IVAC Corporation (1979) 92 CA3d 178 (claim and delivery)

QUIZ

1. Provisional remedies
   a. protect the litigants' rights pending a resolution.
   b. require the lesser tribunal to comply with the law.
   c. provide for money damages.
   d. a and c.

2. An injunction is appropriate when
   a. ordinary remedies are inadequate because the time required renders the issues moot.
   b. ordinary litigation does not provide the type of remedy needed.
   c. the respondent has clean hands.
   d. a and b.

3. The factors considered by federal courts asked to issue injunctions include
   a. whether the legal remedy is adequate.
   b. whether the party wishes to continue pursuing administrative remedies.
   c. whether petitioner can afford a bond.
   d. whether the respondent has clean hands.

4. The factors considered by state courts asked to issue TROs include
   a. whether it is likely that the party seeking the injunction will prove his case after the injunction is granted to preserve the status quo.
   b. whether the respondent has clean hands.
   c. whether the petitioner can afford a bond.
   d. whether the party wishes to continue pursuing administrative remedies.

5. The three types of injunctions
   a. are designed to preserve the status quo.
   b. require increasing amounts of proof.
   c. require a bond in state court.
   d. a and c.

6. A receiver's order specifies his responsibilities because
   a. he will be paid in proportion to his responsibilities.
   b. he is not liable for carrying out the court's orders.
   c. it is meant to keep the parties from fighting.
   d. otherwise he can only manage the business and perform inventories.

7. Claim and delivery can be obtained
   a. only by noticed hearing.
   b. only by noticed hearing and temporary restraining order.
   c. only by noticed hearing, temporary restraining order, and ex parte motion.
   d. only by noticed hearing, temporary restraining order, ex parte motion, and order to show cause.

8. Attachment can be obtained
   a. only by noticed hearing.
   b. only by noticed hearing and temporary restraining order.
   c. only by noticed hearing, temporary restraining order, and ex parte motion.
   d. only by noticed hearing, temporary restraining order, ex parte motion, and order to show cause.

9. The three types of extraordinary writs include
   a. claim and delivery.
   b. claim and delivery and writs of attachment.
   c. writs of administrative mandamus and certiorari.
   d. claim and delivery and writs of mandamus.

10. The three types of injunction, in order, are
   a. TRO, permanent injunction, and writ of mandamus.
   b. TRO, preliminary injunction, and permanent injunction.
   c. TRO, order to show cause, and permanent injunction.
   d. preliminary injunction, TRO, and permanent injunction.

ALTERNATE ASSIGNMENTS

1. *Auntie Irma's v. Rilling Enterprises:* When Ray Rouse was fired from Rilling Enterprises, he took with him the recipes for Rilling Rolls and another cookie still in development. Alice Rilling learns that Monster Cookie Company is planning to promote a new cookie called the Rolling Raft, featuring the same types of ingredients and flavors as the Rilling Roll. Rilling suspects that Rouse has turned over the recipe to Monster Cookie Co. and that Monster Cookie's new cookie is based on the recipe. What type of provisional remedy is appropriate? Will Rilling Enterprises prevail? Why or why not?

   a. Would your answer be different if you knew that the recipe, although secret, is easily determined by any chemist with state-of-the-art equipment? Why or why not?
   b. Would your answer be different if you knew that Rouse had no nondisclosure agreement with Rilling Enterprises? Why or why not?
   c. Would your answer be different if you knew that the Rolling Raft was already in development when Rouse left Rilling Enterprises?

2. *Whetstone v. Brian:* Even though she lost the trial against him, Megan Brian is still concerned that Gregory James is determined to cause her some kind of bodily harm. A witness, Harriet Culbert, was with Brian late last Thursday and confirms that James was skulking around the rear parking area of Brian's offices at that time. The next day, Brian received a muffled telephone threat; a male voice whispered, "I didn't get you before, but I'll get you now! Watch your back, Meggie!"

a. Using judicial council forms, seek an injunction to prevent James from communicating with Brian, or approaching Brian, her home, office, or car.
b. Prepare a drafted complaint for the same relief.

APPENDIX A

DEPOSITION

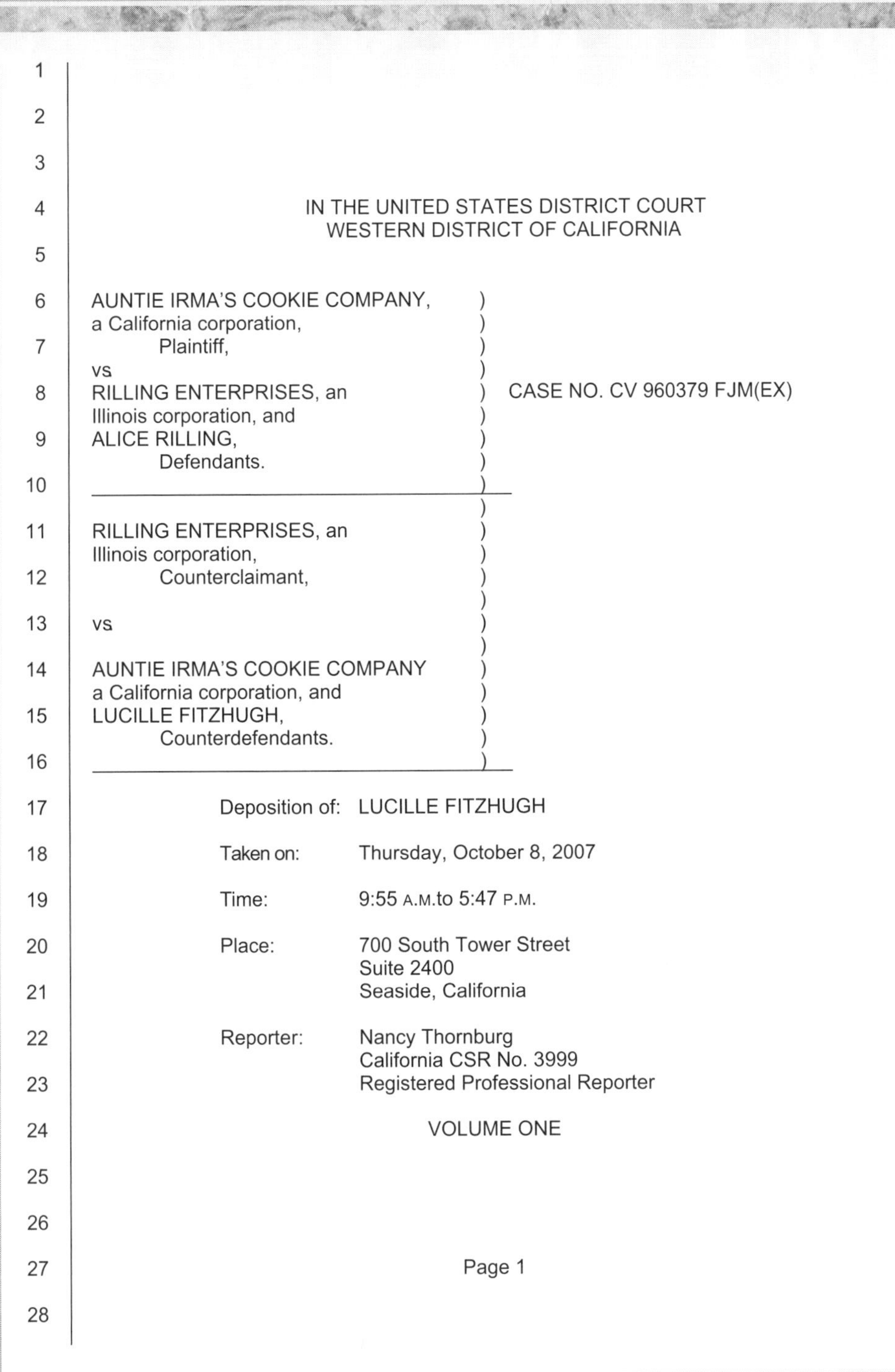

IN THE UNITED STATES DISTRICT COURT
WESTERN DISTRICT OF CALIFORNIA

AUNTIE IRMA'S COOKIE COMPANY, a California corporation, Plaintiff, vs RILLING ENTERPRISES, an Illinois corporation, and ALICE RILLING, Defendants.	CASE NO. CV 960379 FJM(EX)
RILLING ENTERPRISES, an Illinois corporation, Counterclaimant, vs AUNTIE IRMA'S COOKIE COMPANY a California corporation, and LUCILLE FITZHUGH, Counterdefendants.	

Deposition of: LUCILLE FITZHUGH

Taken on: Thursday, October 8, 2007

Time: 9:55 A.M.to 5:47 P.M.

Place: 700 South Tower Street
Suite 2400
Seaside, California

Reporter: Nancy Thornburg
California CSR No. 3999
Registered Professional Reporter

VOLUME ONE

Page 1

VOLUME ONE of the Deposition of LUCILLE FITZHUGH, taken before Nancy Thornburg, a Certified Shorthand Reporter for the State of California, with principal office in the County of Vista, commencing at 9:55 A.M., Thursday, October 8, 2007 in the law offices of Secombe & Riley, 700 South Tower Street, Seaside, California

APPEARANCES OF COUNSEL

FOR PLAINTIFF: AUNTIE IRMA'S COOKIE COMPANY
BY: MARY ELLEN REEDER
LAW OFFICES OF MARY ELLEN REEDER
3911 BENSON STREET
SEASIDE, CALIFORNIA

FOR DEFENDANTS: RILLING ENTERPRISES and
ALICE RILLING
BY: WILLIAM RILEY
SECOMBE & RILEY
700 SOUTH TOWER STREET, SUITE 2400
SEASIDE, CALIFORNIA

****

INDEX

Examinations by	Page
Mr. Riley	3

LUCILLE FITZHUGH,

having been duly sworn, was examined and

testified as follows:

Q BY MR. RILEY:Could you state your name for the record, ma'am.

A Lucille Fitzhugh.

Q Spell that, please.

A L-U-C-I-L-L-E F-I-T-Z-H-U-G-H

Q Ms. Fitzhugh, I'm Bill Riley and I represent Rilling Enterprises and Alice Rilling in this lawsuit.

A Right.

Q Have you ever had your deposition taken before, ma'am?

A No. I haven't.

Q Let's go through a few ground rules to make sure that we conduct ourselves properly today. Do you understand, ma'am, that in the course of this proceeding I'll be asking you questions, and to the extent you are able to and to the best of your ability you'll be responding to those questions?

A Yes.

Q You understand you have just been sworn to tell the truth, ma'am?

A Yes.

Q I'd like you to understand that the laws regarding perjury apply to your testimony today. Do you understand that?

A Yes.

Q If for any reason you don't understand a question of mine, either I mumble or make some nonsensical statement, please bring that to my attention. I'll try and phrase a question that makes sense to you. All right?

A Okay.

Q If you answer a question I'm going to assume that you understood it, okay?

A Yes.
Q At any time if you need to take a break, get another cup of coffee, use the rest room or whatever, you are free to do that.
A Okay.
Q You should understand, ma'am, that although we're sitting here in a law firm's conference room, that the testimony that you give today has the same force and effect as if you were giving it in a courtroom in front of a judge and a jury. Do you understand that?
A Yes.
Q Have you ever been a party to any litigation?
A No.
Q Has Auntie Irma's been a party to any other litigation other than this case?
A No. With probably a collection.
Q Except for collection actions?
A Yes.
Q Is that matters in which Auntie Irma's tried to collect its accounts or matters in which other people tried to collect money, other people—
A Auntie Irma's tried to collect accounts.
Q How many of those matters?
A One.
Q Were you personally involved in that?
A (Unintelligible.)
Q Also, one thing I forgot to mention is in order for the court reporter to accurately transcribe everything that we've done, I need to ask audible questions, you need to provide audible answers. Do you understand that?
A You bet.

MS. REEDER: And I'll add that you need to allow Mr. Riley time to finish his question before you answer it so the court reporter can take it down.

THE WITNESS: Okay.

Q BY MR. RILEY: Ma'am, did you review any documentation before coming here today in preparation for your testimony?

A Yes.

Q What documents did you review?

MS. REEDER: Objection. Workproduct privilege, attorney-client communication. Don't answer.

MR. RILEY: Pardon me?

MS. REEDER: I instructed her not to answer. It's privileged.

Q BY MR. RILEY: Okay. Did any of the documentation that you reviewed refresh your recollection as to any of the events involved in this lawsuit?

A Yes.

Q Okay. What documents were those?

A I don't remember.

Q I'm sorry?

A I don't remember specifically.

Q How long ago was it that you reviewed these documents?

A Yesterday.

Q All right. Where were you when you reviewed them?

A In my office.

Q How long did you review them for?

A For about a couple hours.

Q Did you have a file that you looked through?

A Uh-huh. Yes.

Q Yes. Was it your own file? Was that your own file? Your, Lucille Fitzhugh's file, or was that one of the company's files?
A Yes.
Q I'm sorry, which one? Company or yours?
A No. Company.
Q What types of records were in that file?
A Copies of some correspondence.
Q Any other types of records?
A Agreements.
Q Anything else?
A Literature.
Q What type of literature? Product literature?
A Rilling's literature.
Q Anything else?
A Nothing else I can remember.
Q Within this group of documents then, as you sit here today, you can't remember any particular documents that you looked at yesterday during your two-hour document review; is that correct?
MS. REEDER: That misstates her testimony.
Q BY MR. RILEY: I'm not trying to state her testimony.
Can you remember any particular document that you looked at yesterday when you were reviewing documents to refresh your memory about the events involved in this case?
A I can think of one, a letter from Rilling to Flipper Cookies.
Q Is that a document that has been produced in this case by your company?
A That was produced by Rilling.

Q Any others that—any other documents that you can recall that you reviewed yesterday?
A I just went through—I didn't really review the documents. I was more concerned about dates and things like that.
Q Trying to construct some sort of chronology of events; is that right?
A Yes.
Q Did you make any notes to yourself during that document review?
A No.
Q Are you presently employed, ma'am?
A Yes. I am.
Q By whom?
A By Monster Cookie Company.
Q What is your position with Monster Cookie?
A I am vice president.
Q How long have you been so employed?
A Since August 1st.
Q Of this year?
A (Nodding head.)
Q Where is your office currently? Where do you work?
A I work in Vista.
Q What's the address there?
A 752 Allan Avenue.
Q What are your duties and responsibilities as a vice president of Monster Cookie?
A Hire salespeople and make sales.
Q Okay. What products or product do you sell or service that you sell for Monster Cookie?

Page 7

A We sell franchises for cookie shops, and Private Cookies.
Q What is Private Cookies?
A A Rilling product with a private label sold by mail order.
Q By private label you mean that you sell the cookies to companies that package them for resale under their own trade name?
A Absolutely. So the department store chains sell our cookies under their in-house name. A very lucrative market.
Q That's it as you understand it? Rilling sold Monster Cookie its products, which they use and market by mail order for private label?
A Right. That is correct.
Q What particular Rilling product is sold in Private Cookies by Monster Cookie?
A As far as I know they only—Rilling only has one product.
Q What kind of—
A The Rilling Roll.
Q Do you have any other responsibilities other than hiring salespeople and selling franchises?
A I basically have P and L responsibilities for the western region.
Q What does that mean?
A P and L, profit and loss.
Q You are kind of the head of that division; is that it?
A Yes.
Q What's the western region?
A It's California, all the way through Georgia.
Q Any other responsibilities?
A That is it.
Q Do you have any ownership interest in Monster Cookie?

Page 8

A No.
Q Is Monster Cookie a corporation, to your knowledge?
A Yes.
Q You are not a stockholder?
A No.
Q Do you hold any options or warrants or any rights to purchase stock?
A Not at this point.
Q Is that something you are negotiating for?
A Yes.
Q Who is your—who do you report to at Monster Cookie?
A I report to Earl Marzipan.
Q What is his position?
A President of Monster Cookie.
Q Umm, are you a director of Monster Cookie?
A What do you mean?
Q A member of the board of directors.
A Not at this point.
Q That is also something you are negotiating toward?
A Yes.
Q Do you have an employment agreement, ma'am, with Monster Cookie?
A Not at this point.
Q You are negotiating that, too?
A Yes.
Q What's the—Let me ask the question this way. What's the basis for your employment now?
MS. REEDER: Objection. Vague.

Q BY MR. RILEY: Commission salesperson? Are you on a salary? Hourly wage earner? Do you have a set amount that you are getting?
A I'm on a salary.
Q You are on salary at this point?
A (Nodding head.)
Q Yes?
A Uh-huh. Yes. Salary plus bonuses.
Q Is a bonus based on production in terms of number of sales and so on?
A Yes. Profitability, all those good things.
Q What's the status of your negotiation with respect to an employment agreement and stock ownership and membership on the board of Monster Cookie?
A Negotiating.
Q At the time that you undertook employment with Monster Cookie, was any commitment made to you concerning stock ownership or membership on the board?

MS. REEDER: I've been very patient, and Lucille has been very cooperative, but now I'm going to object to this whole line of questioning as to relevance. Do you have some basis that this is relevant to this litigation?

MR. RILEY: I want to find out—Monster Cookie is relevant to this litigation, and I want to find out the full extent of Ms. Fitzhugh's involvement with Monster Cookie. It goes toward her—a lot of things, including bias and credibility. But there's an agreement I know that's been produced between Auntie Irma's and Monster Cookie, and I believe that it's going to come into play in terms of probable damages, too. I mean, it's clearly likely to lead to the discovery of admissible evidence.

MS. REEDER: I don't see that Lucille's current employment has anything to do with the issues of the lawsuit. If you can show me how that has anything to do with what she's claiming Rilling has done or what Rilling is claiming she's done, then we can spend time on it but—

MR. RILEY: Let's just say that the Monster Cookie/Auntie Irma's relationship is an issue in the lawsuit.

MS. REEDER: But I don't see how. It's not in your pleadings, either as a count or as an affirmative defense.

MR. RILEY: The problem is, we contend that the agreement between Irma's and Monster constitutes a breach of the Monster-Rilling agreement.

MS. REEDER: So what? That's between you and them, not us.

MR. RILEY: Well, the thing is, if we need to sue Monster to stop this agreement, we will do it in this action. If this agreement exists, and if it says what we believe it says, then we will have to add Monster as a party, and seek an injunction. My position on this line of questioning is that, given the wide scope of discovery—anything which may lead to admissible evidence—the claims you have made for damages may be mitigated by the relationship with Monster. I'll concede for purposes of argument that that is not our principal purpose in this deposition at this juncture, but that's where we are going. May I proceed?

MS. REEDER: Can we at least agree that you will conclude the entire deposition in the time frame we discussed? I don't want to get picky here, but you know you're going pretty far afield, and I don't want to subject my client to hours of questioning about claims that may or may not ever be brought.

MR. RILEY: Certainly. I will do my best to speed this along.

Q BY MR. RILEY: Back to my question, ma'am.

Were any commitments made to you by authorized people at Monster Cookie with respect to stock ownership or membership on the board?

A There were other things in the works that had nothing to do with the employment.
Q What are those other things in the works?
A My purchasing the shares. Not necessarily related, only to some extent.
Q Okay. What percentage of the company is available to you for purchase?
A Between 5 and 15 percent.
I will have some water.
MR. RILEY: Sure.
(A discussion was held off the record.)
Q BY MR. RILEY: Is it your understanding, ma'am, that if you do, in fact, purchase these shares of Monster Cookie, you would also be entitled to a seat on the board?
A Yes.
Q How many members are there on the board of directors at Monster Cookie?
A I don't know exactly.
Q Who were you employed by prior to August 1 of this year?
A Auntie Irma's.
Q Is it still in existence?
A Yes.
Q You are no longer employed by that company; is that correct?
A Yes.
Q Do you have any position at all with Auntie Irma's?
A I am president of Auntie Irma's.
Q So you are technically an employee of Auntie Irma's?
A With no pay.
Q Are you a stockholder in Auntie Irma's?
A Yes.

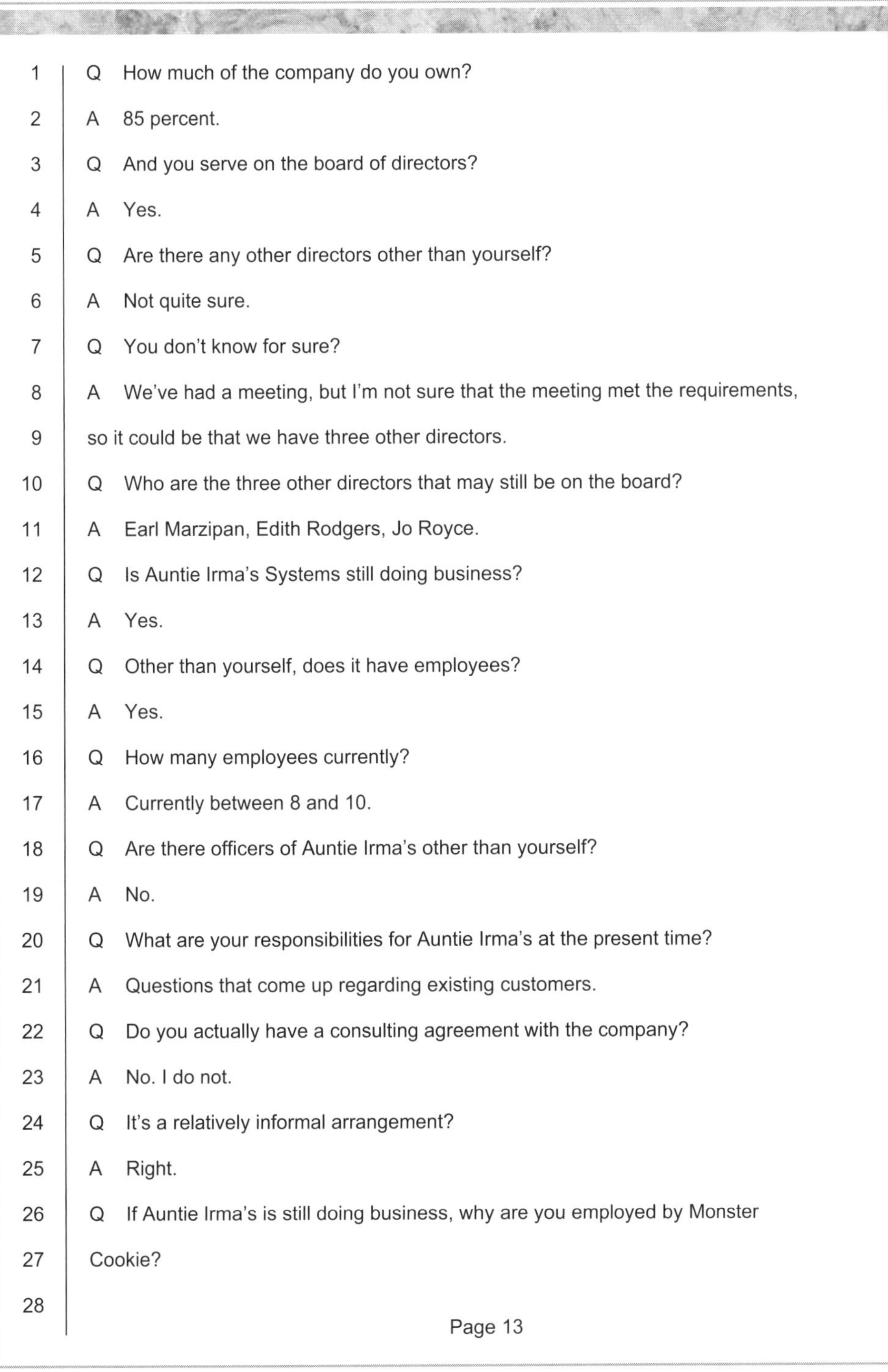
Q How much of the company do you own?
A 85 percent.
Q And you serve on the board of directors?
A Yes.
Q Are there any other directors other than yourself?
A Not quite sure.
Q You don't know for sure?
A We've had a meeting, but I'm not sure that the meeting met the requirements, so it could be that we have three other directors.
Q Who are the three other directors that may still be on the board?
A Earl Marzipan, Edith Rodgers, Jo Royce.
Q Is Auntie Irma's Systems still doing business?
A Yes.
Q Other than yourself, does it have employees?
A Yes.
Q How many employees currently?
A Currently between 8 and 10.
Q Are there officers of Auntie Irma's other than yourself?
A No.
Q What are your responsibilities for Auntie Irma's at the present time?
A Questions that come up regarding existing customers.
Q Do you actually have a consulting agreement with the company?
A No. I do not.
Q It's a relatively informal arrangement?
A Right.
Q If Auntie Irma's is still doing business, why are you employed by Monster Cookie?

Page 13

A Because I have to make a living, and I have to keep the company alive somehow. You people terminated my license, and called up all my customers, offering them sweetheart deals to go to Rilling. Auntie Irma's is a shell now.
Q What is the current business of Auntie Irma's? What does the company engage in?
A We have our local shop, and we have the Lacy Irma cookie line to market through Monster Cookie and other licensees, like the contract with Rilling.
Q As I understand it, the Mega-Monster is the same as the Rilling Roll; is that correct?
A Equivalent.
Q So before the termination by Rilling you were selling the Rilling Roll and the Lacy Irma, is that correct?
A Yes.
Q And now what do you intend?
A We intend to continue to sell the Lacy Irma, but sell the Mega-Monster instead of the Rilling Roll.
Q Will you have the same territory for the Mega-Monster? The U.S.?
A No, there are no limits.
Q Why?
A Because Monster Cookie has a private label agreement with Rilling that has no territorial limit.
Q What product or service is it hoped that Auntie Irma's would provide through Monster Cookie?
A Well, we can provide the Lacy Irma line, which Rilling soon will not be able to do, since they've breached the license agreement. We can provide the Rilling Roll or its equivalent, the Mega-Monster, through Monster Cookie. Since the Monster Cookie license is an unlimited geographical territory, we can sell the

whole package internationally if we want, for less than Rilling's other licensees. In fact, we can compete directly with Rilling with its own product coupled with the Lacy Irma. Alice made a little mistake there, and got too greedy.

Q So in other words, Irma's can continue to do business, and even increase its business by selling the Mega-Monster?

A If Monster Cookie makes it available to Auntie Irma's.

Q Is there some question about that?

A The question of Monster Cookie wanting to get involved with Auntie Irma's, due to Rilling's litigation, and the ability of Auntie Irma's to pay for the product. The termination has crippled the company financially. That's what Alice intended.

Q Has Monster Cookie at any time ever provided Auntie Irma's with the Mega-Cookie product?

A Yes.

Q On how many occasions that you are aware of?

A I can remember, five or six.

Q Over what period of time?

A Since October, more or less, of last year.

Q Your testimony is that at the present time Monster Cookie is considering no longer making its product available to Auntie Irma's; is that correct?

A That is correct.

Q Who is making that decision at Monster Cookie?

A That would be Mr. Marzipan.

Q When was it that you first learned from anyone that Monster Cookie was considering no longer making the Rilling Roll product available to Auntie Irma's?

A From Mr. Marzipan.

Q When?

A When? (Indicating.) I would say a—three months ago. A couple months.
Q Since that time since you first heard of the possibility that Monster Cookie would no longer make the product available, has Monster Cookie, in fact, made the product available?
A I don't think so as far as I can remember. On the basis of paying cash for it. That pretty much might be the only basis that we can get the product, if we can get it on that basis.
Q Did Mr. Marzipan ever tell you any reason why the litigation between Auntie Irma's and Rilling in any way impacted Monster Cookie's ability or willingness to provide product to Auntie Irma's?
A They also have a license from Rilling.
Q And how does that relate to the question of whether Monster Cookie can provide the product to Auntie Irma's?
A They don't want to get involved with Auntie Irma's having problems. That would be a concern.
Q But did he ever explain why it's a concern?
A Not exactly, other than it could impact them unfavorably.
Q Did Monster Cookie supply product to Auntie Irma's, before Auntie Irma's was terminated by Rilling?
A No.
Q Did Monster Cookie and Auntie Irma's enter into any arrangement that you are aware of which would have allowed Monster Cookie to supply product to Auntie Irma's before termination by Rilling?
A No.
Q Is it your testimony, ma'am, that—Well, let me ask you the question this way. Did Auntie Irma's seek the Mega-Monster product as a substitute for the Rilling product?

Page 16

A Yes, after the Rilling product was withdrawn from Auntie Irma's.
Q To your understanding is the Mega-Monster product identical to the Rilling product other than the name of the product?
A It's an older product. It's an older formula than the present one from Rilling.
Q What release is the Monster Cookie product, do you know?
A I believe it's a 42H.
Q And your understanding is that Rilling has a newer formula?
A Yes.
Q What formula is that, if you know?
A 42L.
Q Do you know when the 42L formula became available, if it ever did?
A On a prerelease basis, in the month of August of last year, I was told it would be available and provided to customers on a prerelease basis.
Q What is a prerelease basis? I'm not all that familiar with your industry.
A Prerelease is basically—it could be the product 100 percent, but it has not been put through quality control and may have some minor problems.
Q Do you have any understanding as to which particular Rilling license customers had been promised the 42L formula in August of last year?
A CrackerCookies.
Q To your knowledge has the 42L product ever been released?
A Yes. As far as I know it's in the market. I have seen the literature that is available. It's talked about when, you know, when they go to a prospect; it's talked about as something that Auntie Irma's doesn't have.
Q When you had discussions with Monster Cookie about product to be sold outside of the United States, which discussions occurred before Rilling terminated Auntie Irma's license, could you tell me when those discussions occurred?

Page 17

A From memory, I would say September of last year.
Q So within a couple of months before the termination of the Auntie Irma's license?
A Right.
Q Did Monster Cookie actually make the Mega-Monster product available to Auntie Irma's for those purposes?
A No. They said they would but I didn't need it.
Q You had not completed the sale at that point?
A Right.
Q In September of last year, was it your understanding of the dealer arrangement you had with Rilling that you had the license to sell or make available the Rilling product outside of the United States?
A That was my understanding. Yes.
Q What was your understanding based on?
A Based on the fact that that's what the contract says and that was what I had negotiated.
Q I'll get the contract out in a minute. I may have to get it out now, but as I remember there was a schedule or an exhibit or something attached to the agreement that defined the territory—
A Right.
Q —for your license; do you recall that?
A Yes.
Q And that exhibit said the United States; is that correct?
A That's correct.
Q And at least in my reading of that exhibit there was no other territory delineated in the contract.
Is that your recollection as well?

A Okay. Several contracts. On the master license, which is the one that applied in this particular event, it said that as long as I would put the Auntie Irma's products, okay, together with a Rilling's, I could sell it anywhere in the world. That was my understanding of what that thing said.
If it was purely the Rilling products, the U.S., but if it were an Auntie Irma's product which would use the Rilling as a component, as long as I had the Auntie Irma's product, that I could sell it anywhere in the world.
Q What you call the master agreement, is that the—
A Unlimited license.
Q The unlimited license?
A Yes. And I had been given those assurances by Ms. Rilling.
Q When did she give you those assurances?
A In Seaside about July of last year.
Q And was that a meeting, a face-to-face meeting, that the two of you had?
A Yes.
Q Was anyone else there?
A Yes. Mary Ellen was there.
MR. RILEY: Off the record. We'll take a two-minute break.
(Recess.)

Q BY MR. RILEY: Prior to July of—Well, strike that. Did Auntie Irma's at anytime make any sales outside of the United States of the Rilling product, whether bundled with Auntie Irma's products or otherwise?
A Yes.
Q How many occasions did Auntie Irma's do that?
A Once.
Q When was that?

A Last year, or may be earlier this year.
Q Who was the end user in that instance?
A Sterling Cookies.
Q Where were they located at this time?
A England.
Q You guys sent me a bunch of documents. I don't remember. Were the sales documents relating to that transaction in the documents you produced in this case?
A Yes.

MS. REEDER: I'm not sure that is so. I mean, Lucille gave me a lot of documents. I'm not sure that was included in the ones that were produced.

MR. RILEY: I'm not saying they were or weren't. I don't remember, but is there any particular reason they would not have been?

MS. REEDER: We made a bunch of objections to a lot of requests, and that applies to the customer files.

MR. RILEY: We got some customer files, though.

MS. REEDER: Right. You got customer files of prospects of Auntie Irma's that were usurped, if you will, by Rilling when Rilling started competing directly with Auntie Irma's. You did not get customer files for—

MR. RILEY: All sales.

MS. REEDER: —all sales for customers who were not in controversy, if you will.

Q What product was sold to Sterling Cookies?
A The Auntie Irma's products, which includes the Rilling product.
Q Did Auntie Irma's obtain a nondisclosure agreement from Sterling Cookies in connection with that sale?
A I don't recall. I didn't see the need.

Page 20

Q You didn't see the need? Wasn't that a requirement of the license?
A I guess it was. But our contracts contain nondisclosure terms, which should accomplish the same thing. I don't see why we have to have a separate agreement when the contract will do the trick.
Q Before making the sale to Sterling Cookies, did Auntie Irma's or anyone at Auntie Irma's, you or anybody else, notify anyone at Rilling that you were trying to sell product to Sterling Cookies?
A Pretty sure we did.
Q What do you recall about that?
A I recall that I personally told Alice before and after the sale. Making a sale was something that, you know, we all took pride in, including Alice, so—
Q Do you have a recollection, ma'am, a firm recollection that before you made the sale you told Alice Rilling that you were going to make a sale to Sterling Cookies in England?
A I'm pretty sure that I told them after the sale. I cannot be certain that I told them before. I would feel—I also vaguely recollect that the customer got in contact with Rilling before the sale, as has been customary with a lot of customers.
Q And was there any arrangement made with Rilling, financial arrangements with respect to a prospect in advance—
A As far as I am concerned, I didn't have to make any arrangements.
Q As far as you were concerned, you believed you could make that sale to Sterling royalty free of Rilling; is that correct?
A Absolutely, yes.
Q At the time of the original, or let's say the first agreement, between Auntie Irma's and Rilling, did you have any understanding at that point about Auntie Irma's right to make sales outside the United States of Rilling products?

Page 21

A I was not—I had an understanding that I was not.
Q That you did not have that right; is that correct?
A That is correct.
Q That understanding then changed when the unlimited license deal was signed as far as you were concerned?
A Yes. Exactly. That was part of the negotiating, something that I needed to have.

MS. REEDER: I think Lucille is getting a little tired, and I'm looking forward to a break. Why don't we take an early lunch break, and we can resume in an hour or so.
MR. RILEY: I'm not sure we can get done today if we break now. Are you going to make her available tomorrow to finish?
MS. REEDER: No, I think you should be able to finish today. As I said earlier, you've been dwelling on a lot of irrelevant stuff. We agreed on the one day, and the fact that you've spent it delving into potential claims you may have against someone else on an unrelated matter is your decision. On the other hand, we can stay after 5:00, if you like, to try and finish in the one day.
MR. RILEY: Okay, we'll try. Off the record?
MS. REEDER: Fine.

(The deposition recessed for lunch.)

Page 22

APPENDIX B

LITIGATION OFFICE PROCEDURES

There are as many styles of practice as there are practices. The organization of a litigation office, whether a law firm, corporate office, or public agency, will reflect the style of practice of the attorneys who work there. The paralegal can significantly enhance his usefulness to the firm and its clients, and enhance his own professional experience, by mastering those procedures, and improving them.

There is another truism of the practice of litigation: Whatever can go wrong will go wrong. No matter how insignificant the error may seem, no matter how remote the consequences of it affecting the outcome appear, it will cause problems later on. One of the most important aspects of practice is to anticipate errors, and avoid them at all costs. If an error occurs, then remedial action must be considered and implemented as soon as possible.

The fact that errors can be so dangerous and detrimental has resulted in the development of some office procedures that are fairly common. Awareness of these procedures by the novice paralegal will assist immeasurably in beginning a new paralegal position.

Basic Office Skills

There are several skills that should be mastered before beginning the first paralegal position. As fundamental as it sounds, even a beginning paralegal on the first day of the first paralegal job should know how to answer phones professionally, run a photocopy machine, use expedited delivery services, send a facsimile, scan a document, and access the Internet. These days, even a novice paralegal is expected to know how to log on to online research services, use the major electronic legal and public information research systems, and receive and send electronic mail.

Only a few years ago, law firms would ask whether the applicant for a paralegal job had computer or word-processing expertise. Now it is assumed the applicant has this experience. The question has become what and how many applications programs is the candidate for employment fluent in. The desired programs include word processing, database management, calendaring and docket control, time and billing, spreadsheet programs, and specialized legal programs for document analysis and case management control.

The key to a successful beginning at any law firm, whether the new employee or intern has office experience or not, is to ask for a tour of all of the office machinery and equipment, and to ask about any special procedures that are in use. For example, some firms will have copiers that are programmed to accept codes for clients, so copies are automatically billed to the correct clients; the user will need a list of codes. Other firms have a manual system where copies are written down by client or client number for later tabulation. Other firms may not charge for copies at all. Most firms will have a particular greeting they prefer for incoming callers; the proficient paralegal will either ask about or notice the telephone manner of other office personnel, so the paralegal can answer the telephone properly when the need or occasion arises, even if that is not part of the formal job description.

The paralegal should also ask where and how case and billing files are kept, and how the firm controls file use. For example, some firms use file cards in the main filing system to show who has checked out the file so it may be found quickly if necessary.

Other than the physical production of workproduct (printing, word processing, copying, faxing, etc.), office procedures can generally be broken down into three categories: case files, including correspondence files and evidence maintenance; chronological files; and billing files. These three activities account for virtually all of the functions that the litigation law firm does other than the legal work and services themselves, such as research, consultation, drafting of letters and documents, and representation of clients. The new paralegal should keep these functions in mind, since these are the foundation for a successful performance of the paralegal services.

Case Files

The legal profession is a profession of words. It is also a profession of communication. Lawyers and paralegals are constantly communicating with each other, clients, opposing counsel, the courts, and third parties such as witnesses. It is absolutely imperative that these communications have standard and routine protections and means of preservation.

Most litigation offices have files for each client, kept either alphabetically by client name or numerically by numbers assigned to incoming clients. Case files, when not in use, are almost always kept in a central location, so that all of the case files for the office can be located in one place. Medium and large firms usually have some sort of "out card" system, so the user of a file can place a file card in its place while the file is removed; anyone looking for the file can consult the file card and determine where the file is and who has it. This type of system may be manual or computerized.

Litigation case files are usually divided into at least three types of documents. They are almost always filed with the oldest document on the bottom, with the more recent documents placed in order at the top, in other words in reverse chronological order. That way, newer documents can be filed without undoing the entire file to place them on the bottom. Moreover, the most recent documents are usually the ones that require more frequent reference.

Correspondence Files

Of these three types of case files, the first is correspondence files, which contain all of the correspondence concerning the case. These files will have the client contract, letters to and from the client, demand letters, and correspondence with opposing counsel and the courts. They may also have communications between counsel and the support staff, experts, and consultants. It may become incredibly important to find a document seemingly unimportant at an earlier time, so keeping copies and keeping them filed in proper chronological order are critical.

The correspondence file also typically contains the notes by the attorney taken during telephone or in-person conferences, and any other notes of counsel. Research memoranda may be kept in this file or in a "workproduct" or "research file." Maintaining copies of correspondence can be much more important than it initially seems. A date change may be the subject of a dispute, and one counsel may be required to make a motion to compel, or to continue the trial. The letter confirming that date change will be the principal evidence upon which such a motion will be based. When files are full, they are usually numbered (*Jones v. Smith*, Correspondence, Volume 7), and a sheet is placed on the top of the contents to indicate the comprehensive dates of the documents inside, and that the file is closed. A person searching for a document will know by date whether it is likely to be found there.

There will also be notes of conversations or other communications that may be filed in the correspondence files. For example, a paralegal may confer with her counterpart at another firm about a change in deposition dates. The date, persons involved, and the course of the discussion should be recorded in some sort of note preserved in the file, even if a confirming letter will be sent. Invariably at some point the letter will be lost, not sent, or not filed, so the note may be the only record of the conversation, which may be the only document supporting or opposing a motion to compel or for sanctions.

Pleading Files

The second type of case file is pleading files. These contain the pleadings of the case. They generally also contain all of the documents on pleading paper, and all official communications with the court, even though these are not strictly "pleadings." For example, a pleading file will usually contain the complaint and summons; the answer and cross-complaint; the answer to cross-complaint; and copies of interrogatories, responses to interrogatories, deposition notices, notices of case management conferences from the court, and proofs of service for everything requiring service. Some firms divide these documents into pleadings files containing strictly pleadings, discovery files, and other sorts of official communications. Large, unwieldy documents, such as voluminous deposition transcripts, may be kept in separate, special files for convenience but may be referenced in the pleading index, so someone unfamiliar with the case can locate them efficiently.

The organization, accuracy, and completeness of these files are critical.

Most pleadings files are faced by an index, showing the date of the document, the name of the document, and the source of the document. The documents themselves are separated by sheets with tabbed numbers, so they can easily be located. Thus, an entry might be:

Tab No.	Date	Description	By Party
15	11/23/07	Smith Answer to Jones Cross-complaint	Smith

Consider that the date of the document could be many dates, from the date of signature of the document, to the date of the service of the document, to the date of mailing of the document.

Such files are usually kept in the order that the documents were served or received, not in their actual order by date. Thus, for example, a document dated November 23, 2007 but received November 26, 2007 will be placed in the file after a document produced November 23, 2007 and sent out on November 23, 2007. Each firm will have its own conventions and procedures for proper filing.

Periodic review of such files may reveal a lapse or missing documents. It is not uncommon to discover that some written discovery propounded months before was never responded to, or that a supplemental pleading was never answered. The index of the pleadings files must be complete and accurate enough to disclose such problems.

The pleadings files are the heart of the case. They show the allegations, denials and defenses, and the discovery. As the case progresses to trial, they show the procedural status of the case, as well as the pretrial developments, such as Code of Civil Procedure section 998 offers. It may be quite important to the victorious client after trial to locate and use the 998 demand made months before trial.

Pleadings files that are full are treated the same way as full correspondence files, with the numbered tabs continuing into the new file.

Evidence Files

The third type of case file is the evidence file. The evidence file, sometimes called "client documents file," houses documents—which may be originals—provided by the client to the firm. A client alleging a breach of commercial lease, for example, will provide his counsel with the lease itself, correspondence with the tenant before and after the contract, and before and after the breach. There may be accounting records, ledgers, and cancelled checks. There may also be official notices, such as three-day or 30-day notices, which are required to prove the case.

Evidence may also include physical nondocumentary evidence, such as a shoe damaged in a fall, a bloody shirt, a half-eaten sandwich, or an auto part. (There may also be larger evidence housed in the firms' offices, such as an airline seat, an auto part, or a tree stump.) This physical evidence is usually tagged or labeled in some fashion which does not damage it, and logged in a file.

These three types of files will generally accommodate any case. However, it is not uncommon to find that a particular case demands another type of file, or that some aspect of the case—such as a major summary judgment motion, or pretrial or post-trial motions—require their own separate files, either working files with research and notes, or simply larger files with all of the pertinent documents in one place.

"Chron" Files

Whenever an outgoing communication is prepared, the firm usually keeps at least two hard (paper) copies. One goes in the correspondence file of the case file for the client or matter. The other is kept in the "chron" file, or chronology file, which contains a copy of every outgoing letter or document produced by the firm.

Chron files are usually kept by individual, not by case. Usually every individual who produces outgoing documents will have one. Thus, if the attorney signed the letter, his chron file would contain a copy of it in order with every other letter produced that day, week, month, and year. If the paralegal signed the confirming letter, a copy of that letter would go in the paralegal's chron file, also in order of production. If a case file copy is lost or damaged, a copy can be located in the chronological file of the person who produced it.

The paralegal should make certain that, even if there is no formal policy in the litigation office in which he works, that the paralegal maintains a chron file to retain and document any communications prepared by the paralegal.

Incoming Communications

Just as chron files record outgoing communications, it is important to keep records of incoming communications. As noted earlier, it is important for the paralegal to know simple office procedures such as how the telephone is answered. It is equally as important to know how calls are transferred, and what callers are told when a call is not taken. It is very important to know the method of taking messages and transferring them to the appropriate person.

Most litigation firms not only keep track of incoming messages but retain the carbons or computer records of the telephone messages for an indefinite period. The information kept in these documents can be critical to locate a telephone number years later, or to determine the precise date and time of the message and to whom it was directed.

Billing Files

The other main category of files in litigation offices is billing files. These files contain copies of the actual invoices or statements sent to clients. Clients are usually billed monthly, and the bill usually shows what activity occurred when, how long it took, who performed the service, and how much is being charged. It will also usually show what costs were incurred, and what is being charged for them.

The firm will also maintain the backup documentation for the bills. For example, a paralegal billing a half hour for a particular activity will have prepared a time slip, whether paper or electronic. A record of that time slip will be maintained somewhere. A firm billing a client $715 for a deposition transcript fee will have a copy of the invoice from the court reporter somewhere in its files, filed either by client, vendor, or service type.

These backup documents may be useful for a variety of purposes. A client inquiring about his bill may want to see them; personnel preparing a post-trial motion for fees or costs or both years later may have to provide them to the court and opposing parties. A question about a telephone message last year that cannot be answered for lack of a message book copy may be answered by referring to either an old bill copy or the time slips submitted at that time.

Sometimes paralegals are called upon to respond directly to clients with billing questions, so familiarity with billing files is important. Sometimes paralegals may be asked general questions by the client, and familiarity is also appropriate. Finally, a paralegal billing his time should study old bills and time slips to find out the general type of the firm and how clients are billed for certain services. "Making copies" might be considered clerical work and therefore unbillable; "document review and organization of key documents file" might better communicate the same activity, show the client that the work was billable, and that his case was being worked on.

Case Management

Managing cases is a special art that is personal to the office or even the individual attorney. Most law firms keep some type of intake sheet to record the client's initial contact with the office. This sheet, whether paper or electronic, will indicate generally how the client came to contact the firm and when, the initial facts of the case, and any calendaring deadlines or immediate concerns such as statutes of limitations.

This form may be continued, or other forms may be used to track the progress of the case, such as motions (including the last day to file and/or serve the moving, opposition, and reply papers), discovery (including dates served, dates responses are due, dates given to client to complete draft responses and verifications, etc.), and the trial date (including the 40 or 50 dates it triggers for pretrial activities, etc.). This type of case management is more and more frequently done by computer, especially in multiattorney firms, and may be done by day, week, month, or year.

Some firms use a formal system of assigning paralegals and other professionals to each case; others use a more informal approach. In either event, communications about who is responsible for what and when are extremely important, and every paralegal, novice or experienced, should be fully familiar with the system in use. It is never acceptable to miss a deadline because "It wasn't my job."

Conclusion

Once the basic categories of documents and evidence are understood, much of the mystery about litigation offices will dissolve. The new paralegal, or even the experienced paralegal in a new position, should think carefully about the work of the firm and observe assiduously the way it is managed. The paralegal can then be much more important to the operation of the firm and much more effective as a professional.

ANSWER KEY

For Chapter Objectives, Review Exercises, and Quizzes

1

CHAPTER OBJECTIVES

1. a. First client contact/prelitigation phase
   b. Pleadings
   c. Attacking the pleadings
   d. Discovery
   e. Trial
   f. Post-trial
   g. Appeal

2. Any of the following: private law firms, nonprofit corporations, corporations or other business entities, government agencies.

3. The litigation paralegal's role is to do everything the lawyer can do as well as the lawyer can do it in all phases of the litigation. However, the paralegal cannot appear in court, give legal advice, and negotiate a fee.

REVIEW EXERCISES

Fill in the Blanks

1. Litigation is a process of resolving disputes in the judicial system as defined by cases and statutes.

2. Legal principles; rules that govern the process of the litigation; contracts or torts; civil procedure

3. Any two of the following: Code of Civil Procedure, Rules of Court, Evidence Code, local rules; Federal Rules of Civil Procedure

4. First client contact; filing the pleadings; ascertain the merits of the case

5. a. Names of the parties
   b. Causes of action alleged
   c. Relief sought

6. Because they are defective or contain inappropriate matter

7. Obtain information and evidence for the case

8. Law and motion; evidence; judgment; law; facts

9. a. Attorneys' fees
   b. Right to new trial
   c. Altering the judgment

10. Appeal
11. Government agencies; nonprofit corporations
12. a. Contingency
    b. Hourly
    c. Flat rate
13. a. Partnerships
    b. Corporations
    c. LLPs
14. Any two of the following: family law, personal injury law, labor law, employment law, patent law
15. Profitable; attorneys; paralegals
16. a. Pleadings
    b. Trial
    c. Judgment

QUIZ

1. c.
2. a.
3. a.
4. d.
5. d.
6. c.
7. a.
8. d.
9. a.
10. c.

2

CHAPTER OBJECTIVES

1. Rules of Professional Conduct
   Disbarment, suspension, discipline
2. Business and Professions Code and Rules of Professional Conduct
   Civil penalties to the paralegal
3. Compliance with Business and Professions Code (i.e., combination of education and training and continued professional education)

REVIEW EXERCISES

Fill in the Blanks

1. Giving legal advice without membership in the State Bar of California
2. Truthful advertising properly identified as such
3. They govern referral fees, and fee splitting.
4. They require that attorneys be competent to handle any case they accept.
5. All communications with clients are encouraged.
6. When the client insists on following a course of action that will cause the attorney to violate the professional rules of conduct
7. When the client has not paid his bill or disagrees with cocounsel
8. Commingling of money that belongs to the client with money that belongs to the attorney, prohibited because it is not clear whose money is whose
9. Professionals by education and training who provide services under the supervision of a member of the state bar association
10. Four hours of ethics training every three years; four hours of substantive training every two years

QUIZ

1. d.
2. c.
3. a.
4. c.
5. d.
6. c.
7. d.
8. d.
9. c.
10. a.

CHAPTER OBJECTIVES

1. The client must determine whether he wants this firm to represent him.
2. Any three of the following: meritorious, no conflict, financial issues, competency, attorney not a witness

3. a. Hourly
   b. Contingency
   c. Fixed fee
   d. Combination

4. Substitution of attorneys; all files and documents

REVIEW EXERCISES

Fill in the Blanks

1. Whether the client faces any immediate deadlines. Because the attorney is responsible for protecting the client's interests, and the deadlines may affect the timing of the interview.

2. a. Competence of counsel
   b. Merit of the case
   c. Conflicts of interest
   d. Whether attorney could be a witness
   e. Financial preparation of firm

3. Counsel has a prior relationship and confidential information from an adverse party.

4. Waived by signing a written disclosure.

5. Disqualified; disqualified

6. Competence

7. Fees are not always recoverable, and that fact will affect the economic feasibility of the case.

8. Prevailing party

9. a. Contract provides for fees to be paid
   b. Statute provides for fees to be paid
   c. The litigation was brought in the interests of the public.

10. The fee may be over $1,000; contingency.

11. Anytime they wish.

QUIZ

1. a.

2. b.

3. c.

4. b.

5. d.

6. c.

7. a.

8. b.

9. a.

10. b.

CHAPTER OBJECTIVES

1. Superior courts (civil and criminal trials), courts of appeal (appeals of unlimited civil cases and criminal appeals), supreme court (appeals from the courts of appeal)

2. District courts (trial courts), courts of appeals (appeals from trial courts), U.S. Supreme Court (appeals from courts of appeals)

3. Federal courts have limited jurisdiction, and state courts handle everything else.

REVIEW EXERCISES

Fill in the Blanks

1. Jurisdiction; jurisdiction
2. Substantive; procedural
3. Constitution; Congress; the people
4. District courts
5. U.S. Supreme Court
6. Ninth
7. Superior
8. Unlimited civil; limited civil
9. Courts of appeal; superior court appellate division
10. Small claims courts

QUIZ

1. a.
2. d.
3. c.
4. a.
5. b.
6. b.
7. c.
8. b.
9. c.
10. b.

CHAPTER OBJECTIVES

1. A federal question, disputes between parties of different states with amounts in controversy over $75,000, or exclusive jurisdiction over a particular type of case

2. Unlimited civil case, limited civil case. Amount in controversy

3. Advantageous laws, advantageous procedures, advantageous juries, convenience of parties or counsel

REVIEW EXERCISES

Fill in the Blanks

1. Subject matter jurisdiction
2. Personal jurisdiction
3. Void
4. a. Type of case
   b. Amount of money in dispute
   c. Citizenship of parties
5. a. Federal questions
   b. Disputes between parties of different states or countries with amounts in controversy over $75,000
6. A superior court case with more than $25,000 in controversy; a superior court case with no more than $25,000 in controversy
7. At the beginning of the case
8. Subject matter jurisdiction; subject matter jurisdiction
9. Exclusive jurisdiction
   a. Maritime/admiralty claims
   b. Copyright
   c. Bankruptcy
10. Concurrent
    a. Federal securities
    b. Civil rights

QUIZ

1. b.
2. c.
3. d.
4. a.
5. c.
6. b.
7. c.

8. b.
9. a.
10. d.

CHAPTER OBJECTIVES

1. In personam, in rem, quasi in rem

2. Claim of minimum contacts leading to writ of attachment over property, long-arm statutes over people

3. Motion to quash, special appearance

REVIEW EXERCISES

Fill in the Blanks

1. Borders
2. a. Consent
   b. Mistake
   c. Contract
3. Property
4. Long-arm statutes; contacts; forum
5. Special appearance (or motion to quash)
6. Forum non conveniens
7. Venue
8. Where the property is located
9. Transitory action
   a. Where the wrongful death or injury occurred
   b. Where the contract was entered into
   c. Where the injury to property occurred
10. a. Where the principal office is located
    b. Where the obligation or liability arose
    c. Where the contract was to be performed

QUIZ

1. a.
2. c.
3. b.
4. d.
5. c.

6. d.
7. d.
8. d.
9. b.
10. a.

7

CHAPTER OBJECTIVES

1. The claim for a remedy
2. Complaint, answer, cross-complaint, and demurrer
3. Complaint, answer, counterclaim, third-party complaint, and cross-claim
4. Plaintiff (sues defendant), defendant responds to plaintiff, cross-complainant (a defendant or third party who sues the plaintiff or third parties), cross-defendant (defendant to a cross-complaint)
5. Plaintiff (sues defendant), defendant responds to plaintiff, counterclaimant (a defendant who sues the plaintiff), third-party plaintiff (sues third parties to the original complaint), third-party defendant (defendant to complaint other than original complaint to the action), counterdefendant (defendant to a counterclaim)

REVIEW EXERCISES

Fill in the Blanks

1. a. Claims
   b. Remedies sought
2. a. Admit
   b. Deny
   c. Assert affirmative defenses
3. They determine what evidence can be admitted
4. Federal causes of action
5. The record is important to decide what discovery can be done, what issues will be raised at trial, and what the issues are for an appellate court on appeal.
6. Essential elements; allegations
7. Real parties in interest
8. Standing; capacity
9. Capacity; qualified to do business
10. Joined

QUIZ

1. c.
2. a.
3. d.
4. d.
5. a.
6. a.
7. d.
8. d.
9. b.
10. b.

CHAPTER OBJECTIVES

1. Caption; causes of action, claims, counts, or allegations; prayer
2. Forms for California state courts, optional use for all California pleadings
3. Personal, substituted, notice and acknowledgment, publication

REVIEW EXERCISES

Fill in the Blanks

1. Pleading; caption; court; parties
2. The court has not assigned one yet; it identifies the case
3. Title
4. Any two of the following: tax records, secretary of state, phone book, Internet
5. "Does"
   a. names are unknown at time of pleading.
   b. they are responsible in some way for the damages alleged.
6. Numbered paragraphs, lettered subparagraphs
7. Concise statement of facts for the elements of the cause of action
8. Fill in the blanks and check boxes
9. Concise statement of facts for the elements of the cause of action
10. Fact
11. Notice
12. a. Incorporation by reference—avoid repetition
    b. On or about—pleading dates generally

c. Information and belief—allows pleading without personal knowledge
d. Inconsistent allegations—allow different theories and facts to be pled

13. The law prohibits it

14. Subscription; verification

15. Summons

16. Agents for service of process; secretary of state

17. It is not valid until signed and returned, and the serving party has no way to enforce signature and return

18. Caption

19. a. Counterclaim—against plaintiff(s)
b. Cross-complaint—against codefendant(s)
c. Third-party complaint—against parties new to the action

20. a. There is no "Doe" pleading
b. Facts concerning jurisdiction must be alleged
c. Causes of action are called counts or claims

QUIZ

1. d.
2. d.
3. c.
4. c.
5. b.
6. a.
7. b.
8. a.
9. c.
10. c.

CHAPTER OBJECTIVES

1. Words to the precise effect of: defendant denies each and every allegation of each and every cause of action alleged in the complaint, and denies that plaintiff suffered any injury or damage.

2. a. Admitted
b. Denied
c. Insufficient information to respond, and therefore denied

3. Unverified complaint; verified complaint

REVIEW EXERCISES

Fill in the Blanks

1. 30 days; 20 days
2. Deemed admitted
3. Specially drafted; under oath; verification
4. Negative pregnant
5. Affirmative defenses
6. Affirmative defenses
7. Plea in abatement
8. a. Caption
   b. Denials
   c. Affirmative defenses
9. Hand; mail; proof of service; the plaintiff is already under the jurisdiction of the court
10. Prohibited

QUIZ

1. a.
2. b.
3. b.
4. c.
5. a.
6. b.
7. a.
8. b.
9. a.
10. a.

CHAPTER OBJECTIVES

1. Challenge the sufficiency of the pleading
2. General demurrers attack the court's jurisdiction; special demurrers attack the pleading for lack of capacity, another action pending, defective joinder, uncertainty, and failure to allege whether contract was written or oral.
3. Notice of motion, demurrer challenging the pleading, memorandum of points and authorities arguing reasons to sustain

REVIEW EXERCISES

Fill in the Blanks

1. a. Narrow the issues
   b. Clarify issues at beginning of case
   c. Remove extraneous claims
   d. Set the tone
   e. Questions of validity of causes of action resolved at beginning of case
   f. Limit issues for trial to save money
2. a. Party can (usually) cure by amending
   b. Costs money
3. After time to demurrer has passed
4. All allegations are treated as if true.
5. Judicially noticed
6. It is in the form of a motion
7. Lack of jurisdiction; general
8. Special
9. 30
10. 35 days; as soon as they can be heard on the court's calendar
11. Special demurrers; unlimited
12. Plaintiff has (usually) 20 days to amend the pleading to avoid the issue raised in the demurrer.
13. The pleading cannot be amended, and that aspect of the case is over. That is, if a complaint is dismissed without leave to amend, the case is over.
14. The demurring party must answer, usually within 10 days.
15. a. Notice of motion
    b. Demurrer
    c. Memorandum of points and authorities
16. Motion to strike
17. Motion to dismiss
18. Motion to dismiss
19. Demurrer
20. Demurrer; motion to dismiss

QUIZ

1. d.
2. a.
3. b.
4. c.
5. a.

6. c.
7. c.
8. d.
9. d.
10. d.

CHAPTER OBJECTIVES

1. An amended pleading replaces the entire pleading; an amendment changes individual allegations.

2. Before the pleading is served, before the answer is filed, before the hearing on demurrer

3. A motion is made to the court, required after the answer is filed or after a hearing on demurrer.

REVIEW EXERCISES

Fill in the Blanks

1. Amended pleading

2. a. Before service
   b. Before the answer
   c. Before the hearing on demurrer

3. a. Before service
   b. Before the answer
   c. Before the hearing on demurrer

4. Hearing on demurrers

5. A motion and court order

6. An ex parte application or hearing

7. a. To decide cases on the merits
   b. For judicial economy

8. Doctrine by which amended allegations can be imposed against parties new to the action after the statute of limitations has expired

9. a. The complaint alleged sufficient "Doe" defendants.
   b. The complaint alleged causes of action against the "Doe" defendants.
   c. The pleader was genuinely ignorant of the identities of the "Doe" defendants at the time the complaint was filed.

10. a. Proximity to trial
    b. Prejudice to the other parties
    c. Proximity to trial
    d. Prejudice to the other parties

QUIZ

1. b.
2. a.
3. a.
4. c.
5. d.
6. b.
7. c.
8. d.
9. d.
10. b.

12

CHAPTER OBJECTIVES

1. In the California Code of Civil Procedure (state) and Federal Rules of Civil Procedure (federal)

2. Words to the precise effect that to compute the last day for performance, skip the first day (that triggers the act), and count every day until the last, except if it is a holiday, then the next court day is the date for performance

3. How and when it was served

4. How and when the complaint was filed, and when the court can first hear the demurrer

REVIEW EXERCISES

Fill in the Blanks

1. Calculating and recording the days on which performance is required

2. Dates; client name and case name; nature of the performance; responsible attorney

3. Skip the first day, count all days until the performance is due, except if it is a holiday, and then skip it until the next court day.

4. Claims expire with the expiration of the statute of limitations.

5. The statutory time is suspended until the tolling condition has passed, then resumes. Tolling may result when the party against whom the claim is made is outside the state, is a minor, or the claimant lacks knowledge of the cause of action.

6. a. On the date of service
   b. 10 days from the mailing of the copy of the complaint to the defendant
   c. The date the acknowledgment is signed by the recipient
   d. Last day of last publication

7. 16; 21
8. 30
9. 20
10. 20

QUIZ

1. b.
2. c.
3. b.
4. d.
5. d.
6. b.
7. c.
8. c.
9. c.
10. b.

13

CHAPTER OBJECTIVES

1. a. Interrogatories—written responses under oath
   b. Requests for admissions—admissions and denials under oath
   c. Depositions—oral questions and answers under oath, transcribed
   d. Requests for production of documents and tangible things—documents and things for examination, copying, testing
   e. Independent medical examinations—examinations of claimant by physician or psychotherapist
   f. Expert discovery—disclosure and depositions of experts to be used by the other side at trial, and their reports

2. A discovery plan is an outline of the discovery a party intends to do, and why, based on review of pleadings.

3. Discovery privileges protect the communications between persons to encourage truthfulness. Such communications cannot be discovered.

REVIEW EXERCISES

Fill in the Blanks

1. a. Improve presentation of trial evidence
   b. Focus on issues
   c. Eliminate surprise at trial

2. a. Expensive
   b. Educate opposition
   c. Time consuming

3. A total of 35 interrogatories and 35 requests for admissions can be made; a total of 35 discovery devices may be used

4. Information; contentions; tangible

5. a. Outline essential elements
   b. Determine on what facts and evidence the party will rely
   c. Prepare blueprint for discovery

6. Anything that may lead to the discovery of admissible evidence

7. Encourage full communication between the parties of the privileged relationship

8. Attorney-client; attorney-workproduct

9. 10th day after service; 30th day before trial (except expert discovery—15 days before trial)

10. 30-day cutoff

QUIZ

1. d.
2. a.
3. a.
4. a.
5. a.
6. d.
7. d.
8. a.
9. b.
10. d.

CHAPTER OBJECTIVES

1. Form interrogatories are used to get basic information from respondent, in an unlimited civil case, without using one of the 35 interrogatories permitted.

2. In state court, labeled with propounder and respondent names, set number; numbered consecutively, no introduction or preface, no subparts, separate and independent, definitions capitalized, not compound, signed by attorney; federal court the same but no labels and space for responses.

3. In state court, labeled with propounder and respondent names, set number; numbered consecutively, objections asserted, responses containing all information available to respondent, signed by attorney, verified by respondent; in federal court, placed in space left for response.

REVIEW EXERCISES

Fill in the Blanks

1. Parties; parties
2. a. Inexpensive
   b. All information available to respondent
   c. May be done by paralegals
   d. Allows time for research for response
   e. Can determine legal contentions
3. a. Gamesmanship
   b. Not spontaneous
   c. Evasion
   d. Only propounded to parties
4. The party to whom the interrogatories are propounded, the propounding party, and the set number
5. Cannot
6. Any two of the following: he serves supplementary sets, he obtains a stipulation, he serves a declaration of necessity, he obtains leave of court
7. a. Respond
   b. Fail to respond
   c. Obtain a protective order
8. Interrogatories are propounded with room for the responses; responses are submitted in the spaces left for them
9. Any four of the following: privilege, exceeds scope of discovery, seeks content of documents, burdensome or oppressive, violates format requirements
10. Verify

QUIZ

1. b.
2. d.
3. a.
4. d.
5. a.
6. d.
7. a.
8. d.
9. a.
10. a.

CHAPTER OBJECTIVES

1. Requests for admissions must be separate, independent, and complete statements of facts or contentions to be admitted or denied by the opposing party under oath.

2. Official forms replace drafted requests and have places for specific statements, as well as for admissions of the genuineness of documents.

3. Admitted, denied, or objection

REVIEW EXERCISES

Fill in the Blanks

1. Admission; denial; objection
2. Any one of the following: they are cheap; they obtain unequivocal responses
3. They do not provide information
4. Genuineness of documents
5. Separate; complete; independent
6. Compound; conjunctive; disjunctive
7. Obtain a protective order
8. Subject to a motion to deem them admitted; deemed admitted
9. The responses are improper
10. The requests be repeated before the response

QUIZ

1. d.
2. d.
3. d.
4. d.
5. a.
6. d.
7. b.
8. a.
9. a.
10. d.

16

CHAPTER OBJECTIVES

1. A deposition notice is served by mail or by hand on all of the attorneys (or on the parties without attorneys) to give notice of the date, place, and time of a deposition; the person(s) to be deposed; the means of recordation of the deposition; and, if documents are sought from a party, a description of the documents.

2. A deposition subpoena is served personally; it compels the nonparty-deponent to submit to deposition, on the date and time and at the place indicated, and, if documents are sought from a party, it compels a description of the documents.

3. How to dress, how to conduct herself, what the depositions procedures are, and what to expect when being questioned by the other attorneys

4. To make the transcript manageable by providing an abbreviated version

REVIEW EXERCISES

Fill in the Blanks

1. Oral

2. Any two of the following: they can be taken of any witness, they are spontaneous, they require the witness to commit himself to a particular story, testimony can be preserved for trial, they permit questions about the content of documents

3. Any two of the following: they are expensive, length cannot be controlled, only personal knowledge can be determined

4. Any two of the following: sign the notice, sign the subpoena, sign objections, ask questions at the deposition

5. The initial case conference

6. 15

7. Notice of deposition

8. Subpoena

9. Subpoena duces tecum records only

10. 10 days; no

11. One; unlimited

12. a. Party appearance
    b. Party appearance and records
    c. Nonparty appearance
    d. Nonparty records only
    e. Nonparty appearance and records
    f. Written questions

13. One; unlimited
14. Natural person; main offices
15. State; federal
16. Give the oath, take and transcribe the testimony
17. The consumer is given a chance to object to the production of records
18. The witness, all the lawyers, and all the parties (and the court reporter and video reporter, if any)
19. Object
20. To report the facts in chronological order

QUIZ

1. d.
2. c.
3. d.
4. a.
5. a.
6. d.
7. a.
8. b.
9. b.
10. d.

17

CHAPTER OBJECTIVES

1. Determine what documents are likely to be kept by the opposing party, and how; consider what documents are within the scope of discovery, and draft requests requesting documents by categories described with reasonable particularity.
2. Responses include statements as to whether the requested documents can be produced or will be produced, and any objections to production.
3. In categories as requested, or as they are kept in the course of business with privileged documents removed
4. The documents are copied, with the master set archived for reference. There may be multiple copies made for organization into a master chronology, and into sets relating to each witness and each issue. The documents in each set are indexed for reference.

REVIEW EXERCISES

Fill in the Blanks

1. Tangible
2. Examples such as: documents—originals examined and tested for authenticity; mechanical parts—tested for defects; real estate—surveyed; structures—tested for mold or asbestos; computer disks—examined to determine the date documents were produced; audiotape—examined to determine content of erased material, etc.
3. Subpoena duces tecum
4. Request for production
5. It does not apply.
6. In categories, with reasonable particularity
7. 30 days if demand served by hand, 33 days if served by mail; anytime thereafter
8. A statement that the requested item will or will not be produced, or is unable to be produced, and any objections
9. Seek a protective order; seek a protective order
10. To copy the documents; time is more expensive than paper

QUIZ

1. c.
2. c.
3. d.
4. b.
5. b.
6. d.
7. c.
8. b.
9. a.
10. a.

18

CHAPTER OBJECTIVES

1. When the physical or mental condition of a party is at issue.
2. The date, time, and place of the examination; the examiner's name and specialty; the manner, scope, and nature of the examination; the tests and procedures anticipated; and whether reports are sought.

3. The relevance and importance of the examination to the litigation

4. The paralegal should examine the pleadings and discovery concerning the alleged claims of physical or mental injury, the workproduct of any mental consultants who have reviewed the case, and the records from the treating health care provider; he should research the examiner and consult with the medical consultant hired by the firm. The paralegal should explain the nature of IMEs to the client, review the demand with the client (including the procedures and tests to be performed), and counsel the client with respect to providing necessary information without adding unnecessary commentary.

REVIEW EXERCISES

Fill in the Blanks

1. Any party

2. In the pleadings

3. a. For a second examination
   b. For the examination of any party other than the plaintiff
   c. For a mental IME

4. a. Expense
   b. Risk that examiner may support the opposing party's claims

5. Any responses such as:
   a. Dental examination
   b. Podiatric examination
   c. Optometric examination
   d. Orthopedic examination

6. The examining professional

7. The examining professional cannot testify at trial.

8. His reports

9. Of the danger of potential harm to the party examined due to invasion of privacy; appoint

10. Physical; mental

QUIZ

1. b.

2. c.

3. d.

4. d.

5. c.

6. d.

7. d.

8. d.

9. b.

10. b.

19

CHAPTER OBJECTIVES

1. The name of the party making the demand, the code sections under which it is sought, the date for exchange, and if reports are sought.

2. A consultant is not discoverable, and advises only; an expert is hired to testify at trial.

3. In state court, by a supplemental disclosure within 20 days of initial disclosure, including a supplemental list, a supplemental declaration, relevant reports, and writings of the expert; in federal court, duty to update interrogatory responses regarding experts.

REVIEW EXERCISES

Fill in the Blanks

1. Responses should include examples involving the analysis of the claim or defenses of an opposing party, education of counsel about the technical issues in the case, advice concerning a discovery plan, trial preparation.

2. Responses should include examples involving presentation of testimony, presentation of charts and graphs, presentation of physical evidence, to educate the jury and illustrate the allegations of a party.

3. a. The defendant obtained an IME.
   b. The expert had prepared a report on plaintiff's condition.
   c. Plaintiff demands a copy of the defense medical report.

4. They are generally not otherwise discoverable.

5. Any party; every party; the code (or court)

6. 10 days; 70 days; later

7. Service by mail

8. a. A supplemental list
   b. A supplemental declaration
   c. Reports and writings of the expert

9. He is disclosed and offered for deposition

10. He is not made available for deposition

11. 15 days before trial

12. Notice of deposition; parties

13. Notices the deposition

14. a. The expert identity
    b. A statement of opinions and the information upon which they are based
    c. Any exhibits to be used as a summary of the opinions
    d. Qualifications of the witness, including all publications within the preceding 10 years

e. Compensation rate for oral testimony
f. A list of cases in which the expert testified in the past 4 years

15. a. They are treating physicians
b. by court order

QUIZ

1. c.
2. a.
3. d.
4. d.
5. d.
6. c.
7. d.
8. b.
9. d.
10. d.

20

CHAPTER OBJECTIVES

1. The discovery that is served on parties, the discovery that is obtained from third parties, and the order in which the discovery is to be obtained
2. 10 days after service of the summons and complaint
3. After the initial discovery conference
4. 30 days after hand service, 35 after service by mail
5. 30 days after hand service, 33 after service by mail
6. State court: at least 10 days' notice if served by hand, 15 if served by mail; federal court: a reasonable time before the deposition

REVIEW EXERCISES

Fill in the Blanks

1. Code; court
2. Discovery cutoff; commenced
3. Must be in writing

4. a. Interrogatories
   b. Requests for admission
   c. Production of documents
5. a. Interrogatories
   b. Requests for admission
   c. Production of documents
6. 10; reasonable time
7. 20; time for the consumer to seek a protective order
8. A reasonable time
9. Court order
10. 10; 30

QUIZ

1. b.
2. d.
3. d.
4. d.
5. a.
6. c.
7. b.
8. b.
9. a.
10. b.

21

CHAPTER OBJECTIVES

1. The notice of motion, which sets forth the date, place, time, department of the motion, the nature of the motion, the relief sought, and the documents upon which the motion will be based; the memorandum of points and authorities, which states the facts, the law governing the facts, and the argument to apply the law to the facts to achieve the desired outcome; the supporting documentation, which is usually declarations setting forth written testimony of the facts; a proposed order, which sets forth the relief requested.

2. The memorandum of points and authorities, as described previously, and any supporting documentation such as declarations.

3. The papers are on captioned pleading paper, two-hole punched at the top and stapled together, with footers at the bottom of each page. Papers include a proof of service.

REVIEW EXERCISES

Fill in the Blanks

1. trial; master calendar; law and motion
2. Trial
3. Local rules
4. All parties
5. The notice is defective if the information is incorrect
6. 21; 5
7. The moving party must show that notice to all parties was given timely
8. To allow the parties to decide whether to contest the ruling
9. That the party against whom they are imposed has delayed or displayed bad faith; requests them in writing in the moving papers
10. Ex parte; they can be made without other counsel present;
    a. there is an emergency
    b. evidence might be destroyed
11. 24 hours';
    a. The date
    b. The time
    c. The department
    d. The nature of the motion and relief sought
12. Due in 10 days
13. 45 days after service of the responses if the responses are served by hand, 50 if served by mail; nonexistent
14. Meet and confer; compelling responses
15. Separate statement
    a. The discovery demand in dispute
    b. The response given
    c. The reasons that further response should be ordered
16. Reconsideration
17. Renew
18. Rehearing
19. a. A description of the discovery at issue
    b. The reasons why protective order is justified
20. a. Articulate the issue
    b. Locate supporting law

QUIZ

1. b.
2. b.
3. b.

4. d.
5. a.
6. d.
7. a.
8. d.
9. a.
10. b.

22

CHAPTER OBJECTIVES

1. A motion to dispose of the entire case since there is no dispute of material fact

2. A motion to dispose of one or more causes of action or defenses because, as to those causes of action or defenses, there is no dispute of material fact

3. Notice of motion (giving notice of the hearing and the grounds on which it is sought and what will be relied upon for the motion); a memorandum of points and authorities (setting forth the relevant background, facts, and law); a separate statement of undisputed fact (setting forth the factual issues to be resolved and the supporting evidence); the evidence (supporting the motion); a proposed order (stating the desired outcome of the motion).

REVIEW EXERCISES

Fill in the Blanks

1. a. Can resolve the case
   b. Flush out the assertions and evidence of the other side
2. a. Expensive
   b. Could lose (not often granted)
3. a. The case is over.
   b. The cause(s) of action or defenses adjudicated is no longer part of the case.
4. a. Case continues
   b. Case continues
5. Bench; fact
6. State court requires a separate statement, while federal court may require it
7. 75; 10
8. Trial evidence
9. One material fact

10. Separate statement of disputed facts; references to evidence that disputes at least one material fact

11. Specification of each disputed fact and the evidence supporting it

12. A specification of the precise cause of action adjudicated

13. Law; the judge can determine the law to be applied to the undisputed facts

14. Any three of the following: title, description, body of the notice, memorandum of points and authorities, separate statement

15. The court denying the motion for summary adjudication

QUIZ

1. d.
2. d.
3. d.
4. d.
5. c.
6. c.
7. b.
8. b.
9. b.
10. a.

23

CHAPTER OBJECTIVES

1. The case management judge sets cases for trial in a master calendar jurisdiction, and the trial judge sets the trial date in a direct calendar system.

2. The trial judge sets cases for trial.

3. The party serving the demand/offer proposes to have judgment entered on specific terms.

4. A judicial council form is completed.

REVIEW EXERCISES

Fill in the Blanks

1. Move cases forward, plan for availability of courtrooms and juries, and dispose of cases swiftly

2. Preference; days

3. Presiding judge

4. Mandatory settlement conference; settlement conference statement

5. a. Fees and costs to all other parties
   b. Reimbursement to the county for the court's time

6. That will make a permanent recordation of the terms in case there are disputes later

7. The final result at trial will be less advantageous than the offer/demand, and he could be required to pay expert witness and other costs of the other side

8. Good faith

9. Trial judge

10. Defendant; plaintiff

QUIZ

1. a.
2. a.
3. d.
4. d.
5. a.
6. b.
7. d.
8. b.
9. d.
10. c.

24

CHAPTER OBJECTIVES

1. The case management judge will order cases to mandatory judicial arbitration, which involves the selection of an arbitrator, the arbitration itself, an award, and either entry of judgment or trial de novo.

2. Mediation, neutral evaluation, arbitration

3. A request for a trial following an arbitration award

REVIEW EXERCISES

Fill in the Blanks

1. a. Voluntary judicial
   b. Mandatory judicial
   c. Voluntary nonjudicial

2. American Arbitration Association (AAA) or Judicial Mediation and Arbitration Service (JAMS)

3. The parties agree

4. Courts

5. Court administrator; court administrator

6. a. He represented a party
   b. He had affiliation with an attorney
   c. He has interest in the action

7. Expert discovery; 15

8. The party who intends to offer the transcript serves a notice of intent at least 20 days before the arbitration hearing

9. She will do worse than the arbitration award, not recover her costs and fees, have to pay the other parties' fees and costs, and have to reimburse the county for the cost of the arbitrator

10. Trial by jury

QUIZ

1. a.
2. b.
3. d.
4. b.
5. a.
6. c.
7. d.
8. b.
9. d.
10. b.

25

CHAPTER OBJECTIVES

1. Discovery organization is to accumulate information and evidence; trial organization is to locate and cross-reference.

2. To make sure that testimony and evidence are organized to prove every issue and fact in the case

3. The blueprint of the case, and everything that may be needed at trial

4. Making sure that notices are served, subpoenas are served, and that the witnesses are prepared and ready to testify at the time their testimony is needed

REVIEW EXERCISES

Fill in the Blanks

1. Cost of the case; incurring so many costs that settlement is more difficult
2. Demonstrative evidence; foundation evidence
3. Subpoenaed
4. Notice to appear
5. a. Case management conference statement
   b. Case management or trial-setting conference
   c. Payment of jury fees
6. a. Statement on the first pleading
   b. Specifying at trial-setting conference
7. Any three of the following: deposition testimony, discovery responses, tangible evidence, witness statements, declarations
8. Notice to appear; subpoena duces tecum
9. Subpoena duces tecum; court clerk
10. Impeachment; rehabilitation

QUIZ

1. c.
2. d.
3. d.
4. d.
5. d.
6. d.
7. b.
8. d.
9. d.
10. d.

CHAPTER OBJECTIVES

1. Pretrial conference, opening statements, plaintiff's case-in-chief with plaintiff's direct examination, defendant's cross-examination of plaintiff's witnesses, plaintiff rests, defendant's motions for nonsuit and directed verdict, defendant's case-in-chief, defendant rests, rebuttal by plaintiff and defendant, closing argument by plaintiff, closing argument by defendant, plaintiff's rebuttal closing argument, jury deliberations, verdict

2. A peremptory challenge to the trial judge in state court made at the time the judge is assigned

3. By reference to the witness who will give foundational testimony

REVIEW EXERCISES

Fill in the Blanks

1. Federal; state; trial judge
2. Setting; reset
3. Trailing
4. Peremptory challenge; 15; before counsel leaves the presiding judge's courtroom at trial assignment
5. Judicial council
6. Recuse
7. Pretrial conference
8. Department court clerk
9. He has handled the case since the beginning and is familiar with it
10. Any four of the following: trial brief, exhibits, pretrial motions, jury instructions, witness lists with outline of testimony and time estimates
11. Motions in limine
12. Jury instructions; they are the only way to educate the jury about the law to be applied to the evidence
13. Direct; direct; cross; leading
14. California Civil Instructions; jury instructions
15. Voir dire
16. Peremptory challenges
17. Identification; the clerk; admitted into evidence
18. Directed verdict
19. Plaintiff; defendant; plaintiff
20. Verdict

QUIZ

1. b.
2. d.
3. b.
4. d.
5. c.
6. c.

7. d.
8. d.
9. d.
10. d.

27

CHAPTER OBJECTIVES

1. a. Motion for costs—to claim costs after trial; state court: file 10 days after notice of entry; federal court: file with the clerk, and opposing parties have 10 days to file challenge
b. Motion for judgment NOV—to request the court substitute its judgment for the jury verdict; state court: 15 days from service of notice of entry of judgment by clerk or 15 days of service of notice of entry of judgment by any party, or 180 days from entry of judgment; federal court: within 10 days of entry of judgment
c. Motion for new trial—to get a new trial; state court: 15 days from service of notice of entry of judgment by clerk or 15 days of service of notice of entry of judgment by any party, or 180 days from entry of judgment; federal court: within 10 days of entry of judgment.

2. The judgment states the case name, the trial judge's name, the date of trial and verdict, and the result. The notice of entry of judgment notifies the parties of the date that the judgment was entered.

REVIEW EXERCISES

Fill in the Blanks

1. Judgment book; court clerk
2. All parties; any party or the clerk
3. a–d: Any four of the following: filing fees, jury fees, jury meal expenses, depositions, preparation of demonstrative evidence; services of process; e., f.: any two of the following: expert fees, postage, telephone bills, copying (except for exhibits)
4. State; motion to recover costs; cost bill
5. Federal; 1; 5
6. Motion for judgment notwithstanding the verdict; 15; 15; 180
7. Any four of the following: irregularity in the proceedings, misconduct of the jury, accident, surprise, newly discovered evidence which could not have been discovered prior to trial, excessive or inadequate damages, insufficient evidence to support the verdict, legal error in the trial
8. The jury is polled
9. Jurisdictional

10. Are not extended for service by mail; 60; 60; 60
11. Notwithstanding the verdict
12. The trial judge
13. Nullified
14. For new trial
15. Judgment notwithstanding the directed verdict

QUIZ

1. a.
2. d.
3. c.
4. d.
5. c.
6. c.
7. b.
8. d.
9. d.
10. d.

28

CHAPTER OBJECTIVES

1. California Rules of Court and Federal Rules of Appellate Procedure
2. A notice to the court and the parties that an appellate brief will be filed
3. A request to the clerk to prepare the record of the case to be sent to the appellate court
4. Caption, table of contents, table of authorities, statement of the case, statement of facts, argument, proof of service

REVIEW EXERCISES

Fill in the Blanks

1. Appellate division of the superior court; court of appeal
2. Federal district court; federal district court of appeals

3. Trial court; law

4. a. The judgment be reversed
   b. The judgment be modified
   c. The judgment be affirmed
   d. The case be remanded to the trial court for further action

5. Appellate court; its judgment

6. a. Substantial evidence
   b. Abuse of discretion
   c. Independent judgment

7. Executed; appeal bond (or "undertaking") or stay

8. Notice of appeal; jurisdictional; mailing

9. 60; 30

10. a.–c. Any three of the following: the pleadings, motions and documents filed with the court, court orders, tangible evidence
    d. Transcripts of the proceedings

11. a. Transcript of the proceedings
    b. Any of the following: the pleadings, motions and documents filed with the court, court orders, tangible evidence

12. Stipulated statement; notice to prepare; 10; notice of appeal

13. rule 5

14. Will index and paginate

15. a party

16. Trial court

17. Any four of the following: font size and style, number of words, certification of number of words, cover color, caption, table of contents, table of authorities

18. The record

19. a. The trial court
    b. The appellate court
    c. The Supreme Court of California
    d. The parties

20. Grant; deny

21. Any four of the following: affirm, reverse, deny, retransfer, or decertify a published opinion

22. Unpublished

23. 20; notification from the clerk that the record is completed; 20; 10 days of filing the respondent's brief

24. a. There is a federal question
    b. It is in conflict with the federal courts

25. U.S. Supreme Court

QUIZ

1. a.
2. c.
3. b.
4. b.
5. d.
6. d.
7. b.
8. a.
9. d.
10. d.

CHAPTER OBJECTIVES

1. Writs of mandate/mandamus, prohibition, certiorari
2. Attachment, claim and delivery, receivership
3. Temporary restraining order (TRO), preliminary injunction, permanent injunction
4. Code of Civil Procedure (CCP), Family Code (FC), Business and Professions Code (B&PC), CCP
5. Federal Rules of Civil Procedure (FRCP), Federal Rules of Appellate Procedure (FRAP)

REVIEW EXERCISES

Fill in the Blanks

1. The rights of litigants; lesser tribunals; comply with the law
2. a. There is no remedy available in ordinary litigation
   b. Ordinary litigation does not provide a remedy of the type needed
3. Any five of the following: whether the legal remedy is adequate, whether the party seeking the injunction has exhausted administrative remedies, whether irreparable harm will result in the absence of an injunction, whether the party seeking the injunction is likely to prevail, whether the party seeking the injunction has clean hands, whether the injunction will require supervision by the court, whether the injunction sought is enforceable
4. Bond/undertaking
5. Status quo; trial
6. Stronger

7. Receiver; acts within the power granted in the court's order
8. Attachment
   a. Noticed hearing
   b. Temporary restraining order
   c. Ex parte application
9. Mandamus/mandate
10. Certiorari

QUIZ

1. a.
2. d.
3. a.
4. a.
5. b.
6. b.
7. c.
8. c.
9. c.
10. b.